Real
Cardiff
Three

the changing city

For Kate

1981-2009

Real Cardiff Three

the changing city

peter finch

SEREN

Seren is the book imprint of
Poetry Wales Press Ltd
Nolton Street, Bridgend, Wales
www.serenbooks.com

ISBN 978-1-85411-505-8

A CIP record for this title is available from
the British Library

The publisher works with the financial assistance
of the Welsh Books Council

Printed by Thomson Litho Ltd

Also in the Real Wales series
Editor: Peter Finch:

CONTENTS

SOUTH

WEST

NORTH

BEYOND

POEMS

INTRODUCTION

THE LOZENGE-SHAPED CITY NOW THE BOOM HAS BUST

I'm in the lozenge-shaped city again. Water south, hills north. A city
of rhomboid sprawl. Where else would I be? I'm standing on the
B4487 in bright early-morning sunlight. Traffic low. Birds in inner-
city twitter. This was the Via Julia Maritima once, the paved Roman
route west. A thousand years on it was the stage coach route to
London. Full of ruts and mud. Then it was the hard-topped A48,
when A roads meant something. Newport Road when I was a kid.
Still is. The Africans are walking down it now. The endless displaced.
Heading up beyond Roath Court for the Refugee Council at Phoenix
House. Fewer now that the recession has hit. Polski Sklep[1] having a
hard time. The Czech shop already closed.

We always wondered why in this place there was so much new
housing. Apartments rising like corn right across the boom city.
Concrete mixers. Deliveries of brick. Tower cranes like locusts. Men
in hard hats in every bar. What drew them to this capital? What were
we doing that made them come? Nothing, it turns out. Investors are
blind. Invest where walls rise and your money will climb in step. No
need to sell what you've built. Let the vacant towers glitter. Let their
apartments stand empty, value accumulating as prices soar. Manage
a let if a visitor asks. Sell one to an executive needing a town centre
toehold. Rooms with a water view for singles. Wasp territory. Audi in
the undercroft. Wine in the
rack. Families not needed. No
toy cupboards. No gardens.
No schools.

Now that boom has bust
these investments stand barren.
For Sale. To Let. To Let. Those
not yet completed stay so.
Across the city are half-finished
metal frames, surrounded by
fencing, waiting for the interest
rates to rise once again. Build
has stopped, all but. Apart from

the mega projects like St David's 2, the new stadium for Cardiff City and the scatter of enterprise across the sports village on the Ferry Road. On the hoarding at the north end of St David's 2, our new city of malls and inner-city accommodation, are graffitied the words *More Yuppie Flats Please*. Word on the street is that the blocks inside will stand largely empty. Shells. Unfixed, unfinished walls. A city waiting for the bankers to take control once more.

There have been many visions for this place in which Cardiffians live. Plans for the port to take ocean liners. For the rich to sail for America from Tiger Bay rather than Southampton or London or Liverpool. Passengers would arrive by Great Western. There would have been grand hotels, piers and custom sheds and deep-water berths, but the Severn's giant tidefall defeated them all.

When the Second World War came bombs hit the docks and there was a dangerous scattering across the suburbs but nothing like the devastation that visited Bristol or Swansea or London. Those flattened places were first in line for rebuild. They got the Brutalism and the concrete early. Cardiff, with its drab and dismal streets, slumbered on. Plans for reconstruction, when they came, embraced the spirit of the age. There would be city centre high rise linked by urban motorway. Roads would dominate, flying in on elevated concrete platforms. The city would resemble Metropolis. You wouldn't live here, you'd come here. The centre would stretch north as far as Maindy. Cars stacked in giant parks. Pedestrian walkways woven among them like raffia. This was Buchanan's plan of 1964. Cardiff couldn't afford it. Only the outer distributor roads were built along with some of the centre car

parks.

Buchanan's successor was Ravenseft's Centreplan of 1970. More centre highrise linked by first floor pedestrian decks. Conference centres, offices, malls, concert halls, shops. Everything in the old centre flattened to make way. The 1973 property crash saw that one off.

What Cardiff actually ended up with was piecemeal redevelopment. Smaller scale. One block at a time. St David's Hall. The pedestrianisation of Queen Street. The opening of the St David's Shopping Centre. The bus station redesigned and made more welcoming. The entrance-way to the city from Cardiff Central Rail Station cleared. Trees planted. A new library on Bridge Street. On the site of the old open market and the bend in the Glamorgan canal the arrival of the prestigious Holiday Inn. The building by Brent Walker of the city's own World Trade Centre at the back of Mary Ann Street (now known as the Cardiff International Arena, home to trade shows and concerts by Bob Dylan and the Manic Street Preachers).

By the time the new Cardiff unitary authority was created in 1996, with Russell Goodway in charge, the boom was well underway. Cardiff, the newest European Capital. Cardiff, the world's youngest city. Cardiff reborn, rebuilt, rebranded. Come for the glass and the grass. City of malls and parks. Cardiff with a Bay. City of opportunity and joy. A smogless place of life and light. And come they did. The European Summit in 1997. The Bay's Mermaid Quay in 1998. The Rugby World Cup at the new Millennium Stadium in 1999. The National Assembly the same year. Fireworks everywhere. The MacDonald Holland Hotel created in the former Hodge Building, Cardiff's first high-rise, in 2004. The Parc Plaza in 2005. The Altolusso apartments on Bute Terrace, centrepiece of *Torchwood's* opening credits, in 2005. This was boosterism. Sell the city, turn the place from manufacture to call centre, from exporter to destination. From heavy industrial to financial screen spinner. Come here to make your decisions. Cardiff media city. Cardiff centre for international sports. For opera and the arts. Visit to get pissed. More vertical drinkeries per acre than anywhere else in the western UK.

City centre living returned in 2003 when Fanum House, the for mer AA headquarters on the corner of Queen Street and Station Terrace was renamed The Aspect and its floors sold as apartments with a view (the railtracks and the

prison actually). Immediate access to all the shopping you could ever need. Greggs opened a sandwich shop below.

The centre flourishes. Come here on a match-day to see it at its peak. Street theatre, music, men on tightropes playing violins, Roma bands with clarinet and double bass, student duos with bright guitars, the Red Choir – some of them sitting now – still ushering in freedom outside the covered market, Chinese selling me my name bent in wire, Ninjah in bling and Sgt Pepper Jacket beating rhythm on the street furniture. The *Big Issue* seller with his dog in costume. The Coptic Christians. The Gaza protesters. The shaved heads of the Hari Krishnas weaving through the crowd. More vibrant life on Queen Street than at any previous time in its history.

St David's 2 – the comprehensive redevelopment of those parts of the centre unscathed by previous interventions – hit the concrete mixers in 2004. Not only were the broken wrecks beyond Hills Street and all final centre traces of Victorian Cardiff to be wiped but much of Cardiff's seventies restructuring along Bridge Street and the Hayes would go too. Twenty-five years was as long as Iceland and the new library lasted. St David's, because he is our patron saint and a Welsh symbol the world will recognise. St David's, to be filled with 'garden architecture and animated facades, storytelling public art and a "portrait gallery of Welsh achievement within the Mall" in an imitation of the City Hall statuary'[2]. Cardiff, city of new height. Capital of Wales. Darling of the valleys. Principal shopping magnet for all of western Britain. And in terms of the boom, opened a year too late. Vacant lots waiting for the fall to bottom. The recession has taken the gilt. I went through yesterday. Brave faces. Glass and just that little bit of echo. Promise as yet unfulfilled.

Back on Newport Road it is as if the fifties are still with us. Victorian three-storey housing still in need of a repaint. Bed and breakfast vacancies. Hopeful signs saying that Construction Workers are Welcome. En-suite at no extra charge. Chip shop at the end of Broadway selling Clarks pies. Someone removing their front wall so that they can park their car in their front garden. Couple of kids on skateboards. Nigerian with an iPod. Man on a bike, no helmet. Cardiff as it was, still is.

notes:

1. Polish shop.
2. Quoted from Eric Kuhne, the American architect leading the branding of the new St David's project for Land Securities in 2002, as reported by John Punter in *Capital Cardiff* 1975-2020, UWP, 2006.

Cardiff Walking

In this city you need a different approach. Check the wind first. Know that rain arrives like a flight of tigers from the south west.

Nearly all of this place is hard top. Unmade roads and paths full of brown and grass finished thirty years ago. No longer do you need to scrape your boots.

Cardiff rises. It seems so flat, there in the centre. But it's not. Bay's edge to Boulevard de Nantes climbs imperceptibly but steadily. You can roll a marble at the top of Bute Street and watch it track right back to the Pier Head.

Of poems on walking there are any number but few on urban joy. The unexpected street you've never seen before, the new view of a familiar vista, the plantings in the gardens of others, the paths and driveways fabricated from rock and gravel, brick and hardcore, worn slab concrete, sheets of black polythene below scatters of chipped slate. Anything to hold the green growth back.

Names of houses: Ger y Lan, Brook House, Cartref, Homewood, Red House, The Firs (no firs anywhere), Woodside, Wayside, Westside, Hillcrest, Maes-y-Gareg, Lincoln House, Cymric House, Mount Stuart House, River House, Lake View, Fairwinds, Mallards Reach, Brynhyfryd (no lovelies, no hills), Glamorgan House, Cardiff House, The Rectory, The Vicarage, The Old Post Office, The Old Rectory, The Old Surgery, The Old Vicarage, Ty Newydd, Felin Allt, Ty Ni. Nothing great, little grand. No Fort Apache. Just names to mark these places out from the swamp.

Inner city you are invisible. The further out the more your body lights. Flicker crossing Roath. 60 watts over Rhymney. By the time we reach St Mellons you glow like fire. In these suburban brightnesseses the walker cannot be surreptitious. Covert is not a Cardiff word. Enter a street and no matter how silent you are your first step will make everyone look. Why are you here. What do you want. You can warm your hands on the glowering. Walk on, don't stop.

CENTRAL

A RIVER WALK

The plan is simple enough. With twenty or so post-grads, plus a few
of the intrigued and the encouraged, all new to Cardiff, I'll lead a
walk around the city's past. Stopping and explaining. Pointing
things out. They'll want to locate the city in the scheme of things,
now that they've moved here. From Shanghai, Malaysia, Boston,
and Nottingham. Wales has entered them. By osmosis, through their
feet, through the air. So this is the coal port capital of the capitalist
world. Largest exporter the latter-day empires ever knew. Now
renewed and rebuilt. The shopping destination of choice. How does
it all fit together?

I'm standing on the bank of the Taff at the town end of Sophia
Gardens, on the metalled river path that runs here from the National
Sports Centre just to the north. Opposite is a boarding stage for the
new water taxis, a complex confection of floating platform, safety
fence, and barber's pole hitching post. All classes catered for. Wheels
no disincentive. If you are chair bound or manoeuvring a giant
pneumatic-wheeled baby transporter then this mini-quay will present
no barrier. Pay your ticket and roll.

To the south is Cardiff Bridge carrying four traffic lanes, opened
originally as a stone structure of three arches in 1796[1] but rebuilt,
strengthened and widened on many occasions since. The original
Cardiff Bridge, made of wood and subject to constant erosion by ice
and flood, stood some 300 yards up river. In those days the Cowbridge
road left Cardiff through the West Gate to skirt Blackfriars before
crossing the Taff and then the Turton Brook. The village of Canton was
next. The line of the road followed the Roman Portway, crossing the
Canna, and then later the Ely, at Pont Lai. Still does. Although the
Canna is long lost, the Ely straightened, and the Turton carried below
ground in the corporation drains.

This area was once the Little Park, the Drying Hayes, a place
where cloth from the Castle's fulling mill was laid out on frames.
South was the Cardiff Arms Hotel and the Great Park. South again
were the salt marshes crossed by the swirling meanders of a flood-
prone Taff. I follow the river path, under the bridge and then up,
along Coldstream Terrace first, and then Fitzhamon Embankment.
Tough itinerant streets. Hard core Riverside. These used to be the

Taff Meads – meadows – places of cattle and long grass. Camping grounds for travellers and tinkers. For those passing through. And those spectral campers are still here. To encounter them come after dark when the homeless and the alcoholic gather in Dickensian groups, drawn here by the magnetism of moving water.

I'm walking the new cut, along the Taff in its flood-defenced, man-made channel. This is where the Victorian engineer Isambard Kingdom Brunel put it. The original river bed ran south behind the Cardiff Arms, one of the town's great inns. When eventually it was dry enough to walk on it became parkland. Cardiff Arms Parkland. The name stuck.

Fitzhamon actually is an embankment. You can peer west down Despenser Street and Fitzhamon Lane to see the land sink away. Brook Street bends in here, houses built along the line of the now lost Canna. There's an outlet pipe emerging from the Taff embankment flood defences. A trickle of water sometimes comes from it, they say. But I've never seen anything. Stuffed with dirt and fag packets when I looked in 2003 and still the same in 2007[2].

At the south end of Fitzhamon, Sunday morning, is the Cardiff Farmer's Market. A straggle of food stalls selling 'good food which doesn't cost the earth', local produce, organic, non-corporate, sustainable, green, fairtrade, not an ounce of artificiality, no added preservatives, no e-numbers, real. Farmer's markets are an early twenty-first century obsession. We want non-processed alternatives, stuff that isn't container-shipped, burning carbon as it comes. Local. Nothing from further out than fifty miles. But I spot Manx Kippers, crepes from Brittany, Teifi cheese, Rossmoor oysters, French huile d'olive vierge extra, in fact a whole stall devoted to olives in all their abundant non-Welsh variety, then wild boar and rare breed pork, Lliw Valley smoked fish, English apple juice, fruit pies from Newcastle Emlyn. Fifty flexible miles. And why not?

The market's end is indicated by a large painted steel sculpture of a slice taken through the seeds of mustard, coriander, saffron, nutmeg, cardamom and ginger. Heather Parnell, David Mackie and Andrew Rowe made them. The council paid. Part of their push for regeneration. Lightens the darkness, I guess.

Next to them is an official map for the homeless. It shows the route of the breakfast run, the location of the area's numerous hostels and bears a set of instructions on how to doss out at night. Do not sleep alone, find a place where there are others. Put cardboard below you. Don't drink. Keep your hands and feet well covered. Get something hot inside you before you close your eyes.

The Wood Street river bridge takes me into the lost opportunity of Millennium Plaza and its dominant multiplex. Beyond was once Temperance Town (see *Park Street* – p.41) but now the bus station. This plaza is the south end of the Millennium Stadium. The Empire Pool once stood here (see *The Festival of Britain Steam Rooms* – p.62). Demolished, planners promised, to give us a world-class square from which to behold our world-class stadium. Space and light. Instead they gave us this cramped and jerry-built place. Over the road is the steam-age watertower at the western end of Cardiff Central. You can just make out the huge daffodil that was painted on its side as an outreach unemployment project from the 1970s Charles Street Carnival.

The way back north is along a wooden walkway cantilevered out over the river. The Millennium Stadium hard on my right. Celebratory bricks underfoot. (Come On Wales. Wales Forever. Wales The Best. Wales We Love You. Jason Soley Bracknell Come On

England). Sports were first played on this ground when the Cardiff Arms was demolished[3] in 1878 to make way for the new Angel Hotel. The Marquis of Bute, who owned the land, allowed access for leisure but not trade. People walked. Kicked balls. Threw them. The army was allowed use of the space for training. A 300-capacity sports stand was erected in 1881. They played cricket in it along with the newly imported novelty, baseball. Only later did they stage what has come to be the Welsh national game, rugby. The Marquis sold his interests in 1922 and the land was leased to Cardiff Athletic Club. A cricket ground was created to the north and a larger capacity rugby stadium to the south[4]. To help pay for upkeep a greyhound track was developed on the same site[5]. The last dog ran in 1977. There were soccer matches. The Riverside Soccer Club, forerunner to Cardiff City, played here until 1910 when they moved on to Ninian Park. The Empire Games were here in 1958 with the dog track used for athletics. Speedway went round in a heat of scream and dust. As a diversification Lennox Lewis fought Frank Bruno in 1993. To cap that Prince Naseem Hamed beat Steve Robinson in 1995.

Using Lottery money the new Millennium Stadium was built in 1997. Its magnificent spider from Mars structure with a re-positioned pitch now occupies around two thirds of the whole Arms Park site. The Cardiff Athletic Club pitch remains, physically attached to the north end of the Stadium and with its ground still aligned east-west. Capacity 12,500. Recalcitrant, determined. Home of Cardiff RFC. The Millennium Stadium may be at the Arms Park but will never *be* the Arms Park. History and vested, dogged interest will see to that. Between games at the Millennium Stadium they play recordings of the crowds singing. Amuses the tourists. I can hear them through the river walls as I pass.

Who else has sung here? Gyrating dots in the spotlit distance. Michael Jackson, Sting, The Rolling Stones, David Bowie, U2, Dire Straits, Tina Turner, Manic Street Preachers, Jose Carreras. The Jehovahs, every year, suits, fresh faces, I'm Here For God. 5000 lost among 74,500.

Top end the walkway spills out onto the place where Cowbridge Road and Castle Street meet. Bute's reconstruction of the ancient West Gate opposite, still attached to the side of the Castle. The town wall is long gone. The gate is a portal into nothing. Before Brunel the river Taff flowed across here, edging Lord Bute's mills and swinging in a dramatic meander to push for the sea down what is now Westgate Street.

As I pass the street fills with rugby supporters pouring out from the ground. Traffic is stopped completely. The hoards surge back towards the Glamorgan Staff Club. Here, once, stood Cardiff's medieval quay where they made cannons for the Navy. Shipped them to Portsmouth. Exported coal, lead, cloth and butter. Made ships. The-300 ton *Wellington* was launched in 1813. Built in a yard just back from the Queens Vaults. You could have walked down mud-encrusted St Mary Street and have seen the masts rising above the chimneys.

At the junction of Quay Street and Westgate stands a multi-story 60s concrete car park, built over the site of Blounts Gate. Blount was a keeper on the West-facing town walls of Cardiff. Almost all traces of his empire were either swept away by the scouring Taff or lost through centuries of development. In the car park basement the outline of his place of work is marked.

Sliding into Quay Street is Womanby Street, one of Cardiff's oldest. As it runs back to the Castle it curves slowly. It is as narrow as you'd expect an ancient street to be, and, apart from the preserved Jones Court[6] to the left, has had its history almost completely removed. The ancient taverns – the Horse and Groom, the Red Cow – are demolished. Trinity Chapel is unmarked. Clwb Ifor Bac has had its 'h' stolen. The British Legion, home of the 70s Middle Eight Jazz Club, has long disappeared. The walls are a mass of fly posting. Jason Soudah, The Poppies, Sonic Lodge, Zinc, Viva Machine, Ryland Teifi, Jump The Underground, Pram, Mr Huw, Endaf Presley, Larry Pickleman, Genod Droog, Get Cape Wear Cape, Boom In The Diamond. Everyone their own mc. Everyone is famous now.

Music, drunkenness and violence have been Womanby constants since Scandinavian raiders founded it. If, indeed, it was they who did. Pirates, English, Irish, jazzers, dopers, The Soul Crew, Skinheads. Front of me on Castle Street Bute's nineteenth century Disneyesque-rebuild of Cardiff's Roman pre-history is decked for Christmas. Discrete lighting quietly and dimly erected on the Castle walls by helmeted engineers operating in full compliance with all regulation, relevant documentation completed, registered and filed. Corner of Castle Street, out of Dempsey's rollicking testament to Irish fakery, surge a dozen beer-fuelled rugby fans heading east to the next watering hole. Cardiff, thick and furious, still continues. Over the road and back across the river, with the water taxi stop still empty and unvisited, is the place where I started.

ATOMIC CARDIFF

After Calder Hall opened in 1956 they began to build them up along the river estuary. Atomic giants. Hinkley Point A, Oldbury, Hinkley Point B. Almost another at Aberthaw but they left that creating 1500 megawatts from Tower Colliery coal. There was never one built at Roath, although that didn't stop atoms elsewhere in the city from starting to dance.

When I was a child in the 1950s atomic power was something the *Eagle* told us had been invented by the English. When protons and neutrons meshed power came for free. No more coal to be dug, nor petrol to be burned. This was the future. A whole world lit up like the dial of your luminous Dan Dare watch. Freedom and fame. The Eagle did not touch on real world death. Dan Dare fought only the Mekon and the evil green Martians. There were no Russians where he was. His was a planet where the Nazis had been long defeated and all at home was now green and golden. But things did not continue like that for long.

By the time we got to the nuclear 60s reality had taken control and we were jittering on the eve of destruction. Standing on Queen Street still full of cars and red double deckers, selling *Sanity*. Linking arms in the arcades, dressed in white lying down as if the fallout had got us, civil disobedience on a local scale saying stop and no one listened. Would they send the V-bombers on out from St Athan? Would *Ark Royal* knock their invading planes out of the skies? Would the Bloodhounds[7] on their spinning platforms protect us from incoming intercontinentals? Not a chance. For the first time in my entirely post-war life I experienced it. People were afraid.

At the time of Kennedy and the Cuban stand-off I'd lain in the long grass of Roath Park expecting the Russians to appear overhead any moment. Would I see them? Would their H bombers be beyond the clouds? Or would their dark shapes flick below my lids like midges just before the heat arrived? Silence. Nothing for a long time but the sun and the slow wind. Then I went home.

People feared that electricity and its atom source would wreck us, stuff would seep, mist would cross skies turning green brown and making our skins blister. Out there where walls could stop nothing. Atom rads like Martian rays. Hair falling. Sticklebacks in Roath Brook with three eyes. Redness. Can't sleep. Head swollen. Extra toes.

Electricity did not leak from the sockets and flow across the floor as my grandmother had believed. It came through wires, rubber dressed, made the lamp filaments glow and the tram motors turn. In Cardiff power first arrived in 1884 when the Anglo-American Brush Company (AABC) built a generating plant on the Hayes. Coal trucks on Hills Street. Steam and noise. The building used was once the fish market. It was later rebuilt in the same style in 1936 as the Electricity Showrooms. It's now Habitat, selling poorly-insulated lighting imported from China, upmarket Ikea-like furniture, throws, mugs, prints. AABC's power reached your home by overhead wire and only in the evening. In 1889 the plant closed due to safety fears. Bare power wires were flown into by birds and when the wind was up brushed against buildings.

Power generation moved to briefly to Ninian Park Road and then to a new steam powered plant on Newport Road. Current was direct, hitting the street lights at 2500 volts. The Newport Road plant eventually became a main generator for the South Wales Electricity Board. Roath Power Station. Twin cooling towers. Three-phase current at 6000 volts. Coal. Steam. White smog in sky-rising streams. Closed in the sixties to make way for Sainsbury's. We all went up the hill to watch the towers coming down.

During the Cold War Cardiff feared less than it did during the war with Hitler. The Docks were closing. The city was no longer a target. There was early warning radar along the far east coast of England. We had V Bombers in our eastern skies. Under BHS, west of the Glamorgan Canal on the Friary was rumoured an RSG – Regional Seat of Government. Hotly denied officially by everyone. The *Echo* couldn't track it. The shop staff at BHS kept their mouths shut. CND published comprehensive plans as a foolscap-sized exposé. Sold for one shilling. Police took mine, never gave it back. Perhaps this RSG never actually existed.

Maybe the power wielders would retreat instead to the Pentyrch Royal Observer Core post in a small private paddock off the Mountain Road north of the village. In use between 1961 and 1968. Blast Pressure Indicator pipe missing. Ventilation shaft filled with builders' rubble.

In the 1970s protesters clad in jump suits carried cardboard coffins and paper maché nuke warheads through the city centre. Banners said *Make Cardiff Nuclear Free*. Don't allow it. The target was CP1, the Welsh Office, seat of government nuclear policy in Wales. protesters sat on the steps and sang like the farmers and language protesters before them. Shared a common membership. There was a kinship between cymraeg and hill farming and keeping the grass radiation free. Police cleared everyone. Arrested some. Took away their leaflets. Didn't give them back.

Inspired by Adrian Mitchell poets met to decide on common action. Rise up. Walk to London. Fill the fountains with red paint. Pour metal glue in government door locks. Enter Trafalgar Square. Sit down.

To counter the fear of Soviet incursion and the prospect of burned streets full of Russian bears Cardiff Council allowed development of the Royal Ordnance Factory (ROF) at Llanishen. This place had made munitions during World War Two and was spread over a site that is currently occupied by Llanishen's Parc Ty Glas, the Tax Office, S4C, northern M&S and its retail friends, depots for stationery, breweries, gyms and indoor paintball. A section north of the railway was used to develop parts for Britain's A-bomb from the very outset of that project. Between 1961 and 1987 ROF expanded to employ more than 400 people producing non-fissile components for all UK warheads: free-fall V-force bombs, Polaris and Trident's virulent tips, battlefield nukes, things that glowed, hovered in unreal space, and ended the world when they fell.

Taking Caerphilly Road north to the crematorium, approaching the roundabout with the flower shops for memorial wreaths and heart-wrenched sprays, the factory sat left, glowing behind its chain link fences. In 1981 when the US decided to base cruise at Greenham and the women woke up, ROF Llanishen became at local target for protests, doc wearers, short hair, holding hands, singing. Not everyone could spend their lives for the next nineteen years in Berkshire. Instead they weekended here. ROF planted fast growing conifers. A dense green immediately inside the chain link. Hard to paint on, difficult to get through, impossible to climb.

As part of the end of Cold War fall-out Greenham was denuded of its 96 US Cruise in 1991, the weapons flown back to the Arizona deserts for destruction, no longer needed against a Soviet Union which did not now exist. The Greenham land was returned to the people in 2000 and the protesters left.

ROF Llanishen closed in 1997. Metallic Beryllium had been processed on site from 1961. 367,757 samples of soil and air had been taken at 101 local locations during those 36 years. All clear. Beryllium is used in missiles and inside nuclear reactors. Exposure to it causes acute pneumonitis, contact dermatitis, and respiratory failure. Officially not cancer although Cardiff has a cluster in its northern districts. Connected? Who can tell.

The fifteen acre site in the ownership of the Atomic Weapons Establishment was cleared in the early 2000s. Buildings were demolished. Slabs lifted and toxic drains dug out. Remains of depleted uranium and beryllium removed, taken by road and land buried, licensed and controlled but quietly, at Bedford and Oxford. Safety assessment carried out. Clipboard ticked. Safety goggles. Hard hat. The earth went out by road, trucked, so much hazard-free fly tip. Atomic buzz reducing. Remediation completed July 2001. Handed to developer 2002. Barratt. Renamed St James Mews. Unimaginative orange brick townhouses. Milestone Close. Jubilee Gardens. O'Leary Drive. In the downturn hard to shift. White lime on their perfect surfaces. Sun on their perfect roofs. Dancing atoms in their perfect dust.

In the Bay the Assembly argue UK policy on a new nuclear Trident. They talk in their blogs and their glass corridors. They have no power nor access for pressure but hold opinion like a wrench. Turn it. The clear reaches of our green land will stay that way. No Trident here. No shimmer or trace.

The Z berth at Roath Basin hosts visits by the nuclear fleet. Used to. Alongside Southampton, Liverpool, Gibraltar, Bermuda and Hong Kong. At the X berths at Devonport, Faslane and Barrow in Furness the Navy maintains it nuclear fleet. At the Z berths there are landfalls, war game rehearsals, civic visits. Operational recuperation, material re-supply and personnel changeover. *Resolution, Renown, Repulse, Revenge, Vanguard, Victorious, Vigilant, Vengeance, Swiftsure, Sovereign, Superb, Sceptre, Spartan, Splendid, Trafalgar, Turbulent,*

Trenchant, Tireless, Torbay, Tonypandy, Talent, Triumph. The last came in 1996. Sat for three days on the dock south of Crickhowell House. Sailors ashore in the Bay pubs. Mermaid Quay undeveloped. The whole area still a seedy, failing mess. The Z berth was closed as the Bay developed. But not abandoned. Emergency planning arrangements by local authority in progress pending reinstatement. If the nuclear leaked what would happen? How would the rads be measured? Where would they go? For how long would they seep?

All that remains today, bar an atomic clock at the University, are the beta emitting isotopes of carbon-14 and tritium, a form of hydrogen, processed for medical use at the white clear mirror-gated facility of Amersham International. This is north of the Glamorgan Canal Nature Reserve and Forest Farm and south of the motorway at Whitchurch. There is another radiation cluster here. High leukemia, says one research report. No incidence, says another. "No evidence to substantiate these claims…" says the First Minister. I cycle past, mud and green. Security inside their glass boxes. Radiation badges on their uniforms. The Cold War is over and the Cardiff air is clear but the rads are still around. Atomic continues.

TOP RANK

Billy said skip the black&reds and hearts and go only for the bombers. They'll last all night. They'll sell you out of a plastic bag. Inside jacket. I check the mens looking for a leather hat and a ten bob deal. But there's nothing. I'm walking down the slope into the Rank, bright Friday night, stamp on the back of my hand to get back in. This is 1965. The year Graham Bond made his *Sound of 65* hoochie coochie album and took on the Teds at the Cardiff Capitol. Chuck Berry was the star and the boys in their bright blue and pink drapes and drains, in from the valley backwoods, were screaming down anything that wasn't pure rock'n'roll or American. Mark Winter. Moody Blues. All booed off. Until Bond came on. A squat bomb of a man, one hand on the Hammond the other on the mellotron. Pork pie hat. Dark glasses. *Wade in the Water* like a wave of power. That silenced them.

In the Rank the basement dance floor spreads out like the insider of a liner. Polished wood, upholstered booths, tables screwed to the floor. Kids with suede desert boots, slim ties, tight lapelled Italian jackets. Women in short skirts, white faces, white boots, white lips, dark holes for eyes, hair flowing, every one of them, twist-era bee hives lost, now chasing the straight pure heart of Joan Baez. Above me on the ground floor is C&A Modes, clothing the new generation and most of it in action now in front of me. The store that sold you cord jackets with leather collars, trousers with slice pockets, bells and flares, beltless terylene hipsters, shirts in purple polka dot, colour like there hadn't been since 1939. The new world. Shimmering. I'd made the connection and was slowly gaining speed. The disco thrumming. McCoys. Georgie Fame. Manfred Mann. Someone on the dance floor doing that thing with their fingers. Pulling them down one after the other. *5-4-3-2-1*.

You'd get more blues here than rock, more hi-hat mod beat than pop. The disco used florescent strips that picked up the white lint on your shoulder and made your teeth gleam like torches. The mirror balls spun. Light splashing and slicing. Smoke hot air. Mojos working.

The Rank had started life in 1877 as Livino's Music Hall. Queen Street was still Crockerton, yet to be renamed in honour of the monarch's jubilee. The pillars of the East Gate still stood outside, back towards Boots. The place where the bears danced. The edge of Cardiff where the wannabes collected, where the soil tips mouldered, where the shanty of outlanders drawn by the town's increasing wealth had set their shacks. Wattle, walls of woven straw, held together by rotten rope.

Oswald Stoll, who owned Livino's, employed the architect Frank Matcham to turn his rag-bag hall into something worthy. It opened as the Empire Theatre in 1886. Was destroyed by fire in 1899. Rebuild by Matcham and reopened in 1900 as the Empire Palace. Capacity 1726 people. Sliding roof, wooden benches in the gods. Far more than you could ever get into the mod's Top Rank. Harry Houdini, Dan Leno, Vesta Tilley, Harry Tate, Albert Chevalier, Charles Coburn and Sir Harry Lauder all played on its stage.

The Empire became a cinema when film overtook theatre as the preferred entertainment medium of the masses. This was 1931. The place adopted the name Gaumont in 1954 when the Rank Organisation took over programming. Capacity 2820. More than the Millennium Centre. Ice creams, popcorn, peanuts, barley sugar, American hard gums. Kids stuff on Saturday morning. Jiving in the aisles when *Rock Around The Clock* was shown in 1956. Seats ripped and slashed when they played *Don't Knock The Rock* in 1957. Then suddenly, victim of market shrink and the demon TV, the last film was screened in 1961 and the theatre was demolished. C&A's rainbow clothing store was built in 1962. The basement was retained by Rank and run as a ballroom. A room for the holding of balls. The quaint pre-war nomenclature hovering on into revolutionary times. The drink is flying. The bombers are driving. The ballroom is leaping to *Louie Louie*. Mods like gyrating stick insects, every one of them smoking. Louie Louie, Louie Louie, oh baby me gotta go.

I came here at the start of 1964. Too young to know what any of this was really about but keen to learn. Top Rank were putting live bands into their shows. There was a revolving stage, idea borrowed from the London Palladium. On it was Alexis Korner and Blues Incorporated. Guitar, saxophones, dancing rhythm, powerhouse noise, melancholic blues. Not in the hit parade. Nowhere near. The whole deal with r&b was that it wasn't supposed to be a popular music. This was the place that hipster jazz had taken us. Outside tin pan alley, beyond the Cliff Richard hit machine, never the stuff of Hollywood films or teenage hops where they served soft drinks and everyone sat round the edge of the floor on pre-war chairs. The blues were full of big-legged mamas, mojos, and black cat bones. Rock me baby. Not dance with me but fuck with me. Caught that southbound train, rocked all night, until the dawn. There was a decoding of all this in the back pages of the *Melody Maker*. We all read that. Alexis Korner was the great white British pioneer[8].

I'd bought Korner's first album in Spillers, on the Hayes. *Ace of Clubs. R&B From The Marquee. How Long How Long Blues. I Want To Put A Tiger In Your Tank.* A sort of skiffle-era guitar with sax and amazing blues harmonica playing on top. Nothing like pop music at all. Nothing, actually, anything like the r&b of the British blues boom that would follow it. Purist. Off centre. Jazz-based. Immensely hard to get into. But the only thing available anywhere that had r&b on the label and that you could actually buy in distant provincial Cardiff. And here he was, Alexis and cigar, at Top Rank, Queen Street. No Cyril Davies, his ace harmonic player, formed his own band. No lead voice Long John Baldry, done the same thing. Instead Korner had doubled the sax line up putting in Dave Castle on alto alongside Dick Heckstall-Smith and adding black singer Herbie Goins. The music was a revelation. Early soul, call and response, British Stax. The way a lot things would eventually go.

Top Rank would hit its stride in the 80s and 90s as a venue for visiting bands. Almost anyone who eventually got to be anyone played here. The Who, Simple Minds, Thin Lizzie, Coliseum, Deep Purple, Squeeze, Killing Joke, Sex Pistols, U2, Dave Edmunds, Jeff Beck, Pink Floyd, Elvis Costello and the Attractions, Wreckless Eric. But in 65 it's still high school turning into streetlife, CND simmering, guys in suits and shiny shoes, a dress-code that stopped you from coming in if you looked beat or hip or rough. Beer hot and brown out of pumps with motors attached to them. Cigarette burns in the back of your jacket. Eyes with pupils reduced to dots and arms that jerked like your batteries were only making half a connection. Ice lights. Long walk anywhere always done at high speed. Seemed like that. Top Rank Top Rank. Had a record label named after it. Had to be good. And for a while it was.

But when new market forces took hold as the 1990s turned to the 2000s Top Rank began to dwindle. Audiences fell. C&A closed for redevelopment. Top Rank faltered and then Top Rank fell. When they knocked the building down in 2004 the outlines of the much earlier low-rise two story houses which once lined the street here emerged, briefly, vague shimmers of the long past. The new enterprise that emerged, right on site, Gaumont, Rank and Empire all swallowed, is new millennium forerunner Primark. Deeply cut-price clothing sold with all the chrome, perspex and 2010-glitter of the designer up market. Packed with more customers than ever came here dancing.

The draw of the £2.50 tee shirt and the £5.00 blue denim. Unequalled in space or time.

I go in to replicate my nervous foray here from 1965. The slope has been replaced by an escalator. No-one climbs in 2007. Up or down. You ride. In front of me is a youth in tee and check slacks. Winter outside. He has ink on both arms, scrolling his shoulders. He's pierced his ear lobes and inserted inch and half amber discs like a tribal African. The skin stretched around their outer edges like so much parcel tape. We ride down into lint and cotton heaven. Where the stage once was are rack upon rack of novelty pajamas. Sets with slogans across their fronts. *Game Over Goodnight. Lounge Loafer. Hangover Repair Kit. No 1 Daddy.* £6.00 a throw. In the women's section Primark are

doing 60s black wool coats for £30 and 60s print bow shift dresses for twelve. There's a sort of forty-five year cycle going here as the past keeps re-emerging into the present, subtly altered always, but redolent of the era on which it is based. Alexis Korner would have walked here with his cigarillo and his off key voice. 60s tight trousers. Couldn't do that now. Cigarillos thrown into outer darkness. Blues about as fashionable as Formica.

On Queen Street Plastic Mic Trevor is singing again from the goods doorway at Boots. Sinatra standards. The guy who paints himself white and doesn't move for eight hours has collected a big Saturday crowd. Four black guys are handing out Christian tracts. Amplified pan pipes. Man with a guitar and a practice amp. Girl with a violin. A new generation go by with little black dots for eyes. The world's still buzzing.

THE MARCHIONESS

Who would this be? Charlotte Hickman-Windsor, Marchioness of Bute, died 1800 – first wife of the first Marquis. Frances Coutts, Marchioness of Bute, died 1832 – second wife of the first Marquis. Lady Maria North, Marchioness of Bute, died 1841 – first wife of the second Marquis. Lady Sophia Frederica Christina Rawdon-Hastings, Marchioness of Bute, died 1859 – second wife of the second Marquis. Hon. Gwendolen Mary Anne Fitzalan-Howard, Marchioness of Bute, died 1932 – only wife of the third Marquis.

Augusta Mary Monica Crichton-Stuart, Marchioness of Bute, died 1947 – wife of the fourth Marquis. Lady Eileen Beatrice Forbes, Marchioness of Bute – wife of the fifth Marquis, died 1993. Maybe the first passenger ship, *Marchioness Of Bute*, from Newry to New York, 15 May 1850. Or the second, built for W.G. Morel and Company, launched 1906. Perhaps the Marchioness Of Bute Regal Pelargonium, black flowers fading out to purple. Half the world belongs to Bute.

The Marchioness Of Bute Brains tavern in Frederick Street, Cardiff. Demolished 1980 when the extension to Boots was built. All the streets around there went: Cross Street, Union Street, Frederick Street, Hills Terrace. The St David's precinct rose from their ashes turning Queen Street to Bridge Street into a maze of mall. Went in there recently, Boots, a different force in the land from how it used to be. I found the dispensary where the Marchioness's bar once was. There was a woman with a basket containing twenty-four bottles of cough linctus being questioned politely by white-coated dispensary staff. Upstairs, where the dances had so many attending the floor bowed, was thick with Boots christmas – ribbon, wrapping, calendars, oversize packets containing hand cream and mirrors, talc and deodorant, Simpson's soap, boxed fluffy toys.

Bute left his name like stately litter right across the city. His name, first name, last name, middle name, his titles, the names of his wives, his children, the manors of the family's Glamorgan estates, his properties in Scotland, his managers, his advisors, his engineers, his agents. Dumfries, Crichton, Mountstuart, Tyndall, Corbett, Sneyd, Clark, Collingdon. If you can't work out why the road you are in is called Ninian or Augusta or Colum or Lady Margaret then check the Bute family tree.

The pub was built in the early 1840s, named after the second Marquis[9] to begin with and then, when he remarried in 1845, changed to that of his wife. Lady Sophia, mother of John Crichton-Stuart, the third

Bute, the man who had Burges turn Cardiff Castle into a Victorian Disneyland. The pub was on the corner of Cross Street. Breweries were nearby. But then most of central Cardiff was near a brewery in the nineteenth century. Ragged men drank to stay alive. Covered with dust and dirt from manual toil.

No Walls, the weekly literary club and talking shop, used to meet in the upstairs bar. Poets, doggerel scribblers, versifiers. Even the barman wrote. As a guest, to provide non-provincial avant-garde literary fulfilment they invited the beat generation master George Dowden. In the late sixties there may have been fewer Cardiff pubs with sawdust on their floors but many of the clientele remained wrecked. Depended where you went, naturally, but down here, beyond Queen Street's Taff Vale, and where the paint flaked from porous wall, the working man still held court. Pint in a thick smooth-sided glass. Tieless, shirtless, unshaven, covered in earth or steel dust or coal.

Dowden[10] was an American exiled in Brighton. He was Allen Ginsberg's bibliographer. He'd published a great book, *Letters To English Poets*, in which he told poets Lee Harwood and Paul Matthews just how it all should be. Amanuensis, stylist, man with a beard, bard. Dowden arrived in the wake of other greats: eccentrics, experimentalists and sixties boundary pushers all. Revolutionaries and wild men. Poets who had the pulse beat at their fingertips. Adrian Henri, Alan Jackson, Brian Patten, Jeff Nuttall, C C Hebron, Barry MacSweeney, Chris Torrance, Jim Burns, Peter Mayer, Derek Telling, Bob Cobbing, Thomas A Clark. The Cardiffian Welsh were in awe. Wanting to know how it was on the beat pathways on the other side of the pond. Webb awake. Tom Earley taking notes. Herbert Williams sketching it out for the *South Wales Echo*. Rhydwen Williams writing it up for *Barn*.

Dowden had taken on Ginsberg's breath patterns. His lines went on for as long as they could be recited without drawing new breath. Slabs, chunks. They felt like prose poems. They were conversational, edgy talk, street talk, rich with Pound-like allusion, engaging, tale-telling, followers of the urban line.

He had the audience silence themselves, put a candle on each table, lit them, added incense. Had us Buddha-breathe, follow the air in and then back. Chanted. Om Kaviraj. Say your name. Say it loud. Breathe it out. Gregory, David, Geraint, Fred, Huw, Heather, Sam, Fran. People had come for poems. Not participation. Some of them

---

Bute Spam

3ute™ Place
Mo.unt Stuar2t $9uare
Sanqu4ar 3tree7
Cr.ic8ton H.ou3e
Jam4s $t.reet
Dum.8ries Pl.ace
Sop.5ia Gndsssss
GlossOp Terror
Nin.i.an Perk
Beaut $1r.44t
Be.wt Pk
3ute™ 3oa.d
B.6te Ea5t Duck
Enlarged Mo nu2ent

---

walked out. Give us Ginsberg someone shouted. George gave them Dowden. Not as revolutionary nor as famous but as timelessly American nonetheless.

No Walls put out a broadsheet bracketing him with Tom Kryss, da levy, Douglas Blazek and William Wantling. World gonna change soon. Just you watch. Charles Bukowski would have been there too but he hadn't discovered us yet.

In the street outside where the Marchioness's entrance once was is the south end of an air quality control station[11]. Above it the City's computer controlled information hoarding. *ST MARY STREET CLOSED Late Shopping Winter Wonderland WINDOWS LOADING.* Man with a hand drum and an amplified didgeridoo. Table selling *Socialist Worker.* Supporter on megaphone. Young. Still young. Been doing this since 1975. Twelve students in hip new tee-shirts chain themselves together, heads down. Free Burma they chant. Street preacher with Jesus on an easel waving the good book. Street preacher with a carry amp and a hand-held mic praising the Lord through rap. Oversized watches being sold from a trolley. £5.00 a throw don't bring it back. Drizzle. Crowds. Unabating noise.

I take Dowden home to Llandaff North where he can sleep on my couch. Train back to London tomorrow. Wants to leave here as fast as he came. Marchioness unreconstructed. Never to be. Do you remember it? I ask this of my friend Dave in the shiny 2007 smoke-free Discovery. What was there about it? Down at heel, he says. Smoke and dust. Full of rough men. If it ever got full at all.

CENTRAL HIGH RISE

I was supposed to do this from the sky. Check the shape of Cardiff's sprawl from the height of the clouds. A swoop across Google Earth with added air and lots of noise. But all that went down the pan when the plane I thought I'd lined up failed to arrive. So how else do you look at a city from above? You climb. And to do justice to the project you climb more than once. To facilitate it all I have invented Tall Buildings Day, recruited Jonathan Adams[12] as a fellow traveller and, in true psychogeographic style, planned a climb of as many of Cardiff's skyscrapers as possible. All in the same day if we can.

Wales has come late to sky scraping, much in the way that it has come late to the idea of cities themselves. There's never been an historical need. In Manhattan space was at a premium and the only way on was up. In Paris, where lateral space went on forever, Baron Haussmann's grand design was not to be blurred by the addition of height. The city would resist. Still largely does. London spiked the skies when it needed to. Built a miniature America in Canary Wharf. But for generations Cardiff never got much higher than the industrial age six-floor stand-off between Solomon Andrews and James Howells as they developed the St Mary Street east side. A taller Cardiff structure could sink into the alluvial subsoil, dropping slowly through porous tide-filled shales. Why take the risk?

It took a century, almost, for things to move on. The Gas Board's mirror-sided cube next to the rail line at the southern end of Churchill Way was perhaps the first break with low and dirty. Snelling House. Ten shining stories[13]. But the Newport Road Julian S. Hodge building looking like a fifties take on how Corbusier might do it was the first real Cardiffian point at the clouds. Cardiff the city, Cardiff the capital. In the 1970s, slowly spiking itself, sixteen stories high, out of the gloom.

I meet Jonathan outside Capital Tower just as the fire drill kicks in. Hundreds of the uniformly young are streaming in coffee-carrying, fag-smoking lines to congregate around the water fountain on Kingsway. Capital Tower, once the hated Pearl Building, now houses Admiral Insurance's call centre, Welsh success story. FTSE listed. Recession survivor. CEO a face on TV. They'll sell you any kind of motor policy you want. But not right now.

The building, at eighty metres and twenty-five stories tall, is both Cardiff's and Wales' highest. It is constructed[14] over the ruins of Greyfriars Monastery (1284). Most of that hardcore has been skipped off. In the wall next to reception they've set a stone which came from the remains of Greyfriars House. 1582 it claims hopefully, amid the present day marble and leather.

As we rise in the fast lift in the company of Sian who works for building management, Jonathan is telling me that he's never designed a tall building. Before the recession he was working on plans to redevelop the Sherman Theatre in Senghenydd Road and for the build to be paid for by selling the air space above. Twenty-two stories of city centre living, apartments within sight of City Hall. Forget about TV. Take the elevator down for handy live drama. Like almost all other speculative builds on hold now. The theatre redevelopment still happening but slowed.

Who else is in this place? We climb through their floors like ghosts – Crown Prosecution Service, Gaunt Francis Architects, Elephant (an Admiral nom de plume), The Law Society, NSPCC Cymru, Cory Sports, Cable & Wireless, Portman Travel. Staff café on the penthouse floor. We arrive almost instantly. No ear pop dislocation. Lifts make a building, says Jonathan. Good ones have loads.

Reaching the actual roof has affinities with the way most of us get into our domestic loft spaces. A clamber up concrete service stairs, yellow Slippery Surface notices, then a pull-down vertical metal ladder with a flap at the top. This one is made of mesh and designed to keep out the pigeons. Sky's blue. No wind. The roof, addled with phone masts and relay dishes, has the feel of a domestic felt flattie – low pools of water, a seeping of moss, occasional green sedum, small clouds of gnats. The view, however, is something else. Cardiff unadulterated, unmasked, untabulated, uncompressed, unrolled. Built beneath trees, filled with green spaces, squashed between the Cefn Onn ridge and the Severn estuary. Dotted with the white of higher structures but mostly grey slate roofed low. Steam coming off Celsa on the edge of the Bay water. The Castle, green manicured, walls polished and mended like it was about to be put up for sale. The Millennium Stadium with the new Ninian Park beyond like white crustaceans. Leckwith's green forest in the distance. The centre an untidy mass of pre-recession crane and construction. Cardiff's radials – Lloyd George going south and the red King Edward VII running north, looking like someone had genuinely planned them. On a good day we're told you can see Weston, Bristol, China and then bits of Venus and sightings of Mars. I don't doubt it at all.

The growing Cardiff high-rise scape that surrounds us is mostly rendered in white. Jonathan tells me that planners want to see a larger colour palate in use. Blue, gold, red, green. A city of coloured hats and shirts. Are we taller here than anywhere else in Wales? Sadly, no longer. BT's Stadium House has a pinnacle mast on the roof that goes higher. Swansea's Oceangate at 107 metres is taller and that will soon be beaten by Cardiff's Bay Pointe at 123. If it's built. It's an opportunist game. Developers get planning and then add extra stories if they think they can be readily sold. Well that's what they used to do. The future is now wobbly uncertain.

The Pearl Building was built by Sir John Burnet in 1969 and based on the earlier Alison and Peter Smithson Economist Tower in London (1962). Its sheer bulk, its modernist vertical lines and chamfered angles were anathema to terrace-living Cardiffians. But that was then. The city has shaken itself many times since. Views change. The Pearl's transformation into Capital Tower in

2002[15] with the addition of uniform blinds to all windows, blue film to the glass, a new entrance canopy and access steps plus the sweeping away of bulky plantings to the front have largely worked. The opinions of locals have been similarly updated. Mass change to almost everything now standing to the south of here has reduced Pearl-hatred to memory. We love the lines of concrete. We relish the glitter. We want the skies.

Going back down is like riding an elevator in corporate America. The business suited carrying files. Technician in overalls, earphones in, wrench in hand. Call centre workers with Mohicans. Women with discrete tattoos. Document trolley pushers enter on one floor and leave on another. Life in the air. Hardly anyone goes the whole way down.

We walk back up Newport Road, almost to within touching distance of Longcross Court, the development on the site of medieval preaching cross that once stood here. This is the south end of Heol y Plwcca, present day City Road. Its name a testament to Cardiff's industrial rise. Here we are on the oblong roof of the thirteen-story Eastgate House. Built in 1969 and known then as Heron House (after the development corporation that financed it). At 46 meters its reach may be beaten but its access to the sky is still superb.

Like many of Cardiff's earlier high reachers the building has been reclad and given a sharp aluminium canopy housing a TV embellished reception. Sky news on both screens when we pass. Sport and business. Decline in progress in both camps. Eastgate houses a mix of operations you'd only ever register if you had to use them. Arcane names that underpin the city. Adler Manufacturing. Coface Credit Management UK. Ethnic Business Support Programme Ltd. Biofusion plc. Capita Symonds and Capita Architecture over four floors. Jonathan smiles as we pass through. He works there.

On top, accessed courtesy of Gary, building supervisor, who has pulled down another extending loft ladder and

opened another ceiling hatch, the view of the city core is blocked by the long glass wall of Brunel House[16], the Capital Tower, beyond it, with its blue and green cubed grid of windows, looking like a giant version of an early computer game. The lost and reinvented Cardiff district of Tredegarville spreads below us. This was an estate of grand houses developed by the Morgan family[17] of Tredegar House from 1857 onwards. The Rhymney Railway's Cardiff Parade station stood to the west, Roath Road Wesleyan Methodist on the corner of Newport Road to the east. Both structures now lost. The district is used by dentists, chiropractors, sports injury specialists.

To the north Cardiff runs out under trees towards the white highs of the Heath Hospital and beyond the asbestos-riddled eighteen floors of the Llanishen HMRC[18]. Government Buildings, officially. Forever hated, like the Pearl. For what they are, where they are, how they pollute, how they look. Plans to demolish have been proposed by think tank, the Cardiff Policy Forum. But no one has listened yet.

Around us Newport Road flows like a restrained Wilshire Boulevard. Its development characterised as undisciplined by John Newman[19] in 1995. A man who dislikes the future. The Leslie Halliwell[20] of structures. A lover of tasteful plot and disciplined dialogue, of stone and tradition. Position and past. And he's right, often, but not all the time.

THE MEDIEVAL HIGH

How much nearer to God could we get if we built structures that rose up to meet him? Castellated towers, soaring spires. To medieval Cardiffians the fortified keep on its mound at the Norman Castle would have been a dominant skyline feature. Higher than anything they lived in. But the tower of St John's, the parish church of lords and of masters, rising straight from the barely drained Cardiff subsoil, would have been a worthy competitor with its crenellations seeming to catch the clouds. Erected in 1473 the tower is as old as almost anything extant in the twenty-first century city. The architect was William Hart, according to Rice Merrick's 1578 report, written when the octagonal cages and open battlements of the top were still pretty new. They've been worn by weather, rebuilt, cleaned, remoulded, strengthened, potched, bodged, remade and refixed many times since. They burst skywards in an ascendance of pinnacle on pinnacle, gargoyles at each angle, the water-worn leaves, buds and flowers of the ancient crocketing everywhere.

It's still Tall Building Day when the Captain of the Tower, Bob Hardy, meets us. A Eucharist service ministered by the Rev Keith Kimber and attended by a handful of the faithful is in Friday lunchtime progress. We climb the 149 tower steps up a grey spiral of Lias limestone ashlar in decorous silence. Doors are small, steps narrow, the passage slim. The past was a tiny place. Bob rings bells. There are eleven in this tower. Ten change-ringing bells, one that tolls the time. We climb in the space through which a thousand ringers have moved. The space that the religious past of Cardiff transited. The priests and the martyrs. The clockmakers and clockmenders. The righteous and the rich. The pious and the poor. Officials and servants. The lord and the ordinary. The Latin, the English, the Welsh. They've left the track of their hands on the stained smooth stone of the tower walls.

Bob's talk is of bells and peals and the sounds they make. Grandsire Caters, Plain Bobs, Stedman Caters, a Black Sheep Surprise Royal. It's a world I had no idea I was entering. There's a board on the wall of the ringing chamber that celebrates the Stedman Caters peal of 1954. It took 3 hours and 11 minutes then to ring all the changes. Slow by modern standards, says Bob. We'd shave a few minutes off that.

Each bell has a different sound and the sequences in which they are rung are annotated as music. Columned like the codes that operate computers. I knew someone in school who did this, says Jonathan. Sat between lessons poring over his notebook of listed figures. Can you remember his name, asks Bob? Ringers know ringers. Andrew Bull. Yes, he's one of ours. Bob looks him up and there he is in the list. Still ringing after all these years. Bells are a Freemasonry.

We sit on old wooden benches that have been here for decades. We are surrounded by the appurtenances of a world we've long left. Gold lacquered signboards engraved with the names of long-departed ringers and the peals they achieved. Paul W. Thomas's peal of 5040 Stedman Triples in 1975. Bro. W.B. Kynaston's 1954 peal of 5079 – 'The First Peal To Be Rung In Wales By A Band Of Freemasons'. M. Jack Pryor's 5003 Grandsire Caters in 1964. All celebrated on individual boards. And then the history of it all on a much larger centrepiece which lists peals that go back to Victorian times. To the Glory of God. Of course. But nowhere does it actually say that.

Why do they ring? To call the faithful. To mark the turning of the world. In 1714 to celebrate the coming of King George I to England and the capture of Savannah from the Spanish. In 1767 to welcome to Cardiff the brothers of George III. In 1790 to mark the fact that the town elders had walked the boundaries. In 1794 to honour the British fleet's defeat of the French. In 1797 to mark a victory over the Dutch. In 2000 to see in the millennium. Did they ring for the peace accord in Ireland, victory in the Falklands, the withdrawal from Basra, the winning of the 2008 Grand Slam, the defeat of Centreplan, the coming of the broad-gauge, the draining of the canal, the city's move from Labour to Liberal in 2004, the end of those great city fixtures, David Morgans and then Woolworths? No one recalls.

The bells themselves date from 1708 when the tower had six installed. These were increased to eight in 1814 and then to ten in 1893. They are engraved with the names of the men who cast them and occasionally with aphoristic verses. When they malfunction, they are replaced. 'My sound is good my shape is neat twas Bayley cast me so complete o 1768 o' is on the side of one of earliest.

In the clock room, locked to keep out those who might fall through floors or attempt to make the thing ring when it shouldn't, we view the mechanism built by Gillett and Johnston. The service record, hand done with a biro that is running out of ink, is tacked onto the back of the door. Gillett and Johnston's phone number is given in case of need. Still available, in Croydon, to fix a slipped spring or a broken cog. The original two-hundred-year-old mechanism is in St Fagans.

On top, Cardiff peered at through the Oolitic limestone battlements, is a land of slate roofs and skylights, of fire escapes and graffiti, of places where staff go to smoke and sunbathe, of pools of water and stretches of moss and sedum, and the ventilation mechanisms that extract stale air from the

CLOCK ROOM

THERE HAS BEEN A CLOCK IN THE TOWER FOR OVER 200 YEARS. THE PRESENT CLOCK IS MODERN, REPLACING AN OLDER ONE THAT IS NOW AT THE WELSH FOLK MUSEUM, ST. FAGANS. WE REGRET THAT THE PUBLIC CAN NOT BE ADMITTED TO THIS ROOM.

city's lungs. Close-up the tower looks fragile, held together by metal bands, wrapped with lightning conductor, sat on by crows. The highest pinnacle is surmounted by a golden ball on top of which is perched a golden cockerel. The church itself, running back eastwards from the Tower, has an aisle at least four degrees out of true. To confuse the devil, says Bob. Crap construction, says Jonathan. Building inspection back then was an emerging art.

Below us slick Cardiff shops in the sun. Despite the downturn more stores opening soon. It's what we do.

Bay Scape
Bay Pointe
Bay Pint
Glass Needle
Glass Spindle
Glass Spring
Tower One
Tower Two
Tower Three
Glass Necklace
Glass Arm
Block T
Block B
Mizzen
Genoa
Spinnaker
Burj Al Cymro
Abraj Al Berman
Heritage Gateway
Tredegarville World Financial
The Kardif Spire
The Abertawe Beater
Caerdydd 101

High Rise
Could Have Been

PARK STREET

You come to Park Street when you need to. Most don't. Most Cardiffians can't even tell you where it is, jammed there between Westgate Street and the river. To the north were once the open reaches of the Arms Park. South was Temperance Town, Cardiff's lost district. Temperance Town, just the sort of name you'd like on your birth certificate. It was built by teetotaller Jacob Matthews on land leased from the alcohol-hater, Colonel Wood. There were no pubs, no bars, no back rooms selling penny ale. There was a temperance hall on the corner of Havelock Street and two churches and then housing for several thousand law abiding Christian souls. The area thrived from 1860 until Cardiff Corporation dispersed it by bulldozer just before the Second World War. Was this demolition forward-thinking slum clearance from a council ahead of its time? Could have been. But wasn't. The Great Western Railway's splendid new Cardiff General Station needed better approaches. Temperance Town, erected on land reclaimed from the straightened Taff and infilled with town trash, lacked architectural merit. Its inhabitants were poor and offended the eyes of arriving travellers. They had to go.

The city was building new estates on Sloper Road and in Tremorfa and Ely. Cardiff was growing. Temperance Town's inhabitants were easily dispersed. Originally there were plans to use the cleared space for an exhibition hall, a conference centre and a vast underground car park. But they never happened. Instead the Council built a bus station. In this place, councillors planned, no poverty would ever be seen and arriving rail travellers would encounter only the glory of the affluent with no sightings on any occasion of locals addled by drink, destitution, violence or drugs. There'd be no fast boys with tattoos, no can holders, and no homeless with blankets on their shoulders. Wood Street, the district's central artery, got a 1950s-styled Terminal Building along its southern side. At one end was that renowned addition to Cardiff's café culture, Big Asteys. Of small Asteys there was never a trace. To the north was St David's House. Chinese restaurants, Pound Stretcher, Hyper Value, cheapo cheapo, and offices where pensioners could get passes to ride for free on the buses.

By the time Jonathan and I get here the Park Street world has been totally transformed. Havelock Street's Thomson House, once home of the *Western Mail* and *Echo*, has been flattened. The diggers are still

in action demolishing the boundary walls. Loose warning tape flutters from the corners. I feel like the H.G. Wells's traveller stopping briefly to peer from the seat of the time machine. Since 1860 the Territorial Army Drill Hall, blocking Park Street's run into the river, has been built, demolished, built again and then demolished once more. Temperance Hall has fallen.

But Southgate House remains as does the County Court, standing to the north. This is the anti-church. Hall of divorce. Fill in the form, get the certificate. Sit shaking in front of a beer in the Royal Hotel wondering where it all went wrong. Where the saw mill was and the well and the timber yard they built the Empire Pool in 1958 and then demolished it again in 1998. (See *The Festival of Britain Steam Rooms* on p.62 for more). Millennium Plaza, low-rent steel-clad cinema, and the south end of the Millennium Stadium were erected instead. Fix your eyes on this stuff. It doesn't stay long.

We are actually tackling Stadium House. Tallest building in Wales if you measure to the top of its roof antenna. Not quite as high as Capital Tower if you don't. This place was once the site of the GPO's pre-STD hand-managed telephone exchange. Lines of operators wearing headphones handling customers. Linking the world. An early call centre with bakelite headphones and circular dials. Press Button A caller. And so your money would vanish, never to return. Today it's BT's offices, engineer control centre and reserve data farm. I came here a month ago and asked how visitors might access the top. You won't get up there, mate, said the tattooed receptionist, looking like a boxer. Shook his head in pity. Gave me a number to ring. This was BT, world-leader in telecommunications. When I rang no one ever picked up.

Stadium House was extended and completely reclad in 2002. Next to the white arms of the Mars Lander-like Millennium Stadium it resembled a 60s concrete throwback. Cardiff needed new. Visitors arriving at the Central Station would be appalled. The spirit of

Temperance Town once again. BT employed Percy Thomas to add a glass-fronted entrance and then Parsons Brinckerhoff to over-clad the whole structure in gleaming twenty-first century white. Ace card was the addition of a sky-top array of microwave dishes and the hiding of these behind a necklace of lights. The headband, the crown, the revolving restaurant, the  spinning disc. It glows brightly on the Cardiff night skyline, topped with a forty-two meter spire carrying not an angel but a red light on its god-reaching head.

Nigel has fixed the climb. A BT manager. Friend of a friend. How the world gets on. Jonathan is late, caught up in a Design Commission presentation and then the wonders that are the Railway Station Car Park. You can't park here without opening an account he's told. He rings the number. Quotes his card. Pays an arm and a leg. Then has to key in his reg number. For D press 1, for F press 3, for the number 4 press 5. Half-way through he presses the wrong digit. Communication breakdown. Has to start all over again.

We meet in the front lobby where three security guards eat sandwiches against a backdrop of alarm panels, Health and Safety notices and clipped clip boards that have to be ticked. We go up with Andy Williams, the Audit and Compliance Manager, who is roof trained. Health and Safety rules. Health and Safety chants and sings. How tall is this structure I ask. 15 floors. In the penthouse suite are the staff who manage engineer call-outs. Two screens on each desk. Shirt-sleeves. Headphones. Views out of the windows make Cardiff small and incredibly near. Hi-res detail of the Castle seen from the south. The Beijing Olympics styling of the new arcades of St David's 2 and a full-screen close-up of the Millennium Stadium roof. We can see the stands but not the pitch. Can hear the crowds but never see the ball. In the old Arms Park days, Andy tell us, staff would work Saturdays just to be able to come up here and watch the game. No longer. You see people out there sunbathing sometimes. Flat out on the moving metal roof. Jonathan and Andy break off into a discussion of the ways in which grass pitches might be better managed. Andy favours the American model where, when not in use, the entire field is rolled out of the stadium to stand in the sun. Wary of the cost of Welsh space Jonathan counters with a plan to lift the pitch and haul it up until it reaches the roof. It could fold along the centre line, he suggests. Rise on wires and then unfold again. A Mars Lander, again, beneath the open sky. Instead the grass browns and bogs. Gets replaced pallet by pallet with new growth. Trucked in, hammered down.

The western side of the fifteenth floor is protected by a machine that won't let you pass until your iris has been scanned and recognised. This is the data farm, a reserve for the main operation at BT's Internet Data Centre down in the Bay[21]. BT run Buynet, a credit card clearing operation used by Bosch, Cineworld, O2, Eckoh and Venda. This is the kind of commercially sensitive data that can't be left on a laptop on a train.

Next are the service floors and the roof. Full of service gear, lift housings, ventilation pipes and heat ducts. Up a further metal-runged ladder, is the famous necklace. 78 metres high. Not a revolving restaurant after all but a galvanised-steel assembly housing a mesh of dish and relay and fronted by lights. A collar. A glittering tiara. An international space station tied to earth. The painted mild-steel mast rises through its centre like Strongbow's arrow. Our long distance neighbours complain about this, Andy says. The lights keep them awake at night.

Descending the rocket-fast elevator my ears pop. Only building that's happened in so far. Stadium House. Ten out of ten for looks. Nine for lifts. Two for paranoia. We ought to love you, BT. Right here you look great. You used to be ours. Now you are not.

A CITY OF MALLS

It's a day full of smoke. Ray Smith[22] and I are in the Moulders Arms. We've come up from the Cambrian via the Greyhound and the Salutation. Ray calls this a cultural odyssey. He wants to talk about literature, about writing, about Wales. I've begun my small magazine, *second aeon*. A mix of avant garde and old garde, poetry and pungency, amid the darkness of the city. The *Echo* has featured me as one of the new white hopes. I have no idea what that means. Ray thinks I might be onto something and is determined to join in. He's promised that we'll meet people from the world of drama: actors, writers, directors. He's bandied names – Ray Handy, Christine Pritchard, Olwen Rees. There'll be a National Theatre soon, boy, he tells me. He's read Dedwydd[23]'s *Black Book* and agrees with every dramatic word. We'll take over the New and we'll make Wales sing. As if it didn't already. He's fulsome and fervent. He pulls hard on his beer.

Ray is an actor in the Richard Burton mould. Same considered speech, same cool good looks. And like Burton he too is a writer. I've done poems, roaring things, Anglo-Welsh poems that'll burn your socks off. I'll let you see them. I'm finishing them now. Just a few burnishes left to do. I never see a thing.

Out back someone begins playing a cornet and a banjo joins in. St Louis Blues. In the streets around us – Union Street, Barracks Lane, Frederick Street, Paradise Place – houses are already being deserted. They're boarded up ready for slum clearance. It's the early seventies and Cardiff is getting a conscience. Reconstruction has been delayed for too long. The city is beginning to demolish its back-to-backs, its unsanitary hovels, its houses with walls like J cloths and roofs like string vests. You like this, Ray asks me? He means the jazz. I shake my head. Not really. I'm into the Yardbirds. Rhythm and blues. You know. He does not. I want to talk to him about how I, too, might join the world of directors, lights, and people applauding but am thwarted. A woman with a blonde beehive and big, rattly, plastic bracelets sits at the next table and asks Ray for a light. Attention gone.

The whole of this area south of Queen Street, the heart of the expanded city, will soon become a vacant lot. It's an area that has housed most of the immigrants from Ireland and England and the outer reaches of Wales, those who have provided the labour for a century of capital-building. Live near the job, but now to be moved on.

Over the years the Council have considered many solutions to the problem of redevelopment (see p.10 in this book's introduction for a belt through some of the more far-reaching proposals). It has ended up now with a smaller (in the scale of things) but still pretty dramatic knocking down of most of the urban centre. This gave the stores along the south side of Queen Street the space to move back and then back again. Cardiff suddenly had shopping at a range and depth never imagined possible before. A land of wonder for those who had lived through first the war and then its economic aftermath of falter and lack.

In 1982 the Heron Corporation, in conjunction with a consortium of major retailers, opened the St David's Shopping Centre – Cardiff's first shopping mall. And, if you discount the covered market and the Edwardian arcades which link Duke Street with High Street and St Mary Street with the Hayes, gave the first totally rain-free shopping experience of size in Wales. The whirl of life and drink and jazz had been swept away. Ray had gone on to fame and fortune as Spikings in *Dempsey and Makepeace* and as Charlie Norris in the BBC adaptation of Kingsley Amis's *Old Devils*. The National Theatre had not been built[24]. I had not joined in.

St David's, the mall, was a new way of doing things. When it opened the papers were full of articles praising the glories of this sparkling cultural experience, how the range of goods on offer was unmatchable, how it was clean and endlessly bright, how you could walk in winter without a coat from Park Place to the Hayes, from St John's Square to Charles Street. When the purpose-built concert hall opened a year later, how you could stroll from James Bond at the Queen Street Odeon to Beethoven at St David's Hall. Did you need special shoes to walk the marble floors? No. But that didn't stop some retailers from suggesting that you did.

In 2008, Ray dead 17 years and me still to write my first play, I try to track the old routes. The Mall does not mirror former street patterns in any way. The land has been excavated to well below the depth of Victorian construction. A whole surface has been lost. The Moulders Arms was rebuilt in 1906 and had a separate ladies toilet installed in 1943. The city records tell us that. Little else. There might have been a mark somewhere in all the new build showing its location. But it wasn't famous enough. So there's not.

The Mall's polished walkways have names. St David's Way. Cathedral Walk. Town Wall North. History hangs on only in the engravings along some of those walkways showing where the town wall once ran. Shoppers trek across it in their thousands. The past flickers in memory, do we want it anywhere else?

This place is not the street. Mall life is sanitised. There are no street sellers, marching bands, anarchists, political protesters, drinkers, bikers, skate boarders, horses, roller bladers, preachers,

tract distributors, dogs, leafle-teers, sandwich board men, peddlers, buskers, dancers. No charity junkers. No hot doggers. No flower pushers. No fortune tellers. No rap bands. No sunglass shifters. No balloon sellers. No bubble makers. No pan pipe Peruvians in Red Indian feath-ers. No men with guitars and street amps. In the mall life is retail. Commerce in its clean clothes shines.

The Centre Director is Steven Madeley, a bike man from Nottingham. He came here in the 1980s to study pharmacy and liked the place enough to return. He currently lives in Cowbridge and daily cycles the 18 miles into the city and then the 18 back. In his spare time he competes on two wheels at a national level. Velodromes. Helmets. Lycra. Carbon pro-rocket shoes. He has that wiry look of the super-fit, a man in a suit who, if he saw a shop lifter making a break could certainly catch him up.

We're not keen on the word *mall*, he tells me, we like to follow Cardiff tradition and think of these places as arcades. We're in the Centre management offices up above Debenhams. From the walkways on the roof outside here you can look down through the glass onto St David's Way. Observe its carefully orchestrated mix of curved bench, plant island, and storefront. The walkways are being re-laid with Yana limestone ready for integration with the vast St David's 2 opening to the south. Steven will manage both complexes. St David's is a joint venture between Land Securities and Capital Shopping Centres. Money drives. This is how retail works. St David's attracts more than twenty million customers annually with at least a million per week visiting just before Christmas. A lot of feet along its shining floors. Cardiff – the megastore capital. Cardiff – a real rival to the UK's other cities. If they offer any residual competition then St David's 2 will certainly see them off.

Steven rattles statistics from memory. 400,000 square feet in this complex. Another 1,000,000 to be added. 60 stores here. Another

110 in SD2. 23 restaurants. 1500 staff now. 4000 next year. He estimates that around three-quarters of a billion people have walked through his complex since it was first built.

Are the other Cardiff malls your rivals, I ask. I'm using that M word again. I'm referring to the Capitol Centre and the adjoining Queens Arcade which has an entrance built into the old Glamorgan Canal tunnel. Steven nods. But naturally we co-operate. We try to. Retail works like this. You need to cosy right up to your commercial competitors. Best place to open a new shoe shop is always right next to an existing one. You can't really tell where the boundary between St David's and the Queen's Arcade is, unless you are looking. The shopping experience is paramount never the architecture.

The Centre is a broad church, he tells me. We like to encourage the quirky among the corporate. Shops selling juice and harps next to the names everyone recognises. Mothercare. Boots. Miss Selfridge. Marks and Spencer. Footfall is vital. The whole centre is geared towards increasing that. It's private land, a fact that many Cardiffians do not realise. This means that the Centre decides who comes in and who stays out. No alkies. Plenty of the retired. The time rich drift through here soaking up the calm and the warmth. A group of retired Maltese meet daily on the benches to talk and pass the hours. If you come in here with a samba band in tow then security will ask you to leave. With discretion, of course. Security is strong. Everything is covered by cameras good enough to tell if you've shaved that day or not. Interference with the shopping experience is not tolerated. Walk don't run. Softly drift. This is the future about which J.G. Ballard warned.

Not that there have not been confrontations. Some rubbing up against the weird is inevitable anywhere. Men coming in naked with their clothes in a carrier. Political protesters. Rastas with ghetto blasters. Loud shoppers proclaiming their inalienable rights. All subservient here. They are asked to leave. And if they won't then without fuss bundled.

But why St David's? The saint never came here. Left no mark. Made no converts in the lands where now stands the nation's capital. Wouldn't the Bute Centre be better? Or the Temperance Town Arcades. The Newtown Malls. The Sam Haman Shopping Experience? *St David's* has the better Welsh resonance. Being Welsh is important. We have women in national dress on stilts handing out welsh cakes on our national day. We might soon engrave the anthem into the walkways, says Steven. Being Welsh is good for trade. Good to see that they've worked that out at last.

I leave the way I came, past Jones The Bootmaker, Phones 4U, Crouch the Goldsmiths, Claire's, Warehouse and Clarks. I've no idea of the official name for the walk I'm using. Instinct guides me to the open air. Like airports the Centre offers mild disorientation and an enveloping warmth to hold onto its myriad visitors. They blow like dandelions along the well lit, well ordered passages. They are encouraged. They smile. They return. Now the coal's gone and the steel is going shopping is a manageable replacement. Latte and wild landscape. Fashion and fine beaches. Credit cards and crags. The new Wales. For a while.

CASTLE

Open Google Earth and key in *Cardiff* and you'll arrive right at the main gates. True town centre. The city's geographic core. The Romans thought so too, and the Normans, and the Butes. On Google Earth you can see this council castle in all its roof-top glory. Satellite shot taken some time in 2006. The banks behind the south Roman wall fully excavated, yellow construction crane in-situ, the new eight million pound interpretation centre half built, a building site of historical depth and endless turmoil.

Local authorities do not make good commercial operators. In the long past when I studied the subject a discreet strand of my Municipal Administration postal correspondence course[25] was called *Local Authority Trading and Why This Does Not Work*. Trading involves risk. The recompense for taking risk is reward. Yet reward does not return to the local authority risk taker. It vanishes into central funds. The risk taker therefore does not bother. Cardiff Castle, since it was given to the City by the John Crichton Stuart, the fifth Marquis of Bute in 1947, has belonged to Cardiff Council. For fifty dark years a millstone. But now, in the new, clean and destination city of the third millennium, the beginnings of an asset. The Interpretation Centre opened in 2008. Visitor numbers are already up.

Before the Romans came here in AD55 what existed? Did the invaders found the city? Was it they, building their forts where the Castle now is, who encouraged defeated Silurians to cluster below their stockade's protection? The wooden shacks and lean-tos and fishermen's wattle and daub crowding the well-defended southern walls. Rough habitations that would bend through time to become the cottages of Duke Street and the houses of High Street and the foundries and slaughter houses of Womanby. The High Corner House. The Westgate. The stable blocks. The engine house. The buildings on Broad Street and Smith Street and Duke Street. St Piran's Chapel. The Glove and Shears. The Red Lion. The Ship on Launch.

According to the *Ravenna Cosmography* the Romans might have called this place Tamium. The *Antonine Itinerary* suggests that it was Bovium. Both names could be fantasy. The *Ravenna Cosmography* is an eighth century listing of world place names compiled by an anonymous Italian cleric. The *Antonine Itinerary* is a third century register of stations and distances along the roads of the Roman Empire. The routes are there but the precise locations they mark are open to dispute. Was Bovium the fort itself or a way marker down the road near Queen Street Station? Was Tamium Caerdydd? Or the name of the river? Or was it something the scribing cleric simply misheard? In *Real Cardiff*, the 2002 motherlode, I suggested that they are all wrong and that Cardiff should, in fact, be called Roath. *Rath*, Irish-origin, means fort. Hill fort of the pre-Roman iron age. One by the Taff, another on its mound in the centre of Roath.

John Edwards agrees. He's from that district. Roath born and bred. The name has a ring that *Cardiff* does not. When *Real Cardiff* first appeared I had a lot of calls about this. People suggested that if we were going in for renaming then a far better one for the city would be

Llanrumney. A name of which we could be proud. An academic wrote to support calling the capital Butetown. A difficult connotation, I thought. Someone else wanted to know that since I apparently had these abilities could I rename Rhoose as The Tony Curtis International Airport. Beyond the powers. That place looks like ending up being called something like the

Charlotte Church Air Hub. Best place in the city to drink long yellow pints of cool lager at 7.30am and then fly on twenty-four hour partying to Ibiza. Cardiff, the city that now doesn't, engaging with the world that never did. Sleep, that is.

John Edwards has just finished a twenty-year post heading conservation at the Castle. He's the man around whom most of the changes we can currently see have swung. Interpretation centre, exhibition, restaurant, deeply excavated basement soon to house the Regimental Museum[26], uncovered Roman galleries, walkways running both atop the walls and underneath. The late Lord Mayor, Phil Dunleavy's much-loved moulded plastic mural of city life[27] thankfully now half removed. The medieval earth ramparts dug away and carted off.

To build anew in this place required CADW authorisation for the excavation, the recording of the archaeology, the collection of uncovered artefacts and then the disposal of the remains. Dig it up, catalogue it, take a photo, then lorry it to the dump. It's a way of allowing development and ancient past to co-exist but it's tough on future generations where new archaeological techniques may come into play. New ways of teasing out the past's lost details are now impossible. When they invent the machine that can listen to stones and hear something of what they once heard it won't work here[28]. What's dug out, and to judge by the Google Earth image that's quite a lot, has been carted off.

What did the archaeologists find? Amazing things, it turns out. Post holes showing habitation predating the arrival of the Romans. Proof that something existed before the Mediterranean invaders got here. Some place with a funny name that didn't sound anything like Cardiff. Wooden shafts, flint tools, coarse pottery, a fifteen-metre line of stake holes – evidence of a fence or enclosure. Hundreds and hundreds of sheep bones. Roman coins from all periods including a collection of more than six hundred in the remains of an iron box. Someone's hoard. Evidence of

a fifth Roman fort. A medieval kiln. Peacock tiles. Ram's head jugs.
Wooden tools. Buttons. Buckles. Excavation courtesy of the
Glamorgan Gwent Archaeological Trust.[29] Examples, with photos,
listed on the web. Might have been worth doing after all.

The history of the Castle is actually one of dig and redig. Build and
excavate. Add and remove. Over the centuries most owners have had
a go at instigating change. The shire hall once stood inside the walls.
The Romans had barracks and bath houses. Animals were kept here.
Iron was worked. Walls and roofs came and went. Given the amount
of earth that has been dug up and moved around in the green space
between the Keep and the Black Tower it is surprising that anyone
has been able to discern the site's history at all. But they have.

John points up the complexity of the process, the need to conserve
not only the past but the past's own attempts at conservation. The
third Marquis, the Catholic fantasist, the developer of most of Cardiff
Castle's Disneyesque embellishments marked the site of Blackfriars
(beyond the Castle walls in Bute Park) with low red brick walls. He
also marked the lines of the final Roman stone fort delineating it with
a band of red local stone. These are readily visible on the Castle's
south walls. Check the view from Duke Street. Roman at ground
level, Bute build above. Until 1923 residential housing still stood
across the eastern end of the south moat garden, filling the space
between Castle and road.

Which parts of history do we retain? How do we best show the
storms and raging tides of the flickering past? John takes me to the
top floor of the new centre to watch a wordless film[30] which tells the
story. This wide-screen, fractured and very post-modern race across
two and a half thousand years of history represents the castle as a
shape changer, moving its walls against circumstance, throwing up
towers, bridges, bretaches, barracks, houses, keeps and drawbridges
according to need. Raiders, revolutionaries and reactionaries roar in
constantly from outside. In the darkened chamber the piece plays for
around eight minutes before blinds automatically rise. The twelve
meter cinema turns into something resembling the command deck of
the Starship Enterprise. Outside, through windscreen windows,
appears the Castle. The real one. Motte and Norman Keep. Roman
North Gate beyond.

We walk out across the Castle Green. Little worn by use. No
winos. No one throwing frisbee. No graffiti. You need a ticket to get

in. Cardiffians mostly keep away. There's a play-off here between offering local tax payers free access and damage by overuse. When St Fagans, the former Folk and now renamed Natural History Museum, dropped entrance charges visitor numbers rocketed. But so too did the number of stolen artefacts, damaged exhibits, and scrawled-on buildings. Out there, somewhere on e-bay or on an auction site much like it are bits of our Welsh heritage. Longcase clocks, Welsh sixteenth century clogs. Pay and they are yours. There's talk about how Cardiffians might be offered permits allowing them free or low-cost access. But there's been talk like that for years.

Development won't stop with the opening of the interpretation centre. There are proposals to open the North Gate and allow access directly into Bute Park. Plans are in hand to refill the mill leat and moat on the Castle's western flank. Last time this was done the basement of the Angel Hotel flooded. The leat, the Tan River, once joined the Taff just south of the Angel's car park. The Taff went down Westgate Street at that time. The culvert it was eventually encased in still runs below the Hotel.

According to legend this castle (along with just about every other castle in Wales, and elsewhere, come to that) is riddled below with secret passages and rooms. Tunnels that run to St John's Church, that cross to the abbey of the Greyfriars, that go the whole five miles north to Castell Coch, that snake towards the ancient quay and escape by water, that would take kings and princes in and out without disturbing the attention of the marauding and endlessly upset native Welsh. John tells me, hand on heart, that in his time as Castle Surveyor he has found no trace of these clandestine routes. But then again in the way of these things official denial is no indicator of ultimate reality.

John is working now on restoring the Amstel Hotel in Amsterdam and at Penryn in Cornwall. In an expanding world where yesterday vanishes before your eyes his specialist knowledge is in demand.

I head out to look again at

the dock feeder which runs alongside Boulevard de Nantes. There
was a tunnel here, wasn't there? There was[31].

MARKET

In the wide-shouldered days of the eighties when paperback books
flowed through my hands like tides this place was an epicentre. Not
that anyone ran a press from here or was ever a resident writer. This
was the market, after all. I'd stood outside it many times. St John's
Church end. In the place where the Red Choir now congregate.
Climb the Tower Today. Tea Shop open. *Big Issue*. In the seventies I'd
tried to sell copies of my hand-built poetry journal here. No takers.
Not true, actually. David Callard came by and relieved me of one
copy. But money didn't change hands. He was a contributor.

Inside this 1980s indoor Cardiff Market – green corporation paint
fresh across the metalwork – was the Bear Island Book Exchange,
home of the junked paperback. Still there today. Owner sitting on a
stool eating a pie. Browsers pulling Robert Ludlum and Tom Clancy
from the crowded stacks. A wall of Mills & Boon at the front, like a
room divider. In these knowing, we-don't-ever-read times romance
still shifted. Dark fiction, cult fiction, recent bestsellers liberated
from the retail trade, ex-review. I had these, by the shed. I'd been
writing a regular paperback column for *Wales On Sunday*, in the
broadsheet days before the fall, when the paper said things, wrote in
sentences, delivered argument, expanded minds. John Osmond got
me the job. It might even have paid me a tenner a time, at the start.
That and however many complimentary review copies I could carry.
I carried most of them directly to the market. The deal there was that
he'd buy everything, the good, the indifferent, the bad, one delivery,
one price. I was relieved at a stroke of the undignified task of having
to hump unwanteds back out and lose them somehow in the city's
litter bins. He'd complain. Complaining comes with the territory.
Can't shift that, no call, see. Bring me more fantasy. War books.
Thrillers. I can sell those. Stuff the *Daily Mail* likes. Anything that's
been mentioned on TV. But then he'd pay me. Notes from a wallet-
less backpocket. Just a few.

All was well until the day he opened my big armful box of the latest
gleaming A-formats, took a poke around, and then said I'll buy these.

Jack Jones reprints. Don't want the rest. Sucked on his fag. I took the cash. Enough for a tea and a sandwich. Carted the residue and donated them to a penny whistle player fluting his tunelessness in the passage across the churchyard. Never went back.

There have been markets in Cardiff since the time of the Normans. Livestock. Farm produce. Meat, corn, butter, cheese, poultry, flannel, wool, mead, cloth. The market – the fair – was on High Street, sheltering in the Shambles under the 1330's town hall – the Bothhalle – and running in straggling lines along the street. When the Bothhalle fell down they rebuilt it as the Gild Hall and then when that collapsed in 1747 replaced it with another. The Hall was built in what is now the middle of the street. Traffic passed using the narrow alleys on either side. There were stocks, a water pump, a large cursing stone on which deals were struck. John Evan Thomas's statue of the Second Marquis of Bute stood here for decades before being moved, first to the bottom of St Mary Street, south of the Terminus[32], and later to its present position on a plinth in the skateboard park that is Callaghan Square. In a fit of corporate expansion and administrative glow a fourth Town Hall went up 1853, on the western side of St Mary Street. That remained in use until City Hall opened in 1904.

Attempts were regularly made to contain the sprawling stalls and to clear the roads. In 1823 William Vachell[33] opened a market on land he owned between High Street and Duke Street[34]. The corporation opened their own on former gardens in 1835. The 'New Market' was designed by Edward Haycock. Frontage on St Mary Street next to the County Gaol and gallows[35], rear access from Church Street via the old arcade. Still there today. Initially it sold only meat, fish and poultry. Corn, seed, flour, malt, hops and wool continued to be traded under the Gild Hall until that building's demise. Cardiff markets were now operating outside fair days, selling non-stop through the week. The start of our future. Victorian Cardiff shopped.

In 1886 Solomon Andrews rebuilt and enlarged the market with a four-floor, iron-roofed development which included space for offices and formal shops. This dominated the street and went unmatched until James Howell build his store to a similar size next door. The present market, a further enhancement of the Andrews original, was opened by the Marchioness of Bute (check the plaque at the Trinity Street end) in 1891. Glazed roof, iron trusses. 349 stalls. Balcony. Market manager's office with its own elevated observation platform and clock.

Ashton's (the famous fish seller serviced by staff in rubber boots and hats, stall full of crushed ice, squid, snapper and marble slabs covered with spreads of trout at the St John's Church end, tenants since 1866), C.L. Jones Electrical Spares with bulbs and fuses for anything (including East European torches) on the balcony, pets, meats, cheeses, toys, trophies, vacuum cleaner spares, phone parts, flowers, tea, unrivalled cheese and onion rolls.

Ed Kelly opened his record stall here in 1969. Second-hand mod and soul material, Who, Wilson Pickett, old skiffle, Elvis, copies of Mantovani, Joe Loss, Edward Heath, Sinatra, the 101 Strings, Lawrence Welk, the Big Ben Banjo Band, Big Bill Broonzy now and then. I was here with the rest of young Cardiff unloading lps of ancient beat music (Searchers, Manfreds, Gerry and the Pacemakers) hunting instead for ascendant mind expansion: Fish, Floyd, Dead, Airplane, the new place Dylan had gone. Nothing was ever filed in order. Vinyl in boxes, like Oxfam. Cassettes in cascading sprawls. Ed moved swiftly from his Trinity Street end corner-booth to the present spread nearer St Mary Street. He bought stock and bought more, never seemed to stop. Took over next door. Bought again. Never refused a thing. Grew and grew. Ed was a record collector, a music hall enthusiast and folk singer in the finger in ear tradition. I saw him once at the now boarded-up Locomotive, on

Broadway, singing directly from the *Penguin Book of Australian Verse*. A poem by Banjo Patterson. Was that the right tune, I asked him later. No idea, he said.

The stall today is run by his nephew. Ed died a few years back. It occupies at least half of the southside balcony: boxes, shelves, wall racks, bins. The Bible Depot, evangelical tracts, Sunday school supplies, posters, the good book, cards, is the only thing that stops the music from lapping at Woodie's café beyond. Everything is indexed and in order, data logged, searchable, and purchasable online. Ed Kelly's traditional approach, which allowed for fortuitous random discovery[36], down the pan.

Beyond the Market the St John's churchyard railings are covered with signs protesting against the forthcoming badger cull, protesting against vivisection, complaining about the war. Which war? All wars. There's someone blowing with almost no breath at all into an ancient harmonica. Someone else simply sitting sprawled in front of a begging hat. About fifty pee inside. A place of the people, this. Always was.

UNDERNEATH

The Cardiff Underground. A railink below the surface, like London's, like Moscow's, like the Budapesti metró. It will be the answer to everything. Subways to all places, pipes full of moving light. Let's build one now. The letters pages of Cardiff's evening paper regularly run these requests. Dig into Cardiff's late Triassic mudstone substrata, tunnel the Keuper marls and gravels, slide under the moving Taff. Build a marble station down there under City Hall and another, full of twenty-first century glow and shine, below the Bus Station. That'll fix the traffic. And the parking. At a stroke.

Many know the few examples of underground city that already exist. Or did so once. The canal that went through a tunnel from the Friary down to somewhere south of Next's bargain basement in the Queen Street Arcade. The Dock Feeder that still disappears amid bramble and sapling at the New Theatre end of Boulevard de Nantes. It runs under-cover through the eastern city, down Churchill Way, skirts the Ibis Hotel. Re-emerges briefly at the back of the Big Sleep on Bute Terrace to plough on, below the London main rail line, en route to the Bay. There are, however, many others. Some rumoured, some lost, some still there below basements, behind locked doors, bricked-up arches, barricades to keep out vandals, the curious, the destitute. Cardiff may not exactly be riddled with underground passages – it's hard to dig and stay dug in the clays of a floodplain – but it has its share. Finding them, however, is another matter.

Ben Soffa, it turns out, is an expert. Ben, when he lived in Cardiff, was round the corner from me off Albany. He's an eccentric and I love such people. They don't live on the world, they live inside it. Ben's compulsion is the world beneath our feet. He's a member of Subterranea Britannica, a UK-wide grouping of the likeminded who spend their weekends hunting out blocked-off Victorian railway tunnels, lost mineshafts, city caves, crypts, concreted-over cold war bunkers, forgotten passages, dugouts, drains, souterrains, subways, quarries, oubliettes, and any other man-made or man-used under-ground place. Are they cavers? Some of them. Do they have permits for what they do? Ben smiles. Always, he says.

Ben is down on a family weekend when I meet him. I have just discovered Birdsong[37], a digital radio station that broadcasts nothing but the twittering of birds. We talk amid the chatter of great tits, greenfinches, wrens, swallows, and flycatchers. Sounds of the sky and the sun. Sounds never heard underground. I check Ben's features for the paleness you'd expect from a denizen of the beneath but he looks healthy enough.

We discuss what subterranean Cardiff could actually turn out to be. The still-extant but flooded subway between the Ferry Road peninsular and Penarth (see p.131). The blocked-off 1888 Wenvoe railway tunnel which once carried the Barry Railway's Cadoxton to Trehafod line. The civil defence bunkers at Whitchurch. The Coryton Regional War Rooms. The Wenallt anti-aircraft operations HQ. The Bute Dock Feeder. The caves of the Lesser Garth. The extensive and, in the terms of the underground lost, fairly recently constructed British Telecom Cable Tunnel. Did you ever get access? Ben shakes his head.

The Cable Tunnel was dug in the late 1970s to service the city's expanding need for communications cabling. BT's business at that time was still run by the General Post Office. Hard to imagine now. Stamps and dog licences and phones all in the same bucket. Digital broadcasting and delivery by high-frequency transmitter through dish and tower was still to come. Businesses had air-locked rooms to house their Honeywell computers. Punched cards and magnetic tape carried the data. Operators wore white hats, white coats, and white gloves. Output was on paper that had no end. Continuous, wide, pale, printed on by dot matrix. New block houses were built for storage. The paperless office will be with us any day now predicted the venture capitalists. It still hasn't arrived.

Robert McAlpine were the contractors digging at around the same time BT gave up manual telephone operating for STD[38]. According to Ben the tunnel was four-and-a-half meters wide and bored into the red clay twenty metres down. It ran from Castle Street to the International Arena via BT's then main telephone exchange at Stadium House. They've built the Millennium Stadium next door since. A tunnel branch ran west to Fitzhamon Embankment beyond the Taff.

He switches to talk about the five underground lakes below the Lesser Garth, perched at differing levels, difficult to access unless you are willing to be winched down the dark, sloping shafts that exist beyond the limestone quarry's northern edge (see p.175). Tells me about the ochre colour of the water, the fingers of fungal growth, and the caves that tantalisingly lead off. Quarrying will soon destroy all this. Ben's real enthusiasm, however, is for the remains of the Cold War. The buried bunkers and half-sunk control rooms, the underground storage chambers, the metal-clad meeting rooms and command and control centres dug into the Cardiff earth. These nuclear-proof places are enclosed with pulse resistant wire mesh. They are sanctuaries where the great and the good and the military powerful would go. A respite for when Cardiff's steelworks and Cardiff's port, Cardiff's airbases and, most significant of all, Cardiff's Atomic Weapons Establishment at Llanishen came under targeted Russian attack.

You find these dug-outs by seeing masts in the landscape, bits of ferro-concrete where they shouldn't be, bumps and pathways. Evidence of vehicles where there should be no vehicles. And nothing is marked, ever, on the maps. By chance Ben discovered a dugout above Rhiwbina. This turned out to be the Wenallt anti-aircraft operations rooms, a half-submerged bunker built in the increasing frost of the 1951 Cold War. It can still be partially seen from Wenallt Road, on BT property, south-east of the microwave mast. The site was a vital ops room and later BT's emergency control centre for Wales. It had dormitories, canteen, sick bay, water storage, air filtration, power generators and a pulse-proofed Faraday-caged communications room. It's mostly derelict now. Ben found others. Or, more accurately, the remains of others. The Coryton Regional War Room (Pendywallt Road). Whitchurch Civil Defence Recreational and Training Centre (next to the school, junction of Old Church Road and Tyn-y-Pwll Road). Cold War public air raid shelters at Whitchurch (St Mary's Road, Bishops Road and Kelston Road). More at Pentyrch, Llanishen, Penarth, and Caerau. Dismissed, disused places, stuck on wasteland. Lost behind trees. Overgrown. Broken, graffitied, entrances metal-grilled, rusted, locked.

The Cold War is easily forgotten. It went on for so long and, for the average Cardiffian, nothing actually ever seemed to happen. There were stand-offs at sea. Reports on TV of near-misses between jet fighters. Gun-emplaced barbed-wire borders across Europe. Ditches where tanks faced each other. Out there was darkness and constant threat. But not here. In Cardiff the buses ran and now again there was sun.

In 1957 a war game called *Dutch Treat* assumed a one megaton free-fall bomb at Brawdy and another at Aberporth. Cardiff caught nothing but wind-born nuclear drift. In 1960 *Health Circular Attack* imagined a one and half megaton hitting both Cardiff and Swansea. The cities vanished. In 1978 *Fission Fragments* put missiles into RAF St Athan. By 1982, at the Cold War's height, it was postulated that a bomb on Cardiff would kill everyone in a six mile radius with the entire populations of Pontypridd and Newport suffering third degree burns. Medical help for survivors would not be possible. Ninety percent of medical staff would be dead. Cardiff would cease to be real. The city would be a wreckage of dust, rubble and escaping water. Trees would no longer grow.

In 1987 Reagan and Gorbachev signed the Intermediate Range Nuclear Forces Treaty. In 1991 the USSR broke up into fifteen independent republics. Cold War complete. World free. Cardiff saved.

Threat over? Ben is not convinced. There are still nuclear warheads out there even if they are no longer made in the Welsh capital. Do you think there's anything under this city that you haven't investigated, I ask. Are there secrets still to unravel, caverns full of undiscovered ancient artifacts, the lost grave of Arthur, tunnels connecting business hubs, dark passageways used for clandestine purposes, basements full of rooms that no one has entered for centuries? Possible, says Ben. But improbable. On the other hand if anyone reading this knows of anything, well, do get in touch.

THE GREYFRIARS TUNNEL

Most buildings have secrets. The older the place is then the greater the mystery. Pubs in particular can be addled with the presence of spectres, the sightings of ghosts and the discovery of passageways behind walls, lost doors found in deep cellars, tunnels leaving via trap doors and heading who knows where. Anything built before 1900 is suspect. Check, for example, the Church Inn in Llanishen. Fourteenth century origins. Bricked-up tunnel leading to St Isan's Church over the road discovered during twentieth century renovations. There's another which allegedly runs under the Angel Hotel. Dozens snake below Cardiff Castle (see p.53), Castell Coch, St John's Church, lost St Mary's, below Blackfriars and Greyfriars. In bends and dives to the site of Cock's Tower. Below the river. Running from Roath to Crockerton and back. From the Mansion House to City Hall. From the Custom House to the Jail. There are so many that it is hard to see how Cardiff fails to subside.

Officially none of these passages exists. Mostly true. But look hard and you'll still find traces. Irritants that won't become reality. A 1922 *Western Mail* report tells the story of a tunnel uncovered running from the south side of the Bute Dock Feeder. This was about half way along its length between the bridge by the water fountain on Kingsway and the vanishing of the waterway under cover at its intersection with Park Place. This tunnel ran south towards the castle at an angle of 17 degrees. The report is very precise about that. The tunnel's walls were made of river pebbles with arches constructed of lias limestone. The building of the feeder in 1834 had cut across it and the tunnel entrance was now sealed by an iron door.

Contemporary investigation carried out by the Architect to the Bute Estate, J.P. Grant, uncovered a passage of around two and half feet wide running for almost 400 feet at a depth of about ten below the road. His examination of the passage's floor slabs and arch work led him to date construction at sometime in the thirteenth century.

A Gilbert de Clare escape route from his Castle to Greyfriars. If not that then a mid-sixteenth century construct and the work of Sir William Herbert. Early twentieth century archaeological dating techniques were nothing if not wildly imprecise. Herbert's great house stood on the site of Greyfriars until at least the nineteen sixties. Greyfriars was built in 1262 and Herbert House in 1550. Both now wiped from the Cardiff surface. Brick and foundation excavated and removed. A bit of recording but not much. Nothing left but photographs and even those dim and grainy grey.

The *Mail* reports discuss evil doings, robberies and the hiding in these secret tunnels of bags of jewellery and sacks of coin. Police are reported as taking an interest in the excavations. There's no mention of a conclusion. When the excavations were complete and subsequently filled-in what remained? Could the tunnel still be there? Fenced off by Health and Safety. Yellow tape across its entrance. Known only to pipe layers and drainage engineers. Key to its locked door in a manager's desk somewhere, forgotten. When Queen Street was known as Crockerton and there was no Boulevard de Nantes the space south of the feeder was filled with the Castle gardens. Gooseberries, beans, cabbage. Chances are the nineteen sixties redevelopment of this whole area have seen off what once was. No CADW then. No inspections. If you came across something interesting that might get in the way of building then you tried hard not to mention it. Dig on.

I've gone back and crawled over these bits of artificial river bank. Land drains from the former Council offices[39] (now Park Plaza Hotel & Resort) emerge from the undergrowth. Thin things. No signs, even in winter, of any door or cut or infill. No tunnel. Nothing. Passage past, passage lost.

THE FESTIVAL OF BRITAIN STEAM ROOMS

Northmore and I are feeling rough. We have Chiquito with us although to judge by the amount he is saying that might only be in spirit. We've had a night in the wine shop in the Wyndham Arcade, Chiquito and I on sweet Spanish Sauternes, Northmore on some sort of Bulgarian red. We were heading for the Mike Harries Jazz Club in the upstairs bar of the New Tredegar, but never made it. Diverted by lethargy and laughter and the spinning of the bottle to find out who'd pay next. There was sleep at some point, but not much of it, at Northmore's flat in Tudor Road. Flat is an exaggeration. Two rooms, no bath, use of a cold water washroom down the hall. Northmore had been there for six months. It was all he could afford.

He liked jazz, did Northmore, in the way that others did rugby or darts. It took over his life. Cool Miles, Dizzy chanting salt peanuts. Parker, Coltrane, Monk and Mingus. *Mingus, Mingus, Mingus. Mingus Oh Yeah.* Mingus was king. We'd got back and he'd spun stuff about saints and sinners[40] and jive ass slippers[41] and then played us tracks with Mingus leading on bass like this giant instrument was some sort of electric guitar[42]. Listen to this guy talking, Northmore was shouting. Mingus rambling and roaring over the music like a hipster on speed.

In the morning we'd all felt so bad that there was only one thing for it. Cleanse the brain with steam. Massage the hangover with heat. Hit it where it hurts. That idea had brought us here, in the low Cardiff drizzle. Outside the orange brick-fronted Festival of Britain styled fifties piece of Welsh glory that was the Empire Pool.

The Pool, a last hurrah for Empire and a strange one for Wales, had opened in 1958 when the Empire Games came to Wales. Nigeria vs. Bechuanaland. Honduras vs. Gibraltar. The Cook Islands against Ceylon. Rowers from the Falklands outdistancing those from Canada. Australia rules. But not quite. The pool was as big as anything I'd ever seen indoors. Swimming a width was the same as swimming a length at the pool in Guildford Crescent, the pool the Empire replaced.

The facility at Guildford Crescent, squashed between the West Dock Feeder and the Taff Vale railtrack, began life in 1862 as a Turkish Baths. The eastern habit of sitting around fat and bald with a towel over your waist and with steam hot enough to extract nose hair streaming around you had long been seen as a way of improving the body without muscular effort. You lay supine and were pummelled by a masseur with hands like shovels. You sat in spaces full of boiling heat. You plunged into ice pools. Returned to sit in warms rooms where ex-pat Czechs with limbs missing and Hungarians with moustaches like squirrels read damp newspapers and talked to each other of chess and life.

The squashed, brick dowdiness that was the Guildford Baths was where a almost a whole century of Cardiff school children were taken to learn to swim and not drown. Walked there through the city streets in long snaking lines. Hung their clothes on metal frames, donned their towelling trunks and dived on in. Turkish practises belong to adults. They operated in a different part of the white-tiled echoing building. You never even looked in.

The Empire, by contrast, was a palace of open vistas. Built by the river, south of the Arms Park, visible from the railway, lapped by the bus station. Accessible to all. In the fifties this area *was* the fifties. An architectural city infill that looked as if it had come directly from Dan Dare. British post-war modernism. Brick. Slow curving arch. Big Astey's like a space station, rows of concrete bus shelters like Martian pods. The triumphant thirty-five-foot high mosaic *An Eye For the People*[43] cascading down the side of the *Mail* and *Echo* offices in Havelock Street as if Picasso had planned it. St David's House lining the north side of Wood Street like low-rise Corbusier. Fifties, when change started. Once again.

Northmore, Chiquito and I got there eight years later. 1966. The summer before the Summer. Summer of love that was. When the beads and the smiles made the planet blink, for just a moment. But that hadn't happened yet.

Inside we did the circuit. Slowly. Warm room, warmer room, hot steam room then cold plunge. Ten minutes in the pore-opening sauna. Refuse the massage for fear of what it might involve. Bronzed giant with a half grin and pads on his hands. Soap. Towels. Ring in his ear. Try the aerotone bath where water pulsed around you like an early Jacuzzi. Warm shower. Dry. Lounge around in your white rented dressing gown, served beans on toast and tea, hangover in retreat, almost gone.

In Turkey itself in the Suleymaniye baths at Istanbul, where I went in later life, I discovered the steam to be cooler than Cardiff's, the massage vigorous but delivered without threat and a total lack of beans. In 1966 Janis Joplin has just met Big Brother and Nancy's boots are still walking. Dion has got back with the Belmonts. Frank Zappa has created the Mothers and released an album called *Freak Out*. Nobody in Cardiff yet knows what that means.

The Empire Pool offered far more than simply swimming and massage. There were cafes, a hall for exercise, baths in which to wash (for those whose houses lacked them and, for your money, fuller of water than anything I'd ever seen at home. My mother allowed three inches of luke warm. These came with eighteen of boiling. 1/3d). There was even a traditional Jewish Mikvah bath. This offered ritual purification and used rain water collected in a special tank on the roof. The Empire Pool was demolished in 1998 to make space for the south entrance to the Millennium Stadium. Its replacement is the Cardiff International, an Olympian standard complex on the Ferry Road peninsula. You can see its twentieth century blue checkerboard windows glistening from the link road. Can't walk there easily. Out of town. I've no idea how the Czechs and Hungarians get on.

In 1966 we go to the Cambrian[44]. Half of dark. Chips in Caroline Street. A walk home through the bustle. Things that have changed – many. Things that haven't – still some.

LIBRARY

I'm standing in Trinity Street, south of the covered Victorian Market. I've got the secretary of Victorian Society with me, Elaine Davey. We're trying to work out which part of the Old Library is the extension. The 1896 extension, built at the apogee of Empire when the world still glowed. It's hard to discern. The steps here, which lead to the great tiled corridor, show wear from the feet of generations of Cardiffians. Readers, researchers, borrowers, buskers, red choristers, smokers, sellers of *Sanity*, political intellectuals, poetry pamphleteers, hawkers of philosophical magazines, shoppers, sleepers, women with bags, men chasing a free place somewhere in from the coal coloured rain. A centre of Cardiff life. Used to be.

The Library – between the Market and Queen Street – accessed from Roath by a walk through Alders and the Queen Street Arcade[45] or from Canton past the Castle and the high of High Street. The Library, the city's heart. South, below a scroll encrusted bust of Minerva, stood Café Latrine, the Hayes Island home of John Tripp's alfresco drinking club[46]. Beyond were open air fruit stalls, carts selling spuds, and the statue of John Batchelor[47], Friend of Freedom, crowned with something, always. Traffic cones now, paper bags then. Around him shoppers tramped, traffic flowed. This is Victoria Place. Was then, still is. Unsigned, not named on maps, listed only in guide books. Its centrepiece is the Hayes Island Snack Bar selling tea so strong it could dissolve spoons and rolls thick with onion and

pungent cheese. Before development as a café this was the Cardiff
Tramways Parcel Office. Men with uniform hats and hand carts,
watches on chains below their expanding chests. Above, on the walls
of Habitat, is the city's first giant street TV – news and sport broadcast constantly to flâneurs, shoppers and passers-through whether
they like it or not.

This place is another Cardiff pulse, a beat in the city's blood. A
point around which the town has always whirled, within its ancient
walls, below its Castle, in the shadow of its church. Here time bends
and circles. You can hear it turning. The Red Choir are to the north,
praising the working class. To the south the Samba Band with their
myriad drummers beating. East are a trio of student violinists
playing Mozart. West is a lone headscarfed new European. She plays
a slow polka on a battered accordion. There's a hat but inside it not
much money.

We decide eventually that the south end has to be newer, and when
I look it up that's what it turns out to be. Only the wall facing St
John's churchyard is from Edwin Seward's 1882 original. The others
arrived between 1887 and 1896, as the enterprise extended itself,
yellow brick, white shafts of Portland, yellow blocks of Ham Hill
stone. The whole building tapers south. The façade is fronted now by
a glass entrance porch, embellished with the commercial trappings of
the Cardiff Visitor Centre. Postcards of ladies in Welsh costume. The
lamps of miners. Souvenir coal. Tea towels carrying the national
anthem. The ancient iconography living on.

This 2009 Library, emptied of its books, still retains palpable

Victorian grandeur. Its halls
are used to ready the ground
for a future Cardiff Museum.
Shows about sport, immigra-
tion, childhood, enterprise,
people, transport, industry,
place. Upstairs are hireable
reception rooms and,
unaccountably, the Welsh
office of the Boxing Board of
Control. Jim Driscoll and Joe
Calzaghe, you've walked these
halls. Next door, in the original

library space, now renamed The Exhibition, is Que Pasa – *bar, café, olé* – flickering TV screens, cocktail drinkery, couldn't call it a pub.

Cardiff has had a public library since 1860 when a voluntary reading room housing 49 books and a set of newspapers opened above the entrance to the new Royal Arcade. When the corporation took over two years later it added a lending library and a museum and moved operations to the former YMCA building at 79 St Mary Street. This was at the time of Cardiff's first industrial boom. Demand rapidly outstripped supply. A competition[48] to design a new library to be built on corporation land in Trinity Street[49] was won by James, Seward and Thomas. The building and its almost immediately added extension initially housed the Cardiff Museum (Roman and Celtic artefacts in the basement, coins, bones, fragments of meteors that landed on Penylan, the belt buckle of a Silurian king), the Science and Art Schools, and the new Free Library, open to all. The Schools moved out in 1890 and the museum collections as soon as the National opened in Cathays Park in 1910. On the Library's facades can be seen late-Victorian carved figures[50] representing the reader, the scribe, study and rhetoric. They are high up. Few look. Most passers-by in 2009 don't know what rhetoric is. If you look closely you can also see memorials to Caxton, Wynkyn de Worde, Robert Estienne, Johann Fust, Peter Schoeffer, Thomas Vautrollier, and Andre Wechel. Pioneers of movable type. Men who took print to the world. The Bill Gates of their lost age. Their letterpress unlikely to return.

In the early part of the twentieth century the Library at Cardiff fought a bitter battle with the collections housed at the University of Aberystwyth. Both enterprises had been assiduously acquiring Welsh material and manuscripts with a view to gaining status as the National Library of Wales. Nation building was in progress. Prestige was to be won. Government money was in the wind. In the end, 1907, Cardiff got the Museum and Aber the Library. Cardiff's collection of ancient books and rare manuscripts including the *Book of Aneirin*, an early *Book of Hours* and copious pedigrees, court rolls and heraldic manuscripts, languished. Little known, little loved, today their future is uncertain.

The Cardiff Library moved out in 1988 to the new liftless Shingler Risdon and Associates polygonal slab-concrete wonder in Bridge Street. Next to Iceland. On the site of one of Fry's dusty back-room stores that sold Harrison Marks nude books and copies of *Parade* and *Titbits*. In 2007 the St David's 2 diggers made their move and the grey concrete was demolished. The Library moved its quarter of a million item collection to a temporary large-scale portacabin home on a site adjacent to the old WNO John Street offices, top of Bute Street. A billboard depicting the giant spines of the most borrowed books line its sides. Anything Welsh? Dennis Morgan's *The Illustrated History of Cardiff's Suburbs*.

The twenty-first century replacement, the sixth, a library for an age where the book is doomed, copyright in retreat and digitisation flashing through the wifi air like a samurai conqueror, stands in the former Holiday Inn car park. Six stories, green, sedum, living roof patrolled by a hawk shared with the Millennium Stadium. This is a place of education, entertainment and dining. Colour coded with shelves that float. One hundred computer terminals. Borrowable DVDs. Silent grand piano heard only on headphones. Fiction, prose, music collection, children's collection, Capitol Collection of history and Wales. Areas for live storytelling and book launches and poetry. Three restaurants grace the ground floor – commercial quid pro quo

– Wagamamas, Strada, Gourmet Burger. Best civic building in Cardiff for a hundred years, Trevor Gough says. He's Leisure Services Director and has line of sight, just about, to this stunning place from his eyrie office in the Bay's County Hall. This place resembles a set from *Flash Gordon*. Flying walkways, slate floors, concrete climbing around a dazzling atrium. The artist Neil Canning's huge abstract expressionist landscapes a shimmering backdrop. The structure has been built by Laing O'Rourke in a green, blue and glass checker board style with a brass-coloured façade facing the rain from the south. The new Library arrives in the wake of the worst economic depression since 1929. Thank Ballinger[51] we've got it. If build decisions were being made right now then the books would stay in their tin boxes on John Street.

Titles the library rarely lends:

A History of Minor Roads in Wales.
A Guide to the Sub-Post Offices of the British Isles.
The Joy of Splott
The Book of Marmalade
Highlights In The History of Concrete
Bombproof Your Horse
Weeds In A Changing World
How To Avoid Huge Ships
Did Lewis Carroll Visit Llanrumney?
Dining Posture In Ancient Roath
Caerphilly Cheese Problems Solved
Wanted[52]

Now you know which they are, confound statistics, go borrow.

WYNDHAM ARCADE

Northmore and I were at the east end of the Wyndham Arcade. Potato stalls behind us. A misspelled sprawl of cabbages and carrots sold by men with strong, hairy arms. Apples in boxes. Veg in brown paper bags. Shoppers with string bags and woven baskets. Runner beans wrapped in newspaper. A sawdust barrel full of pomegranates. Oranges in bright stacks. Both of us were full to the top with Lawrence Durrell, Arthur Rimbaud, Alexander Trocchi, Colin Wilson, Henry Miller. Bohemians. Wanderers. Rimbaud gone to the wall by 21. Durrell's *Black Book* unobtainable. Miller unacceptable in polite society. Spent his pages roaring at the world, spinning lists of who knew what the score was and where to look next. Goethe, Nietzsche, Joyce, Dostoevsky, Whitman rolling among the clouds in the violet light of the stars. 'Forward without pity, without compassion, without love, without forgiveness. Ask no quarter and give none! More battle-ships, more poison gas, more high explosives! More gonococci! More streptococci! More bombing machines! More and more of it[53]. What does this mean? Who knows. But it certainly sounded glorious.

I had *The Air-Conditioned Nightmare* paperback Panther in my reefer jacket pocket. Northmore had the banned *Sexus* under wraps at home. From the stores of Cardiff they were selling Arthur Hailey's *Hotel* by the shedload. Where did that tale get you? Jazz on the player. *Don't Let Them Drop That Atomic Bomb*. Cardiff, in your smog filled skies, behind your war battered shades, below your failing roofs, how are you dealing with this? Twenty years on the Cardiff world was still post-War largely unreconstructed. The Hayes canal had gone. The Prince of Wales Theatre on St Mary Street was showing *Nudes In The Snow* and other episodes where the black and white naked strolled, red-pointed breasts bouncing, beach balls across their pubic spreads. Something else had to be happening. We'd seen its traces. Literary vapour trails across a mundane world.

Could we find it? Dances taught. Hands held. Eyes stretched. Chests lifted. Consciousnesses expanded. Minds directed. Astrophysics explained. Electronics directed. Poetry paraded. God believed. Books devoured. Histories recounted. Countries conquered. Wine poured. Holborn lit. Beat bashed. Bop blown. Colours calibrated. Worlds whirled. Cylinders recalibrated. Hair dyed. Smoke cleared. At long last. Universes known.

Northmore's plan was to conquer the world. To reach out and grasp it. Take it all on. In the Arcade we entered the Army and Navy Stores. Facing the Christian Bookstore which filled its windows with literature laced with Christ. Lulled you in with the promise of new worlds. Smiled at you. Spun you. Gave you hope. Gave you the old god again. Northmore, rich with his first soiled wage packet from the steelworks, appalled at the prospect of a life of endless dirty toil, was looking for out. Make hip. Kit yourself. Take on the wilds of the city and then set out to take on the wilds of the world. He ordered knee-high boots. Moulded soles. Great lace-up things with a hundred eyelets. Skinhead decades ahead of his time. He bought bush-shirts with multiple pockets. A khaki cap from the Italian Army which had fur flaps for your ears and a buttonable pocket inside the lid for the storage of coins. Proof-cotton trousers splashed with camouflage, straps at the ankles, pockets on the thighs. Compass in a box. Leather gloves with great flaring arm protectors, like a motorcyclist's. Pack for his books. Canvas webbing belt. Waterproof ground sheet, eyelets, punch studs, wrapped over your head and draped you when storms stuck. He looked like a mercenary when he wanted to look like a hipster. Waterproof. Sold all his Ventures and Shadows records[54] to the second-hand

shop on City Road. Raised enough for a decent bowie knife. Protection. Added that to his pack.

The Arcade slid us back towards the buses. Northmore laden. Me the owner of a new red bandana. Wrap it round my neck. Couldn't afford the cords I fancied. My battered fawn desert boots dyed vermillion. Hip tee-shirt covered in red stars. Mod era end in real sight. Sat upstairs, watched the grey city roll by. Memory in monochrome. Northmore fading like a ghost.

Cardiff was never a place to do this sort of thing. In the growth of the new Welsh world culture was yet to arrive. This was a provincial backwater where grit crunched beneath your shoes. Northmore left. Went out of memory about the same time that Yeah Yeah[55] topped the charts. Haven't seen him since.

The store remains although moved to the Arcade's opposite side. Bailey's Army & Navy Store selling twenty-first century Regatta Action Trousers, Germany Army Moleskins, green scrim scarves, web-tex combat vests and dog tags complete with silencers. Matalan, Primark and Peacocks have caught the cheap trade. Bailey's surplus is now a specialist. Fishermen. Tomboys. Hunters. Vigilantes. Mercenaries. Free defenders. Men with knives and guns. If there was a private Welsh army practising up on the hills they'd join it. Whatever the cause. They wouldn't care.

SOPHIA

I've got myself onto the ledge and I can hear Eric Burdon doing it.
Little tough man. Italian suit, hippy hair outgrowth at the back, mod
crew cut still framing the front. Face like he'd take money from you
with menaces. Voice like a delta growl. On stage at the Pavilion.
Tickets some rocket high price, acoustics like my bathroom. The
bass and the thump of the drums coming through the orange brick
walls. All you needed to recognise the song. Please, don't let me be
misunderstood. We gotta get out of this place. The hypnotic swirling
of Alan Price's organ. House of the song so long the radio almost
never played it. House of the rising rising sun.

Back then Cardiff youth never had dough. Old Cardiff did so little
to entertain. Nothing was ever for nothing. When they put the
Ideal Home exhibitions on here annually they still charged. These
were shows that promoted new style of fifties living. G-Plan
furniture. Free standing gas cookers with dish warmers over the
burners. Inflatable arm chairs. Chrome Italian stools. Lamps made
from wine bottles. Gas pokers that took the strain out of lighting
the coal fire. Kitchen knives that never needed sharpening.
Effortless potato chippers, insert spud and press. Oxo as a hot
drink of choice. Shows half the size of present-day free Ikea. You
paid, you went in, they sold you stuff.

Cardiff then was full of low street light, dark unswept roads,
buildings that loomed grey and soot covered from a hundred years
of industrial effluent. Traffic lights that changed so slowly but were

gloriously so few. Belisha
beacons pulsing their yellow
light through the gloom.

Sophia Gardens were one of
the early parks. Opened in 1857
on land donated by the Bute
Estate and named after Sophia,
wife of the Second Marquis.
The Marchioness herself only
visited once. The grounds had
drinking fountains, flower beds,
a band stand, and paths for
perambulation. In 1951 the

Council opened the Sophia Gardens Pavilion – a post-war palace of the people, a point at the future. Skylon for Cardiff. Concrete, brick and style. The opening concert starred Danny Kaye. Charles Groves and the Bournemouth Municipal Orchestra played here. So did Black Sabbath and Pink Floyd. There were boxing matches, gala dances, great exhibitions. From that outside ledge I heard Manfred Mann tear the place apart with Smokestack Lightning. Couldn't do it on record. Had to be live. In the great snow of 1982 the weight of the falling brought in the roof. Filled the hall with slush. Too costly to fix. The Pavilion was abandoned and later what was left pulled down. Such a short life. The tree house we built in woods around the old well at Penylan lasted longer.

The Gardens became the home of Glamorgan County Cricket Club. Donated land for the site of the first all-Wales National Sports Centre. Had roads built upon them, around them, across them. Had space carved from the turf for surfaced car parks. Held visiting circuses in great tents. Held corporate canvas-protected jollies with fizzing drink served by waiters in white. Buffalo Bill's Wild West Show came here in 1891. Horses, wagons, Indians, lassoes, feathers, guns. Couldn't do it now. Too much public risk. Not enough room. The fate of corporate spaces. You chip into them, bit by bit, year on year. Path, access road, hut, conveniences, café, necessary administrative building. Change of use by stealth. Blink and the green is gone.

LIMNOLOGICAL CITY

Limnological – as if this place were a lake. It's Jennie's word. How she studies the city. Cardiff the urban pool. The tide is going out now. Let's see what the sea has left. Jennie Savage comes from Southampton but had a Welsh grandfather, so she's connected. She used to listen to Radio Wales in his garden shed when she was a kid. Came here to study art under John Gingell and somehow stayed. If there's an artist who has really made something of Cardiff then it is she. Mapped the city, drew the landscape, talked the culture, copied the structure, turned the suburbs into a giant radio, brought in local people and their fragmented memories and made them one. In 2004[56] she pulled together artists from a wide range of disciplines to map what urbanity Cardiff has. Walkers, cyclists, runners, cartographers, performers, players, photographers, micro movers, pencil shifters, singers, chancers, map historians, river trackers, dancers, web programmers, photoshoppers, philosophers, spiritual adventurers and street thinkers. In 2005 she ran *Star Radio*[57] out of a shop in Clifton Street. In 2003 she set up *Anecdotal City*, a project which collected and organised the recorded lives of city residents. Citywide radio with unconventional broadcast. The resultant archive is large[58]. It is where Jennie has amassed her distinctive voices, her idiosyncratic reference points. Her concrete markers in the limnological city.

This obsession with the minutiae of life, for naming it, tracking it, and keeping it from harm, is the perfect art for an age in which internet data drowns us. The world is awash with itself. Jennie makes order where she can. She tells me that once she built a searchable database of every single item in her house on Rhymney Street. Click and find. Belt, pot, bed sheet, notebook, ticket stub, can of beans, settee. What is the history of these things? How do they relate? What narratives do they reveal? The frozen time of Georges Perec's *Life, A Users Manual* softened with technology an visual style. Jennie Savage, the one who makes the invisible visible, rolled out like a map of the stars.

In the city the inhabitants phone each other constantly. Wake speaking. Walk speaking. Wait speaking. Never cease. They photograph their own minutiae. The cast of their skins. The look of their faces. They send the results to each other across the Bluetooth air. Streams of imperfection and pixels poorly resolved. We sit in Bar One, south end of the Millennium Centre, images pointlessly wi-fied through our pores. The city pulses data without cease. I eat a professionally microwaved to 180 degrees 50g Cheddar cheese-filled, pinkish-red Cara potato (heavy cropper, smooth tubers, suitable for long storage, blight resistant), side salad of rocket and lambs lettuce and shaved onion. Half a cherry tomato. Knife and fork rolled into a white serviette. Table served by a ubiquitous Pole. Dark hair. Smile. Jennie has parsnip soup, roll. Could be butter. Not sure.

Jennie has photographed that Cathays street of hers alongside the railway everyday for a year. Another archive[59]. The piles of data she creates crowd around. Is this psychogeography, I ask? She shakes her head. That's an esoteric term created by a cabal of men. I shouldn't have enquired.

This collection, direction, and elevation of data that she engages in, a consuming passion, can spread like a virus. Already I am mentally listing the spoons in the café cutlery holder, recording the chalk board menu, noting the colours of the coats worn by diners, tracking their movements, listing the things they have brought in with them. Listening as their conversations drift by. And that's the link back to the narrative world. Organise what you hear. Let the city tell its own story.

Cardiff is the city of arcades. If we believe our own city tourism promotional push. No other city has them. (They do). These are Cardiff's unique Victorian and Edwardian attractions. (They're not). Cardiff invented them. (It didn't). We have dozens. (We don't). There are lots. (There are).

Arcades are Jennie's current obsession. With financial help from the St David's 2 development Cardiff's arcades are being given the data capture, anecdotal cluster, multiple interpretation history, cut and paste, scrawl and measure Savage treatment. St David's 2, as developers of a huge new mall modelled as a system of enlarged arcades, have a vested interest. Already she and I have walked the length of them talking into her black-helmeted tape mic. How do these passageways make you feel? What parts of your past life were spent here? The Arcades follow the lines of the ancient burgage[60] plots, they link the open spaces once occupied by Cardiff's mesh of courts. They are aboriginal creases. Our ancient lines. They run between street and street. Lit by skylight. Saved from weather. Guarded by entrance gate. Kept free of skateboarders, street traders, the unwanted and the unwashed.

Jennie wants to know why I find these passages so interesting. What makes them work? How are they different? They lack mall shopping's floor to roof entrances. Arcade stores have regular doors and low walls below their windows. The space you stand in outside and the space within used for retail are distinct. In the malls such

separation has with purpose been removed. Arcade traders are almost all small independents. Hang-ons from an earlier age. Places where the shop keepers know their goods and understand their customers. Are personable. Remember you from the last time you came in. Talk to you when you shop. Troutmark Books. New York Deli. Cameraland. Capitol Books. Madam Fromage. Things Welsh. Ian Allen trainspotters paradise. Shops selling old coins, b&w signed star photos, boots, bags, 50s clothes, dj turntables. Jokes. Sheet music. Christian memorabilia. Martial arts ninja stars. Spices. Sweets. Knick knackery. Stuff you want. Stuff you don't need.

Siop y Triban used to be in the Wyndham. The legendary store where Harri Webb held court. Oram and Ward selling marquees and flags. Zen Arts was on the bend in the Duke Street, selling bonsai, dispensing fortunes. City Radio in the Morgan. 12 inch vinyl rock and roll past. Psychedelia flowering.

I tell her some of this. Her tape takes it down. The results will be spliced and fragmented then rebroadcast to arcade visitors wearing special headphones. Arcade present, arcade past.

The earliest was the Royal, linking St Mary Street with the Hayes. It was designed by James and Price for the Cardiff Arcade Company and opened in 1858. The 1896 Morgan, originally known as the New Central Arcade, and slightly to the north, was part of Edwin Seward's vision for Cardiff. He'd been to Paris and seen that city of glorious shopping passages and wanted to rebuild it here.

Seward, a partner in the firm Seward and Thomas, was closely involved in the great Industrial, Fine Art and Maritime exhibition[61] held in Cardiff in 1896 and was the architect of many of Cardiff's great public buildings. These included the Central Library in the Hayes and the Coal Exchange in Mount Stuart Square. Seward. The man who had a dream. Arcades blossomed across the city. The High Street in 1885, the Castle Arcade in 1887, the Wyndham in 1887 and the Duke Street in 1902. The stubby and forgotten Dominions, once full of film distributors, joining Queen Street with Crockherbtown Lane, opened in 1921. The now lost Andrews in the same decade. The coal metropolis of dust and dark became a lit city of covered malls.

In her investigations Jennie has discovered at least two further Cardiff cities – one above the arcades and the other below. Passageways, workshops, storerooms, meeting places – a warren of

corridors run. South of the
Morgan Arcade lie abandoned
furniture repair shops, lost
storerooms, boarded cellars,
service passages that mirror
the arcades themselves. Above
are cobwebbed rooms, halls
full of wrecked fitments, places
where once women sat with
sewing machines and stacks of
cloth and men with pens,
checklists and bills of lading, a
world of dust and disrepair.

The Cardiff Arcades are in the hands of three companies, all
outsiders. The property developers Helical Bar who own the Morgan
and the Royal. Urban City who have Castle, Duke and High Street.
Nick Come who owns the Wyndham Arcade. These guys balance
rent with need, commerce with concern, let the spaces largely to
independents, try to keep the nationals out.

Jennie Savage's expansive *Arcades Project*[62] still runs as I write. She
has drawn inspiration from the author and philosopher Walter
Benjamin who created the great pre-war *Passagenwerk*, the arcades of
Paris as artwork and mirror of man. Benjamin saw these arcades as
standing at a junction in modern society. Their place and space, the
way they worked, the rise of the middle classes who used them and
the new consumerism which they engendered represented turning
points for western culture. Society was now prosperous enough for
the emergence of the flâneur – Baudelaire's urban stroller, the man
who observes and is observed, who is simultaneously inside and
outside, is part of and is detached. The modernist personified. The
object observed by the flâneur becomes changed by the very act of
the flâneur observing. In Paris the practice flourished. Benjamin
followed it. Why was this observer-participant here? What were his
motivations? Was he himself the life on the streets he was observing?

Already Jennie's Project has seen the Cardiff Arcades used as
cinemas, recording studios, cultural trailways, historical maps and
collectors of the unclassifiable and fragmented meanderings of the
city's multiple lives. Jennie will assemble, categorize and order, record
and archive and then magnificently make visible. The components

are mounting up: The Portable Cinema. The Museum of the Moment. The Site-Specific Mobile Phone Video. The Exploring of Arcade Architecture Through Drawing. The Auto-Portrait. The Description of a Building Site. The Million Moments. The bridges. The dialogues. The connections. The imaginations. The manifestations. The reminiscences. The bewilderment.

Where next? Somewhere else? Is the Cardiff map now worn too thin? We shall see.

notes:

1. Cardiff Bridge, known to almost all Cardiffians as Canton Bridge, was built on its present site by a contractor from Brecon, Mr Parry, who was paid £3000 for job. That less £300 for the material of the old bridge which he largely re-used. The new bridge was opened in 1796, destroyed by flood in 1827, rebuilt 1859, widened 1877, widened again in 1931. Drunks jump off it and there have been numerous suicides.
2. See *Real Cardiff Two*, p 88-93 for the story of the tracking of this lost river.
3. The Cardiff Arms Hotel stuck out into Angel Street (now Castle Street) and was demolished as part of a council drive for road widening.
4. This was adopted as the National Rugby Stadium in 1953.
5. Opened 1937.
6. Jones Court was one of Cardiff's many one room up, one down groups of Victorian workers' housing. Built in 1830 by the 2nd Marquis of Bute for Irish immigrants constructing the new West Dock it languished for many years as the depot for Cardiff's street cleaners before being restored in 1982 and re-used as commercial offices.
7. The Bristol Bloodhound, a British Surface-to-Air (SAM) missile of the 1950s.
8. Alexis Korner 1928-1984 *the founding father of the British blues*. Born to an Austrian father and a Greek mother. Brought up in France and Switzerland. Moved to London in 1940.
9. John Crichton-Stuart, Second Marquis of Bute – 1793-1848.
10. Still there in 2009. Aged, leg lost to disease, but still writing.
11. Cardiff A – ST 184765 – 3.5 – Cardiff centre. Urban city centre. Pedestrianised – street (Frederick Street), 190 m from major road.
12. Jonathan Adams, architect of the Wales Millennium Centre
13. Now the 81 room budget designer Big Sleep Hotel on Bute Terrace.
14. See p.81, *Real Cardiff*, The Pearl.
15. The work of Gaunt Francis, Architects, who have offices in the same building.
16. 58 meters, sixteen stories.
17. Most of Cardiff was originally owned by three landowners – The Morgan family of Tredegar House, The Marquis of Bute of Cardiff Castle and the Windsor Clive family at St Fagan's. Bute's holdings were by far the largest.
18. HMRC – Her Majesty's Revenue and Customs.
19. *Pevsner Architectural Guides – The Buildings of Wales – Glamorgan*. Newman, John. Penguin, 1995.
20. Leslie Halliwell (1929-1989) British motion picture historian – founder of *Halliwell's Film Guides* – a man famous for his dislike of almost everything.
21. See p.138 *Ely Fields* in *Real Cardiff Two* (Seren, 2004).
22. Ray Smith (1936-1991). Rhondda thespian. Star of numerous TV series.

23. Dedwydd Jones, dramatist, author, son of Major Francis Jones, Queen's Herald Extraordinary of Wales, author the infamous *Black Books on the Welsh Theatre* which called for an end to the Welsh Arts Council and the immediate creation of the National Theatre.

24. As a physical entity it still hasn't although following Arts Council intervention in 2007 a national producing company now exists.

25. Cyclostyled manuals sent monthly by Royal Mail. Essays marked by a retired councillor in Manchester.

26. Welsh Regiment Museum (41st/69th Foot) previously housed in the Black and Barbican Towers.

27. A 1983 sculpture mural depicting scenes of the Roman occupation completed by Frank Abraham within the lower gallery to the south neo-Roman wall.

28. This is not as fanciful as it may sound. Today we have machines that can look underground without disturbing the surface. Instruments that can detect soil composition without excavation and others that can identify built-on ground from surface boulder. None of these existed fifty years ago.

29. http://www.ggat.org.uk/excav_P1020_CardiffCastle_Intro.htm

30. Created by David and Lynn Willrich (DJW Ltd), Bella Johnson director, with music David Mitcham played by the BBC National Orchestra of Wales and the Morriston Orpheus Choir.

31. See page 57.

32. The Terminus pub, later Sam's Bar. Now known as Zync, a 'trendy salsa bar in Cardiff's café quarter'. Buses finishing their runs down St Mary Street knew the stop as the Monument.

33. Son of Charles Vachell, druggist, after whom Charles Street was named.

34. Vachell's market had an entrance on High Street and on Duke Street. It was well used by country people who would bring in produce by horse-drawn sledge due to the poor condition of local roads.

35. Dic Penderyn was publically hanged here in 1831 for his alleged part in the Merthyr riots. The Drop, the street entrance to the place of execution was roughly where the St Mary Street entrance to the present market now is.

36. This was how I first uncovered Jackson Browne, who had somehow passed me by. Bought *The Flying Burrito Brothers* here, on a whim. Got *Mingus Mingus Mingus* from the middle of a stack of Maria Callas.

37. Birdsong broadcast eighteen hours daily by Digital One who runs Britain's digital radio network in the space left by collapsed OneWord channel. Recorded in the Wiltshire garden of the company's chairman, Quentin Howard, the tape is a repeating loop recorded in 1992. When a commercial operator again buys the frequency *Birdsong* will cease.

38. STD – Subscriber Trunk Dialling. Before the arrival of this innovation anything other than a local call had to be connected by an operator.

39. In the days before the DVLA in Swansea these were Glamorgan County Council's Licensing Department. I worked there, for a time. In 1964 Thomas Woodward came in and I sold him a provisional licence. In 1965 he changed his name to Tom Jones.

40. Charlie Mingus – *The Black Saint and the Sinner Lady* – Impulse, NYC 1963.

41. The *Shoes of the Fisherman's Wife Are Some Jive Ass Slippers*, 1965, released on *Let My Children Hear Music*, 1971.

42. Charlie Mingus – *Goodbye Pork Pie Hat* – On *Mingus Ah Um* – Impulse NYC 1959.

43. *An Eye For The People* by the late Ray Howard Jones was installed in 1959 and fell unopposed to the developers bulldozers in 2008.

44. Now known as Kitty Flynn's, corner of St Mary Street.

45. Closed and replaced with the present Queens Arcade which opened in 1994.

46. Stuff of legend. According to Peter Read's one act play *John Tripp's Tragic Cabaret* other members were Robert Minhinnick, Peter Finch and Nigel Jenkins.

47. The Liberal politician and industrialist (1820-1883) in bronze, paid for by well wishers, made by James Milo ap Griffith in 1885.
48. The contest attracted 127 entries.
49. Occupied at the time by Zion Chapel and the houses clustered around Winstone Court.
50. Carved by W. Taylor of William Clarke, Llandaff.
51. Sir John Ballinger (1860-1933) Victorian head librarian at Cardiff and then the first National Librarian at Aberystwyth. Might have stayed local if Cardiff had won.
52. *Wanted For Writing Poetry* – Peter Finch, Second Aeon, 1966. His first book.
53. Henry Miller, *Tropic of Cancer*. Obelisk Press, Paris 1934. First published in Great. Britain by John Calder (died last year, occasional poet, met him toting a case full of books store to store in the 1980s bad times) 1963.
54. See also Llanrumney Hall, *Real Cardiff Two*
55. *Yeah Yeah* – Georgie Fame. The British Mose Allison. By 1968 lost it. Somehow never followed up.
56. *The Mapping Projects* (http://www.jenniesavage.co.uk/maps/maptext.html) a series of investigations which culminated in a Chapter Arts Centre weekend involving Stefan Caddick, Mike Pearson, Simon Whitehead, Saul Albert, Lottie Child, Heike Roms, Ivan Pope, Derek McCormack, Neil Jenkins, Simon Pope, and Phil Babot.
57. *Star* – Splott, Tremorfa, Adamsdown, Roath – an acronym from the names of Cardiff's eastern inner city working class districts. *Star Radio* was broadcast as random encounter, empowerment as art, the working-class voice as historical, academic document. Radio as a walking event. Chatter as DVD. Theory as fiction. Conversation as content. Content as history. The resulting archive was exhibited at the National Museum of Wales adding validity to street cred and cementing the work into the national psyche.
58. Check http://www.anecdotalcity.com/
59. In 1997 for her degree show.
60. A b   surgage was an enclosed field, rented to freemen (burgesses). In medieval towns such plots were built upon. Their lines remain in parts of Cardiff centre today.
61. Held on land at Cathays Park donated by the Marquis of Bute the exhibition promoted local resources and the trade and industries of Cardiff. It included a canal and a lake and a model working dairy, a biscuit factory and, unaccountably for Cardiff, a replica of Shakespeare's house. The exhibition ran for six months and received over a million visitors.
62. Check http://www.arcadesproject.org/

EAST

BOUNDARY OF THE TOWN

The eastern edge of Cardiff was once a line running up Castle Road, the thoroughfare that connected the Long Cross with the Crwys. Preaching crosses both, markers for travellers, outdoor places where ancient Christianity flourished. The faithful would gather before the preacher. The rain would fall. God's will would be done. Both crosses are now lost. The Crwys somewhere under Gladstone School, the Long Cross in the foundations of Longcross Court at the Newport Road junction. Until 1875 the Borough stretched no further than here. The well-to-do Tredegarville, built on the lands of the Morgan family, buffered this border from the town's ancient core. To the east lay fields and farms that stretched for an empty mile until you came to the hamlet of Roath.

Castle Road, once known as Heol y Plwcca when it was no more than a muddy lane, was renamed City Road when Cardiff won that status in 1905. It originally led to the gallows on the edge of the Little Heath[1]. This was Death Junction, the place where Albany, Richmond and City Road now meet[2]. City Road was never lined by great houses, was never decorous, nor powerful. It was always a ragged and itinerant place, a borderland where change was endemic. Even today, with the actual city border moved east by eight miles, City Road still feels like a frontier.

Lloyd Robson and I are making a film for the Open University. Lloyd, Robert Mitchum obsessive, seeker for truths in the flickering literary changes of Allen Ginsberg and William Burroughs and among the sonic inventions of the Bauhaus, Bukowski and Allen Fisher, is the link man. Selected for his street cred and age. I'm the grey-haired reality check. Used to be the renegade. World's caught up. The working title for the film is *The Making of the Contemporary UK*. City Road is an exemplar of ethnicity and constant change.

We start in the Taste Buds Café and will walk the road end to end talking of change and culture and whatever comes to mind. Director Chris Guiver[3] has us wired for sound. His speciality is shooting from a distance, wrong side of the junction, from behind buses, around cars, out of crowds, other side of the road. Documentary vérité. You keep talking, forget he's there.

Lloyd used to live near here, in what, in another life, might have been a cold-water brownstone apartment but in this one was a bedsit opposite the Mackintosh Institute. The Mac, the faux-castellated and originally eighteenth century mansion that has been known variously as Plas Newydd, Roath Lodge and Roath Castle. It is currently a community centre, a bowls and tennis club, an oasis in a terraced sea. When we arrive it is in the process of being refurbished. There are men on ladders pointing,  plastering, painting. The glory of the family home of the Mackintosh of Mackintosh[4] is being restored. We stand outside decoding a Welsh road sign which warns against parking. Do you speak Welsh, Chris asks Lloyd? I does and I doesn't, he replies. I speaks Cardiff. Kairdif. That's the Welsh language round yere.

City Road itself has to be one of the most ethnically varied places in the UK. It certainly offers the richest mix of eateries anywhere in Wales. They surround us on every side: Tenkaichi Sushi, Halal Ambala Takeaway, Topoli Persian, Troy Turkish, City Balti, Mezza Luna Moroccan, The Bollywood Lounge, Swallow Chinese, Lambe Stores For Your African & Continental Foods, Polski Sklep, City Pizza, Lilo Grill House, Radhuny Mexican, American & Polynesian at The Hawaiian, Fornos Mediterranean Sandwiches, burgers, chips, pizzas, things with spice and things with sauce and things with rich brown gravy.

The Hawaiian[5] is a monstrosity. Clad in 3-D block the colour and size of those used to build the pyramids it sits there like an escapee from strip mall America. Beyond it stands the brutal 60s tower block of Coleg Glan Hafren where dispossessed youth learn hairdressing and aromatherapy. Would Solomon Andrews have cared? The nineti-eth century entrepreneur and operator of Cardiff's first horse-drawn buses had his garage next door. The original brick arches are still in place. Lewis Motors now. A twenty-first century Andrews would have been running Little Chef along the lines of the Hawaiian.

In the lane that runs back alongside the Gaiety – cinema for decades, then bingo, finally the Spin Ten Pin (now closed) – Lloyd

shows us just how creative graffiti can get. Stencils have been used to mark up the permutation poem: *Someone The Truth Let The People Be What About it. What about it the truth. Let the people be someone. Let the people be truth. What about it someone.* Our territory, I tell him. We know this stuff. Kashmir[6] Motors stands beyond. *Sometimes it's easier to find roses in the sea.* Some creative with a working knowledge of apostrophes has put that up.

On the wall of the Park Conservative Club (obligatory portrait of Margaret Thatcher along with a photo of David Cameron inside) is a plaque commemorating the road's centenary celebrations on 10th July, 2005. Unveiled by Rodney Berman, Liberal Council leader. The old order back. Socialism nowhere to be seen.

City Road was once famous for its car showrooms. Dozens, in line. Shops that had room for no more than two Ford Prefects did business next to open lots selling hundreds. There were stickers on the dials reading 'The mileage shown for this car is an approximation only'. BSA House shifted motorbikes and Reliant three-wheelers. Showrooms sold Rovers. Forecourts were chock with Hillmans and Austins. Cash preferred. No guarantees. At this price, guv? Almost all have now moved on.

At the Newport Road end was once installed the city's first automatic food dispenser. This illuminated box the size of a Smeg fridge would deliver a carton of milk in exchange for 6d[7]. Crowds formed to watch the novelty. Grown men who had never drunk milk since they lived with their mothers were to be seen inserting coins and cheering when the machine delivered. Click, thum-thunk. There they'd be, opening the hopper and marvelling. Removing the wax-coated cardboard cartons and holding them up to the light. Full-top cream delivered out of hours. The audacity of the age.

So why is the street like this? Chris gets us to talk. John, the sound man, has inserted new batteries. We've been going for hours. We're standing outside a store which has an flyer in the window advertising a vacancy for a Nigerian Cook (UK work permit essential). Inner city, fellowship of brothers, easy spirit, low cost, surrounded by a mesh of rentable rooms, beds to crash in. This is the road where in summer I've seen locals cooking over braziers on the pavement, kids dancing to beat boxes, men squatting on their haunches, spitting, playing cards.

Poet's Corner, the pub, is now PCs. Cardiff's poets don't go there. The streets to the east are called Cowper, Wordsworth, Southey, Byron, Milton, Shakespeare. Connecting them is Castle Lane. The past just about hanging on.

Then we're back on Newport Road again, on the corner where once stood the Wiltshire and Dorset Bank. Solomon Andrews' house was at no 47 and at no 49 the conical-towered Clark's College which taught typing and coached entrants to the Civil Service. The past. All swept. Keep your eye on the present. It doesn't hang about long.

HODGE

A name to reckon with. Was once. The car loan salesman made good. Made it so good that he built the first Cardiff skyscraper. The first tall thing we'd ever had in this city. Up there before the Pearl was. It looked like a block of flats but we were so in awe of the man and his financial audacity that nobody said. This was on Newport Road. Roath Road that was. Built among a line of grand houses, on the site of Elmsfield. The past doing things well that we struggle with today.

Julian S. Hodge was the grandvisier who wanted to give Cardiff its own bank and its own cathedral. The bank he managed but the cathedral is still waiting. The Catholic Church held back from accepting his proffered £3 million. The new St David's, and what a place that could have been, was never built. The Church was suspicious. Glory be to God and Hodge sort of stuck in the craw. In an earlier era there would have been no such reluctance.

The Hodge Building was constructed in the early sixties to house the financier's growing empire. He'd run a string of car insurance, hire purchase and other loan companies which had led to the founding of the Commercial Bank of Wales in 1971. In County Hall, where I was, up on the red tarmac of King Edward VII Avenue, we had a flyer enclosed with our payslips. Bank with Hodge. You Won't Regret It.

In the canteen lunchtime Trevor explained to me that Julian Hodge was the only lifelong socialist he'd ever come across who owned six motors and a mansion in Jersey. Trevor was hot on the politics of capitalism. He was the man who'd explained to me how it all worked, how to get on, how to control what you had. In the pits when the inspectors came round you let them count all the shovels and tick them on their clipboards and then you took the same shovels out by a back door and over the mountain to the next pit where the inspectors could count them again. Same with banks, Trevor said. Prophetic man. Trevor ran most of the office sweepstakes, did the ticketing for annual Christmas dance, and could supply household appurtenances at a fraction of their shop price. So long as they were items used by the NCB that was. Most of the staff had kitchens full of tin mugs and sheds laden with stout-handled picks and shovels. Martin Williams had a back fence to his terraced house made out of pit props. Further up the valley someone Trevor had once owed money to heated their house with the reserve boiler lifted from the pithead baths. Open a Hodge account, advised Trevor. Conform, stay unnoticed. But I never did.

The Hodge Building served down the years as home to a variety of financial and commercial institutions including one of the successors to the Glamorgan County that Trevor and I once worked for, South Glamorgan. Around it the grand villas sequentially failed to be replaced by a mix of high rise and red-brick office. Behind this complex lay the art college at Howard Gardens. Place of paint and beards and wild visual adventures. A Cardiff base for the flickering avant garde. Terry Setch, Ian Grainger, Ceri Richards, Peter Prendergast, Ivor Davies, Glenys Cour. Home of Anthony Howells and his adventures in what was officially described as Time-Based Studies. Art that required the clock to move. Performances. Videoed constantly and recycled as *Grey Suit,* a VHS magazine. Cardiff Art in Time. Ifor Thomas inside a cardboard box reading poetry. Howells himself climbing in and out of a wardrobe in the company of a high-heeled model. Both progressively removing their clothing. Her reduced to stockings, him to ancient interlock underwear. When they'd finished they sat in dressing gowns while the crowd applauded.

Today Hodge is no more. The philanthropist dead and his bank, never to run the Welsh world, managed by others. It sits on a quiet corner at Windsor Place. His building on the Roath Road has changed hands. Stickered vehicle pillars run along the pavement. Rwy'n Caru Ciwdod[8]. A pull in for arrivals. The structure has been refurbished, rebuilt with new access, new marble, a new pool and health suite, new acres of light. The great glass mural depicting Hodge's sixties Cardiff complete with East Moors Steelworks has been kept as a back drop. The tower is now the Macdonald Holland. The building renamed Holland House. Never Dutch, hardly a house either. Four-star high rise. A city hotel. Royal opening in 2004. Lloyds TSB, the last tenants, synchronously still chasing the ghosts of money as I write.

Jonathan Adams and I are deep into Tall Buildings Day. How many of Cardiff's many highs can we do. We've already climbed The Capital Tower (p.33), the medieval heights of St John's Church (p.37), Tredegarville's Eastgate House (p.36), the Bute Street flats (p.133) and BT's higher than you are Welsh skyscraper at Stadium House (p.59). Now we are tackling where it all began. Hodge that was. Still Hodge for those who knew Cardiff then.

Stuart Emberlin, deputy manager, takes us to the top late afternoon. He's had a hell of day so far. We should have been here at three but got entranced by Shahida atop Loudoun (see p.133) and it's now well gone four. The Hotel has been rebranded the Mercure[9], part of the Accor group, who also own Ibis, Etap, Novotel, and the Mercure Lodge on East Tyndall Street. The hotel trade shifts in the commercial winds. Downturn is slow in hitting, the place is full. The fifteenth floor once held the penthouse suite of the developer, Rightacres. Recently vacated. Mercure plan more bedrooms. 165 will rise to 180.

So long as demand stays good.

From the top, access by far the easiest of any tall building we've done today, steps and a door, there are views of the Crown Courts, and the prison, the fire station, and the port. Working cranes along the blue of water. Touchable. The graveyard[10] on the corner of Moria Terrace and Moria Place, where the 1849 cholera victims clustered, is now a bright

splash of basketball courts and
pathways, the green lung of an
urban park.

From this vantage the 1854
prison looks like a block of
converted warehouses. Only the
walls distinguish it from
surrounding development.
Inner courtyards are shrunk by
the addition of new cells, new
blocks, extra facilities. Remand
is big business. Jonathan thinks
the place restricts city develop-

ment. But its location is handy for those who have to visit. Do your
guests worry, I ask Stuart. He shakes his head.

On Roath Road that was I head back, walking towards Newport
again. The capital that is Cardiff is so contained. I pass them, the
landmarks, the famous Cardiff things. The now sold for redevelopment church of James the Great; the Royal Infirmary, site of the Long
Cross; the Four Elms entrance to Green Lane, now Broadway; the
once dignified but now ragged and turned to multi-use houses of
Newport Road; the lost blacksmiths; the great house of Roath Court,
now a place of funerals; then home. I get there in twenty minutes.
Without a plane I've seen the city from above. Does it look like
Google Earth? It does.

THE GARDENS

I'm passing the flour again, the two-kilo bag on the pavement outside
the phone box on the north-east corner of the gardens, cracked open,
rained on, step spread, moved by the winds. So much paste untaken
by animals, ignored by birds, uninfested, unscraped up, made into
biscuit, tortilla, unrisen bread. None of this happens. The flour stays.
It's slowly shrinking as precipitation takes it to street drain and to
road crack. Makes it pulp and mush. Was going to photograph this
from inception to reduction to final dissolution. Make an essay on the
way time moves. How it is on the dark days. How it is when the light
shines. How it will end up for all of us. Flour in our veins. Riddling

our skin. Didn't. Stood looking as the traffic rolled. Went back again weeks on. Flour still there. Passed yesterday, only a few streaks. Looked once more today, maybe a mark on the tarmac hard to tell. Was I ever here? Tomorrow we'll all be gone.

In the phone box are three girls in primary colours, 60s retro-pattern discs and bars, hoop earrings, hair in black shining spikes, tattoos on their legs and in spirals climbing out of their belts. They're shouting at the receiver, into the receiver, onto the receiver, all three of them, none of them know this receiver word. It's a handset maybe or if it's not that it's a phone. Everything shifts as age pushes it. Booth box boom bang bang. They're shouting yeah yeah and fuck and high-pitched god oh my god. And this boy is hovering around them but they don't see him. But they can sense him. Just haven't looked. He's outside the box high on Carling or something banging the booth's glass sides. Fist. Side of foot. Fist again. Don't. Does. Spray of glass like crushed ice. Who worries. Yeah yeah. Handset left hanging talking to itself. Boom tschsch tschsch boom fucking boom bang bang.

Go through the park where the new cut takes the pulsing brook straight preventing overload. Nothing flooded here since the early fifties. Almost sixty years of functionality and good drainage. End to that soon. Men take small dogs off leads. Light falls through leaves. Mallard in pairs meditate on the water.

In the annual carnival the small park fills with stalls. There a pasting table with a portable hot plate on it and some Iceland burgers, another with old books taken out of the attic, one with broken jigsaws and games no one wants, and then a table of drinks no cans just those soft-sided sugar-squash tasteless from the pound shop. Push a straw in through the fragile lid. Suck if you dare. You can enter the raffle somewhere win a can of sardines or a potted plant. Man with a scrawled card hanging round his neck *Guess My Age. 10p.* No mention of what the prize could be. I try it. Put down 74. In the river they've let loose five-hundred yellow Mothercare plastic ducks all of them with numbers. Kids in bright wellingtons push at them with sticks. Ducks catch on stones, tangle in the weeds, sink. There's a father in up to his mid-calf trousers. An eight year old fallen over completely, crying. Burger smoke. Bouncy castle. Tiny trace of old pop from a radio. People you've never seen ever ventured from their local houses standing here in the sunlight belonging. Fat man with a pipe sucking. Woman with a straw hat in a wheel chair. St John's

Ambulance arm-band sitting on a fold-out chair under the rowan. Anyone broken anything? Not yet.

Across the lawn, where one of the lost tributaries of the Nant Brook flowed where the grass is now close-cropped and there's flowering cherry planted, the Asians are playing football. *No Ball Games No Cycling Keep Your Dog On A Lead Deep Water Danger No Bathing.* In this over-controlled oasis where regulation is culturally or genetically ignored no one's got a music machine blaring or a bonfire burning but they are whacking their football and the plant life is suffering. Lots of force. Seven of the players shouting across their improvised pitch an eighth up a tree screaming encouragement. A goal. Another goal. Dog barks, vanishes into the plantings, chasing something. Sweet wrappers. Sunday. I learned to walk on this very grass. I've a memory down there at the bottom of the bucket that has me encouraged by my mother's urging taking a step and another step and one more then half falling forward into my father's open arms. Football bangs across the same stretch. Same weeds. Same sunlight. Same grass. Is this memory real or was it put there by listening to the memories of others? Memory of a memory. Bent by fog. I walk on. Another goal takes place on the cherry lawn.

The benches have names on them[11]. Plaques. Metal memorials fixed to vandal-proof metal seating. Green painted struts look like wood but can't be carved or sliced or broken by karate kicking or jumping from alcoholic heights. These benches don't sit on the hard-top pathways but are bolted into the land with foot-long spikes. The ground around them is littered with a detritus of crushed sweet, gum and cigarette. The people they remember all came here, all delighted in sunlight, walked their dogs plastic bags tied to their wrists, ball-throwers under their arms, came in all weathers, sat and read papers here, passed time, enjoyed time, wasted time, loved this place. In the churchyard which backs onto the park the stone memorials have been largely removed for safety, for clarity, and for the clearing of the past that the living regularly do. Our dead, if they are marked at all, and there are so many of them, are now recalled on roadsides, in gardens, on metal tags next to trees, on seats that others use. Sitting on a bench dedicated to a person I once knew well is a man drinking a can of black label, feet out, face like a beacon, alright mate? All right. Yes.

At the gate the keeper in baseball hat and jeans is locking a padlock into a heavy chain. It's dusk, light pale in the northern sky. He has three further gates to visit, all of them with clock signs showing closing time. The engine is running in his car. Old white Nissan. Dog in front. In the growing dark, inside, the park is full. Youths by the dozen. Girls in white jeans in lines on the benches. Boys with attitude and cans. Most smoking, kicking their legs around, mauling the branches of the young birches, breaking the buds off, dancing on the bench ends, rolling on their heels, turning on imaginary skateboards, spitting, mouthing, milling, pulling their caps into new sideways angles, smoothing the curve of the peaks, staring into the air, into the eyes of their fellows, into the ground. The locked park at night is their park. They graffiti the path top, write their names onto the boles of trees. Some of them I can see in the distance hauling themselves over the spikes of the railings. One of them carries a bike. Another a bag. They'll be here until beyond midnight. Weather won't stop them. The darkness is a joy. They'll sit like addicts. Waiting for the smack to arrive. Gatekeeper says it isn't his concern. Why should it be. Be gone in the morning. Trash and buggered plants less hassle than a night-watchman. Points himself at Newport Road. Gone.

River is in flood, high as the bridge. The two channels are almost one, a great acre of brown water pushes towards the River Rumney where this stream outfalls. The upstream end of the artificial island where the channels divide is concrete faced like the prow of an ironclad ship. Moulded. Ferro. But, unsettled by seventy years of flood and frost, it has tilted, becoming separated from the land it protects. The river is now eroding the land behind it. It wouldn't take much to effect a repair, couple of bags of mortar, stone infill dredged up from stream bottom. Push it all in place. Half a day from a man with a pick and another with a shovel. But nothing is done and the erosion grows. It's the kind of thing that when this place was a country village would have been mended by neigh-bours. Man with a terrier on a long lead watches. Think they'll ever fix it, I ask? Nah, he says.

Day after Boxing Day. Half the district still on leave taking their kids and themselves for a walk to escape the Christmas cabin fever. Small ones on bikes and in plastic peddle carts. Silver scooters. Electric cars. Balls. Dogs. No access to the gardens. Gates all remain padlocked in the slow sun. At the Church Terrace end a Council notice, A4 printed, done in WORD and then laminated, hole punched and plastic twine strung to the gate railings. *Park Closed Due To Frost*. A brother to this notice strung on the Mill Park next door, been there for months, *Gate Temporarily Closed Due To Slippery Surface*. In the Council offices they repeat the mantra O God my God protect us from litigation and risk. Do not let anyone sue. Inside the Keepers hut closed and metal doored. The ancient toilets rotting in the unvisited dark.

Early spring sun low through the crocus. A long low planting beside the river. White, yellow, orange like a honey bee. Trampled by dogs, by walkers. Squashed by children. But they always grow back.

The silver band has been booked by the council to play hymns and arias and songs that Tom Jones made famous but without the words. They sit in a uniformed half circle up beyond the rose beds. Their van is parked right on the entrance pathway, got it into the park through the gate without difficulty. And why not. Essential delivery. Pensioners swaying. Couples lying full out among the daisies. Kids chasing each other. Why Why Why Delilah. National anthem of south-east Wales.

In the history of St Margaret's Church[12] there's a note that shows that when burials outgrew the ancient lime-washed circular church-yard the elders bought new land. On the slope running softly down to Park's southern end. 1865. That was before there was a park. And before the houses. All this was unbroken green. Even then there were more dead than the land could manage. They put a new wall in and loaded the recent departed into pristine softly sloping ground[13]. Kids drink along it now. Girls at night sitting in rows behind the trees that remain. Council took the others out. Lines of sight restored so there's nowhere for the recalcitrants to hide. Doesn't work. Went by last Sunday. A dozen in a row drinking and smoking. Lad with his Peugeot on the grass, hiphop sounding through the open window. Thum thum. The dead dancing underground.

Checked for the flour again today. Months on. I can still see some faint marks. Maybe. Bright light from the herbaceous. Asters, Cynara, Rudbeckia, Salvia, Hollyhock, Delphinium, Phlox. Someone on a bench reading. Woman with a giant-wheeled buggy. Pensioned clergy-man from the St Teilo's apartments moving so slowly passed the rose trellis. Mother and son throwing a Frisbee. Small dog walking. Child on a toddler bike with outriders, and bells and ribbons, empty lager can in the basket on the back. Everything growing again.

THE ARRIVAL OF WINE IN CARDIFF

My aunt got me into this. She was the only wine drinker I knew. This was 1955 and she was listening to *Cherry Pink and Apple Blossom White*[14] on the radio in her room. Last year it had been *Sh-Boom (Life Could Be A Dream)*[15] but I hardly remembered that. We were at our rambling family house in Ty Draw, four up three down. There were chickens in a coop out the back. Down the lane someone kept a pig. My aunt had a bullfight poster on her wall and a pair of castanets hanging on a tack. She was painting her nails. An untipped Senior Service was burning in a glass ashtray, a half-drunk glass of red stood to the side. So continental. No one else in our family had ever drunk wine before. Do you want to taste it? I did. Not sweet, not bitter. Why would anyone like this? At 8 years old how would I know?

Cardiff had not exactly rushed to embrace the grape and the vine. The city had been a brewing centre for decades – Brains, Hancocks, Crosswells, Ely, Rhymney. Bitter did the working man's trick. Women took stout. For health. My grandmother swore by black and sweet Milk Stout Mackeson. An invalid beer. It looks good, it tastes good and by golly it does you good. Guinness is good for you. Out of the darkness comes light. Guinness gives you strength. These brewers knew how to push their wares. If you were really run down then you could get a doctor to prescribe dark ale, although this had never actually happened to anyone we knew. At the chemists you could buy fortified medicinal wine. In City Road they had a sign in their window among the Beechams Pills and bottles of red embrocation. For Strength and Stamina. How ill do you have to be, I asked my mother. Very.

The only place they actually sold wine was at something called an off licence half way along Wellfield Road. My father explained that this meant you could buy alcohol there but were not allowed to consume it. In the shop, that is. What you did in the street outside was up to you. There were no further off licences in the east of the city other than those attached to pubs. Why would you want to drink at home, said my father. Unless it was to top up what you'd drunk in the pub first. The Wellfield Road establishment sold stuff in squat ovals with pictures of grapes on the labels, in opaque bottles, in dark bottles, in green bottles, in bottles covered with net, in bottles sitting in raffia baskets. Their trade was a steady surreptitious shuffle. Cleaned up. My aunt was a big wine drinker, so she said. Made you sophisticated. Kept you slim. She had a gold cigarette holder and a cache of continental film magazines which showed naked women displaying their breasts but with their pubic bushes airbrushed out. For years I imagined that this was how all women were. Pink. When I discovered otherwise it was quite a shock.

When I eventually began to visit pubs in search of enlightenment, wine was nowhere to be seen. Men drank beer in heavy glasses. Pint of light. Pint of mild. Lager was sold in small green Carlsberg bottles and very expensive. Women, if there were any in our company, would drink gin and lime or vodka and orange or that bohemian favourite, Dubonnet and lemonade. If Henri de Toulouse-Lautrec had visited Cardiff then that's what he would have drunk, wouldn't he?

When wine did make a public house appearance it was in the form of a single bottle which the barman had always opened earlier and kept fresh, when he remembered, by stuffing the cork back into the neck. There was never a selection. You want wine you got wine. And men never drank it, only women. This was 1963. *Hey Paula, Walk Like A Man, You Can't Sit Down*[16]. And of course The Beatles, who came from nowhere and changed the world.

But then people began to turn up with the stuff at parties. In the Wyndham Arcade they'd opened a Wine Shop, a drinking venue which did not sell beer. Half a bitter? Try the Cambrian round the corner. At the Wine Shop you sat around an upturned barrel. Wine came by the bottle and you poured the glasses yourself. Behind the counter they had a set of bull fighting posters. My aunt had been ahead of her time. There was a sombrero and a stringless guitar hanging on the wall. Everyone smoked. The wine of choice was Spanish sauternes – sugar yellow – I came to think that this was what all wine should taste like, a high syrupy sweetness to which viniculture should aspire. The activity began to spread.

Norman Schwenk, American, poet, high priest of the Sherman Theatre's film club, showed me how to get wine for free. Turn up at gallery openings where red and white were given out to private viewers, along with cheese and pineapple chunks on sticks. Do you need an invitation? Say you've had one but left it home. At the Welsh Arts Council gallery in Museum Place they were showing Bruce Lacey's machines, robotic art works which moved, the Womaniser, an iron lung with legs and sets of inflating rubber-gloved hands along its chest. Plans on the walls. Assemblages of lost clockwork and metal drums. We rolled in and took the proffered red. Went back for white. And then for more. No charge. The state was obviously great. Art was wonderful too.

The party problem was the cork. Why couldn't wine come with screw caps like sherry? At the corner of City Road and Albany the grocer offered low alcohol cooking sherry refills straight from the barrel. You took in your empty, got it filled, rescrewed the cap. All at bargain prices. But you needed to be desperate to drink a whole bottle. Were we desperate? Not yet.

Opening wine was hard. You needed a corkscrew. No-one ever had one. No-one really knew how they should be used. Attempts were made to open bottles by cracking their necks off but this was never the preferred approach. Bottles could and did completely shatter deluging the neck cracker with sticky fluid. Fragments of glass entered the contents of the bottle making drinking like Russian roulette. The better approach was to press the cork down hard so that it ended up floating in fragments inside. Drinking was still difficult and subject to sudden rushes of liquid as you attempted to pour. And the resulting drink was usually emulsified with fragments of cork which stuck to your tongue. Accessible, alcoholic, sophisticated, ah yes, but not yet actually enjoyable.

Pubs were now advancing the vino cause by offering choice. Red and white. Ask for a glass of that staple of the uncertain, rosé, and the barman would make up a half and half mixture while you watched. Bottles were displayed in a glass-fronted case. I'd always imagined that drink would be dispensed more easily via a large optic but this never caught on. Wine came by the glass and during the 1970s there was only one size, small. The enormous 42D cup wine goblets of recent times were unimaginable.

Socially wine was advancing. If you had any cultural aspiration at all then you needed to be able to talk about them over a glass of red. Beer wasn't enough. Libation of the masses. Beer and its working class belly would not do.

The really big breakthrough was when wine started to show up in boxes. Cardiffians already used to the wonders of the Party Seven – giant tins of beer which, once opened, could rarely be successfully closed again – took to wine by the box with abandon. Boxes lacked the faux sophisticated trappings of year, vineyard and taste. Range was limited. But they were marketed as a reasonable priced way to get drunk on the great new alcoholic treat of the 70s, and, to the applause of a whole generation, opened without a corkscrew. Push in the plug and turn. Out came the wine. Magic.

Wine was on a roll. It appeared en mass on the shelves of our ever enlarging supermarkets – Bulls Blood, Blue Nun, Black Tower, Chianti, Liebfraumilch, Mateus Rosé, ready-mixed sangria. Households acquired corkscrews, men learned how they worked. Tales went the rounds about not mixing colours in order to stay sober, using white to clean up red wine carpet stains and urban myths about rugby players who could down whole bottles in one gulp and still remain standing.

'Red red wine, go to my head, make me forget'. You'd hear this in the Cardiff night clubs although few of the smashed singing along to it had reached their spaced-out states by wine alone.

The rest is easy history. Red wine is once again good for the heart and the arteries. Most Tesco's have a larger wine section than WH Smiths does for books. Threshers and Oddbins are endemic. All corner shops have more wine for sale than biscuits. The Wellfield Wine Shop is, however, no longer with us. Replaced by a branch of Oddbins at the Globe Centre. Cabernet Sauvignon, Pinot Noir, Merlot and Chardonnay roll off drinkers tongues. Franz Ferdinand on their iPods. No bullfight posters on their walls.

THE CREATIVE EAST

In my *Super Red Book Cardiff*, a sort of Cardiff A to Z, there's no mention of this. There's a list of roads and places key-coded onto flat street maps. The water courses are marked in blue. Parkland is done in dots with hills and outcrops missing. Yet whichever way you look at it there's no mention of creativity. Cardiff the creative hub. City of art. City of design. Capital of culture. The place where these industries flower. Some places in the city have had this description thrust upon them. Mount Stuart Square, media hotbed, streets full of young men with beards and women carrying cameras. Market Road, Canton, thick with dramatists, performers, youth with dyed hair, strange shoes and script-filled laptops. Pierhead Street running rich with parliamentarians, grand dames, aria-hummers, stage directors, composers, first violinists, gangs in evening suits, men with silk scarves, women in heels and pearls, technicians carrying lights and sheets of scenery, fresh shaven AMs, hats, scarves.

Received wisdom puts Cardiff's creative focal point somewhere in mid-Pontcanna. On those streets are poets and painters in daily dialogue. Composers passing time flâneuring among the leaves. Dramatists in the cafes, fixing their plotlines. Dialogue leaping, in two languages, through the very air. Check Le Gallois on Romilly Crescent, epicure epicentre for the thinking man. Drink wine at the legendary Cameo, the eye of the needle through which all creatives will, at some time of other, have to pass. Visit Café Brava, the Conway, Cibo, Ana Bela Café-Bistro. Is this Wales or San Francisco? You choose.

The west of the city clearly has the edge. There are pubs in quantity. Ale in torrent. The roads bend in engaging curves. Architecture changes house to house, one design never dominates. These streets were beyond Bute's uniform design enforcing estate managers. Builders built what they wanted. Style came first.

Back east, where worker's Roath buffeted up against aspiring Penylan, things were flat by comparison. Fewer pubs, fewer eateries, regulation streets in regulation order. The prim Edwardian terraces of Sandringham, Westville, Kimberley, Amesbury and Ilton rose quietly up the hill as if life had been beaten to silence inside them. Around the end of Waterloo Gardens, where the Roath Brook slips unnoticed under the road, are a cluster of shops. Originally grocer, post office, butcher, dairy. Then mini-mart, post office, butcher, empty. Last year corner shop, post office, empty, hairdresser. I spot a tendency developing. Soon this will be estate agents, flowers, still empty, rebuilt as housing. But the east bucks the trend. The corner shop fills. The post office gets completely rebuilt to accommodate its unending snake of pensioners. The hairdressers booms. The vacant butchers reopens as Waterloo Gardens Teahouse[17]. Upmarket. Russian Caravan tea. Darjeeling. White Silver Needle Organic. Oolong Iron Goddess of Mercy. Dragon's Well. Ancient Emerald

Lily Organic Fair Trade. Ceylon. Kenyan. Coffee only served with reluctance. Cakes from Gluten-free heaven. Poetry readings. Style and content. Art on the walls.

Actually the district is far less culturally Spartan than early impressions might give. Despite a richness in street names redolent of the Boer War – Mafeking, Ladysmith, Kimberley – kids drinking in the parks and some vandalising of the bus shelter violence, so far, is largely absent. This is not a place where's there's much granulated car window and house break-in, riotous assembly and never-ending road-hump. It is more dog walker and child buggy, retired TV producers taking the air, violinists in the parks, joggers with iPods and parked Audi Quattros.

The house on Westville Road I'm visiting you wouldn't know was there unless you were looking. It's an unassuming terrace, built in 1909 on former Tredegar land[18]. Hard red brick, bathstone bays, slate roof – all in generous Edwardian proportion. David Griffiths lives here. How many David Griffiths are there in Wales? But this is David Wyn Griffiths, portrait painter. He's a man I first met in 1971 when he turned up at the Duffryn Close home of John Idris Jones, my publisher. John Jones Cardiff Ltd. 70s manufacturer of dragon tote bags[19], publisher of translations, guides to Welsh teas and books of verse. I was the shaky young poet on the verge of his first real publication. *The End of the Vision.* John Idris stood relaxed in the lounge with a girl on his arm. One he later picked up and turned upside down, just to show he could do it. Her skirt falling to her waist, revealing her knickers. David Griffiths arrived with a camera and took several moody shots of me sitting on the sofa smoking a Woodbine. Back cover shots. The book is long gone. But if you are interested then I could maybe still get you a copy.

David's studio is out back. It was once a coach house and later a garage, full of oily cans, old sacks, and broken machinery. Amid the dusty detritus David established his creative space. Painters need light. Need constancy. Flickering change, the moving sun, the passing cloud, these makers of shadow are all enemies. David did what he could to minimise them. He put in heaters, knocked through walls, added unobtrusive roof lights. People don't know this place is here and I like that, he tells me.

David paints people. Portraits. So, too, did his grandfather. He shows me Liverpool Welsh businessman Griffith Robert Griffiths' accomplished portrait of his father, David's great grand-father. Grandfather Griffiths had painted Gladstone and had been hung alongside Fantin-Latour at Liverpool's Walker Gallery. Grandson Griffiths has continued the tradition.

David was brought up speaking ragged Welsh in Pwllheli. At school he had Latin crammed into him and didn't enjoy the experience. Felt that neither of these two great languages actually had a future. Smiles. Freely admits now that he got that wrong. At fifteen, heading for a parent-driven and uninspiring career in law he did an about turn and went to the Slade. Never considered the courts again. David is telling me this as I sit, him sketching, breaking off to take the occasional reference photograph, or for us to have tea. There's loads of tea. In his studio the subject sits before a carefully placed mirror. Watches the artist as he works.

The face has always drawn me, says David. He'd decided to try making a living from his work while employed as a teacher in Birmingham. He'd placed an advert in the local press, *commissions undertaken*, and, amazingly, got one to do a portrait of the headmaster. What he produced was liked and, as a bonus, he was also paid. Everything fell into place after that.

Back in Pwllheli David had visited the art gallery at Plas Glyn-y-Weddw, just down the coast at Llanbedrog. This 1856 Dower house[20] had, at the turn of the century, been developed by Cardiff's Solomon Andrews[21] as a sort of entertainment centre offering dancing, food and art. One of Andrews' horse-dawn trams ran along the sand dunes back to the town, much in the style of those that connected Cardiff's Splott with Grangetown. Andrews would visit Christies in London at the end of auction and buy up any unsold pseudo great masters that remained. These he'd use to cover the walls at Plas Glyn-y-Weddw. People buy anything when they are far from home. His investment provided a steady return.

David had met businesswoman and direct descendant of Solomon

Andrews, Mary Yapp. In 1965 they opened the David Griffiths Gallery in Albany Road, Cardiff. Griffiths creative zip, Yapp business head. The Gallery became the Albany Gallery when David decided to spend more of his time painting and less in management in 1967.

Both enterprises thrived. The Albany representing many of the Welsh greats, including Kyffin Williams. David painting what seems like half the great and the good of the western world. Back at the house on Westville and around the walls of the studio hang distinctive almost pointillistic portraits of George Melly, Enoch Powell, Kyffin Williams, George Thomas, Bryn Terfel and James Callaghan. Faces meshed up from a net of colour. These are largely rejects, David tells me. I have many rejects. I stack them upstairs. They're all burnable. He makes five or six versions for each work. Each sequentially correcting something – a misplacement of hands, a failure of detail around the eyes. The final finished piece goes to the buyer. The earlier preliminaries stay here. I turn my head to gaze at Joe Calzaghe, Beryl Rubens, the sister of the author Bernice, with her violin, Rowan Williams, Charles. They've been here, says David. Trekked up Westville. Sir Geraint Evans, Peter Prendergast, Archbishop Barry Morgan, Sir Kyffin Williams. Not Charles. I went to him.

In terms of portraiture David is the most successful painter Wales has. Painting Charles, the Prince, first at the time of the Investiture and then again thirty-three years later, made him. As artists go David is no bohemian. He plays the piano. Bach, Mozart. Works from eleven until the light goes. Does landscapes as an escape. Painted the 80-year old Rev Canon Bartle Jenkins, late of the home[22] for retired clergy at the end of Church Terrace, simply because he had a kind face. The Canon's portrait sits at my feet. White surpliced, green stole, glasses. I'd see him in the Gardens, nodded good morning as he crossed the end of my street. There is something extremely satisfying about art recognising where you are. The wellspring of place.

In David's portraits the soul is captured, an image of it. The faces watch you, half smile, stare into an ever-present present. The painter Will Roberts is shown sketching the face of David Griffiths as Griffiths himself paints Roberts. The images circle.

Back at the Waterloo Teahouse Chief Brewer Kasim Ali makes steam. Betty Skovbro's photographs of dogs and their owners, taken in Roath Mill gardens, hang on the walls. Dogs smiling, owners enamoured. I take Darjeeling. With milk. It's not all yours, Pontcanna.

BRANCH

We're standing at the edge of Celtic Road at Gabalfa. The van is round the corner on Kenfig. If these were shunting yards once then all sign has now turned to dust. John Briggs is explaining that what you need to do here is set the camera depth of field to F8 and take the park railings so they recall rail tracks. Get the path in shot so it leads the eye off into the distance. This is a day of railways but neither of us are trainspotters. What we are engaged in is an act of pure psychogeography. I have in my hand a mid-1950s Burrow's *Pointer Guide Map of Cardiff*, an early sort of A-Z, with a gazetteer and black and white pages outlining the tiny capital that Cardiff had then just become. The adverts celebrate it. Wales' Most Select Ballroom – The Victoria, Cowbridge Road East. Cathays Motor Services – 20 Minute Fast Battery Charging. Quick Service At Astey's Snack Bars – Nos 2 and 109 Queen Street. Buy Melocremo Sherry at Fulton Dunlop – Duke Street and Windsor Road. With The Aid of *The Pointer* Any Important Street, Public Building, or Feature of Interest May Be Instantly Found. We're using it to walk the rail line that once went from the marshalling yards here to the third of Cardiff's great docks, the Roath.

The Roath Branch Line was a Taff Vale Railway innovation, laid in 1887 to get the steam coal from the Rhondda to the Cardiff staithes and to feed the twin-cooling towered power station on Newport Road[23]. The Branch left the main valley lines just south of Llandaff to muster in a great comb of sidings to the south east of Gabalfa. No Estate when they were built, just woodland and fields. These were wait-order places where coal sat in the owners' wagons until an order for it came through. No lack of those. Trains went down the double tracks the five miles to the sea[24] every half an hour.

The sidings were large, running back from St Mark's Church almost to College Road, space enough for 2240

wagons. Who owned them: Cory, Amalgamated Anthracite, Fernhill, Welsh Navigation, Ebbw Vale, Llanbradach, Welsh Associated Collieries, Stephenson Clarke, Ocean. A sea of ten-ton trucks, five planks high, with end-tip doors. When the Roath Dock trade eventually finished in 1968 the yards and their wagons hung on. British Rail, the nationalised owners, sold the land to the council who developed part of the track bed as the new Eastern Avenue. Stewart Burgess[25], an engineer with Sir Robert McAlpine, who built the highway, told me that the great quantities of earth dug from the Avenue cutting were used as infill at the sidings. The new Eastern joined the older Western immediately south of the yards under what is now Gabalfa Flyover. Days were filled with moving mud-filled lorries and dumper trucks. Excavate from one spot, landfill at another. Each day rusted and empty wagons, thousands of them, still filling the yards and disowned by British Rail[26] were rolled down their tracks. Were any of them somehow not moved and are still there deep under the playing fields and houses that now lie above? Stewart is not saying.

On this walk along a line that no longer exists we'll look for remains. Forty years since its passing. In human terms not that long. Names carved in trees can hang around for a lifetime. Bomb damage to my Southminster Road roof is still visible. The marks left by canal barge tow ropes remain in the underpass at Kingsway. A railway is a big thing, full of smoke and dirt. We hunt the grass at the Celtic Road playing field, check Silver Birch Close. Nothing.

At the back of the Allensbank allotments we don't find anything either. No artefacts, not even a path or a shed or a plot following the line of the vanished track. The map shows it but it's no longer here. John is taking photographs at a prodigious rate. During our passage along the flyover underpass he's taken pictures of almost all the graffiti. His favourite is a text reading 'that's as useful as a crab in a bottle', urban poetry spray-painted onto the path in front of a bench. We pass the old Whitchurch Road trolley bus terminus at St Mark's Avenue and take the lane that parallels the allotments. Today this is a trainless haven of peace and verdant tranquillity. Acres of tilled earth, plots black with years of rich composting, cabbages in rows, bean stakes, the bulbs of onions, troughs of leeks, small apple trees, lines of carrots, lettuces marshalled like rows of wagons. Allotments have been part of the city landscape since 1908 when the council offered its first slices of land to urban gardeners. A ten perch plot at Sloper

Road could then be had for a shilling a year. It's still cheap today. £30 annually will let you join Mr Digwell. Cap on head. Trowel in hand. How long is a perch? Five and a half yards. In Saxon times twenty average human feet. The allotments alongside which we walk are the Soberton & Allensbank. There are others at Leckwith Droves, Flaxland, South Rise, Chalet Gardens and Pontcanna Permanent, places as foreign sounding to non-allotment gardening native Cardiffians as the sometimes glimpsed bus destinations of Draethen and Drope.

Stimulated by all this quiet, natural productivity John is telling me about American County Fairs. All The Milk You Can Drink for 50 cents. Giant Cake sales. Home made sweet stalls. Log chopping. Huge vegetable contests. Sounds like something you could find at Builth. Here there's a large woman tilling her dark earth with a hoe. A man with a pipe and trousers in his socks leaning on a push bike to which has been tied carrier bags of brassica and bits of oddly-shaped wood. A couple on their knees in the distance, praying softly, planting rows.

South of the allotments the Roath Branch ran in a cutting let into the side of Penylan Hill. We go down Wedal Road over which are two bridges. One carries the connecting path between the two halves of the cemetery – the older and complete western section in which I once waited in vain for the funeral of my aunt to arrive and the eastern half, still used, in which she was actually buried. The other has trains on it. A two-car passes before our eyes, Arriva north to Heath and Caerphilly. Evidence of rail. First we've seen but nothing at all to do with the Branch. Before nationalisation this Arriva line used to be the Rhymney, the Roath was Taff Vale.

On Penylan Road, where the new Boleyn Court Executive Detached Apartments have recently been completed, is a metal road bridge. This is rust pocked and full of rivets, TVR origins evident in its side flutings, a rail bridge over tracks long gone in a cutting that has vanished. On the southern side a gas pipe carries a metal plate that once protected it from corrosive engine outpourings. Evidence of smoke washed away by forty years of rain. John uses a complete 36-shot roll of film in celebration. So there was a Roath railway. Once.

Walking the lanes of Cardiff, and this piece of railway map tracking largely involves that, shows another side to the city. The lanes are a hot bed for low-key enterprise. Small time car sales. Unlabeled vehicle repair. Light engineering. Bricoleurs. Men sitting in chairs

drinking tea. Radios playing. Storage and supply. Someone has
pulled their back wall down and is using the now hard-topped rear
garden to flog old Fords and Peugeots. There are multiple spanner
racks and men in oil-covered once-blue overalls visible through
part-open garage doors. A lane-facing outbuilding is full of boxed
electrical goods. Could be DIY and stored Christmas presents but
I have my doubts.

South of Waterloo Road the lane descends from the hill towards
the coastal flats. Once salt marsh then farmland and brick work now
the shopping parks of Newport Road. Buildings must lead to people,
says John, shooting a retired oldster standing outside his Willie Seager
bungalow. Sir William Seager was a nineteenth century shipowner
and Liberal MP who did good works. These cottages, rebuilt now on
the old railway route, are his legacy.

At the Harlequins sports ground where the track once branched
towards Roath Power Station we hear a train hoot and the distant
rush of carriages over tracks. Ghosts returning? No, the London
mainline is just south of us over Newport Road. We track through
Splott across parkland, Celsa's steel mill in the distance. Last slice of
industrial Cardiff, now painted bright blue and shiny white and
enveloped in clean white steam. The route, with track along it now,
runs to the Tidal Sidings depot.

These are owned by EWS and here there is an actual engine. John
gets particularly excited and wants to photograph this Class 08, bog-
standard, Diesel Shunter, silent and maroon, at siding top near the
offices. The depot has a huge notice at its entrance – Cardiff Tidal
Freight Centre No Unauthorised Entry. The offices, late twentieth
century, flat-roofed brick, are full of railwaymen in oily orange cover-
alls. Most of them are eating: pies, take out curries, beans in bowls.
Be all right mate, one tells me, but the boss is here. If you're spotters
you'll have to go, see, company policy. We're not spotters. Heaven
forbid. Paul Cleverdon, the man in change, looking a bit like Keith
Allen in manager M&S slacks and white shirt, is as helpful as we
could want. Tells us about the history, shows me the Great Western
Region map still there on the office wall. Explains about the Quail
Track[27] maps which show all local rail, gets his and makes a photo-
copy, talks about the steel still shifted by his trains at Celsa and the
scrap brought in from the mainline. Can we photograph the engine?
Against company policy, sorry. If you'd been spotters you'd have

been out of here immediately. John explains that we are historians. Calling us psychogeographers would certainly have blown it. How about a shot of the track? Paul Cleverdon shakes his head.

The 1890s Grosvenor Hotel, a giant Brains pub on the corner of South Park Road, looks on its last legs. John tells me that on Newport Station there is a sign which reads 'Only English, Welsh or Scottish People can use this door'. Difficult if you are Irish. We parallel the EWS track through the long reaches of the Portmanmoor Road Industrial Estate. Actual track now. Roath Branch brought back to life as the Cross Docks Link. The estate is a mass of mixed enterprise. Princes Soft Drinks, Westdale Press, Yamato Transport, Premier Upholstery, Enfys Limited. At the south end are the docks. A line of cherry pickers in a yard standing like a mechanical forest. John came here photographing for his books on Cardiff. For *Before The Deluge* and *Taken In Time*. The pavements run with road dirt, the roads with artics tugging endless freight. The thrum of heavy traffic is a feature this place would be barren without.

Ahead the red dragon of the *Western Mail's* printing plant emerging from behind a mass of recently planted trees. Below, an EWS shunter hauls a line of trucks carrying fresh-rolled steel billets, bound for the rolling mill. Still hot, you can feel it on your skin as the train vanishes below the roadway.

I stare out at the roundabout. Huge and green, planted with weeping beech and alder. A forest in the centre of all that's left of Cardiff's past industrial age. That's far enough today. Find the Roath where it crosses into ABP's docks tomorrow.

notes:

1. The Great Heath and the Little Heath were once open tracts of common land running from the town of Cardiff to the hills of Caerphilly. Their final remnant is the park land that sits at the centre of the Cardiff suburb of Heath.

2. See p.22 *Real Cardiff.*

3. Chris Guiver, from Scotland via Hampshire, Nassau, Antigua and Malaysia, has made films for the BBC and Channel 4. He now works for Evans Woolfe Media in Twickenham making educational films for broadcast and for individuals. His forte is the dynamic mix of subject and background with directorial instruction feathered in from a distance.

4. The house passed by marriage to the ownership of the Scot, the Mackintosh of Mackintosh, who developed the district building saleable terraces of worker's housing. The names of his family members and historical origins are celebrated in those of the district streets: Donald Street, Inverness Place, Strathnairn Street, Glenroy Street, Kincraig Street, Mackintosh Place.

5. When I went past, mid-2009, the Hawaiian had changed its name but not its exterior style.

6· But when I return the following day to take a reference photograph the word 'Kashmir' has been removed. City Road constant change, rolling on.

7. 2.5p.

8. I Love the Tribe.

9. Mercure Holland House Hotel and Spa.

10. Land donated by Bute in 1848. Some original gravestones preserved as part of the park wall.

11. Francine Moule 1948-2006 who loved Penylan; Terence W. Thomas 1933-2003; Carmen Bellsmythe 1956-2001; Babs and Bunny Williams 1911-2002; Mary Edith Dobbs 1935-2000; Gus Evans Postmaster of Waterloo Gardens Post Office 1962-1986; Mary Patricia Cronin 1935-2003;

12. *St Margate's Miscellany*, Diane A Walker, Cardiff 1998.

13. The join of the old wall to the new is still visible behind the Church at the start of Church Terrace. The ancient and circular church yard wall suddenly bends straight. A piece of waste-land between the old northern boundary wall and the nearby brook was levelled and the churchyard enlarged.

14. Dámaso Pérez Prado, El Rey del Mambo, *king of the Afro-Cuban beat. All was still calm. Rock and Roll arrived with a mind numbing vengeance the following year.*

15. Sung by the Crew Cuts, all in matching jumpers.

16. *Hey Paula* – Paul & Paula, *Walk Like A Man* – The Four Seasons, *You Can't Sit Down* – The Dovells.

71. http://www.waterlootea.com/

18. As ground landlord Tredegar appointed W. Scott as his architect and imposed strict control over the look and shape of housing development. For Penylan this was to be largely respectable middle-class residences where the most that builders might do to differentiate their work would be to change the detail of terracotta embellishments or the design of the leaded glass in the front doors.

19. When the British beat boom of the 1960s gave us reusable carriers with Union Jacks on their sides, JJC came up with one that used the Welsh dragon. Sales soared.

20. A large estate house occupied by the widow of the late owner. In this case by Lady Elizabeth Love Jones Parry of the Madryn Estate.

21. Solomon Andrews purchased Plas Glyn-y-Weddw in 1896. The house was converted into an Art Gallery and the stable-yard roofed over to form a ballroom which was also used for afternoon teas. Trips by tram to Llanbedrog for the beach and to the house and grounds, and for the evening dances organised by F. E. Young, became a feature of a holiday at Pwllheli.

22. Built in the 1870s as a home for fallen girls. Next door was a home for fallen women.

23. The power station cooling towers were finally demolished in 1972 to make way for, among

other things, the Colchester Avenue branch of Sainsbury's.

24. The Roath Branch ran in an arc from Gabalfa, behind Whitchurch Road, the bottom of Roath Park Lake, and along behind the houses of lower Penylan. It eventually crossed Newport Road near the Harlequins and plunged through that place where Splott and Tremorfa still rub roughly at each other. It reached the eastern edge of the Docks where Portmanmoor Road turns into Ocean Way.

25. Stewart M. Burgess is currently Principal Engineer for Caerphilly Council.

26. Wagons? What wagons?

27. The Quail Mapping Company, specialists in track diagrams.

SOUTH

ROATH DOCK

We arrive from the east, just the way the railway did. The Roath Branch tracks came in along the border with Tremorfa. The south end of Splott. Swansea Street. Long gone now. Enid Street, Layard Street, Cornelia Street, Caerphilly Street, Roath Moor Road. Them too. A whole district lost. The Portmanmoor Road Industrial Estate has swept all away. The Dock Gate is just to the west of Cardiff's Heliport. *Hofrenfa* it says on the road sign. The police used to fly their Twin Squirrels from here until 2008. Chasing dope across the south of the city. Filling the air with roaring blades and the night lanes with beams of light. Today they use Eurocopters out of St Athan, to the west. Splott is reached only after they've crossed the great badlands of Ely. Cormac McCarthy country but without the sun. The Heliport is owned by the Council who are intent on selling it on[1]. VIPs land here for the matches at the Millennium Stadium, concerts at the WMC, the big poker games. The Heliport is big enough to manage 180 flights a day. Around £30 a time to put your bird on the apron. £10 to leave it here overnight.

At the gate the guard directs us to the port office. ABP's shining HQ out on the south end of Queen Alexandra. Cardiff's port is vast. Much larger than you'd think. It's hidden from the majority of the population who see little more than a line of cranes out there on the flats. They run south-east, away from the shining glow of the redeveloped Bay. For most of the nineteenth and more than half of the twentieth Bute's docks dominated Cardiff. They were the reason we

were what we were. Cardiff – coal metropolis, steel town, a capital of the British industrial revolution, a polluter of the whole Severn estuary, a home for sailors and gangers and cutters and longshoremen and women of the day and of the night from all over the world.

Post war all that ended, although the seeds of the decline had begun long before. The newly flooded Inner

Harbour and the Barrage and the money-milking property development that have spun into place since 1980 have turned south Cardiff
into an irresistible magnet of a different kind. They've been aided by
the arrival of at least three landmark Welsh national institutions (the
Assembly, the Millennium Centre, and within shouting distance the
Stadium). On the back have come cinemas, restaurants, a sports
village, an Olympic swimming pool, a snow dome, and high-rising,
white and green sided apartments beyond number. They cluster to
bask in the southern light. The working docks, if they ever existed in
the minds of the incomers, are recalled only by pieces of ancient
machinery, cemented to the ground. Street furniture. Sculptural toys.
Steel buckets and mechanical shovels. Black hooks and links and once
rusted pulleys. Unmoving cranes fixed to a skyline that's been painted
in. The dirt of industry has moved on.

Yet here we are, John and I, loping along Longships Road in his
appallingly-named Bongo Frendee, a sort of contemporary VW
camper van, made by Mazda. We're right in the centre of the vast
acres that are Cardiff's still working docks. There are three of them:
The Queen Alexandra, The Roath Dock and The Roath Basin.
Dockland. Surrounded by industry, still on the go, much of it. Steel
being imported by Celsa, oil to the Texaco depot, liquid bulks, sand,
wood by the shed load, and scrap metal, going out the other way.
We drive. Walking in the docks is discouraged. The safety record is
better when everyone moves on wheels.

John likes to take the part of the street photographer, in the great
Cartier-Bresson tradition. Wait for the moment, take the shot. But
this time he has to set things up. Two cameras slung round his neck,
a discreet Pentax, and then a box the size of an Easter egg, his
beloved Mamiya C330 twin lens reflex. Good at rendering architectural details, he tells me. I'll let you have a go if you like. John works
in black and white, on film, thinks digital is heresy[2], but is not averse
to scanning in his developed negs and photoshopping them into
shape at home. He's been hanging around with writers since he took
pics of John Berryman in the sixties. Back home he has boxes of these
people, grainy, growling and great, somehow all looking like they
work with words. John's writers have this thing about their eyes. He's
done the big things American photographers often do – hitched the
southern states, followed Highway Sixty-One, done the Zimmerman
trail knocking on Dylan's door. Yet somehow he always finds his way

back to the south Wales drizzle. Not today though. This time we've got sun.

Railways ran this place. At their height the entire acreage of Cardiff's five docks were covered by smoke and track. Taff Vale, Rhymney, Cardiff, LMS, and LNWR. They all came here, renting each other running rights, leasing sidings to exporters, to importers, to warehouses, to factors and fixers, connecting up to private lines. Letting the train take the strain. There was hardly any other way it could be done. Some enterprises ran their own engines. Many had private wagons. But most used the locomotive power of the big operators. Why buy when you can rent? There were more sleepers here per acre than anywhere else in Wales. Anywhere in Britain some claimed. How much is left? If there's anything then it's pretty invisible.

John and I meet Ian Meredith, head of port security for the whole of south Wales – Newport, Cardiff, Barry, Port Talbot, Swansea. The days of coming here with a yellow vest and a paper permit and then wandering where you liked are over. 9/11 saw to that. Today visitors must be checked, recorded, badged and escorted. We're at Security Level One, says Ian. No known threats. But that can change. Ian's an ex-navy man who served on 42 destroyers, Royal Yacht Guard, Gulf, Far East, Med, America, invalided out, and regretting the loss. Navy's gone down the pan. They like to think we still rule the waves but it's a myth. Ian shakes his head. He's also an amateur photographer, which helps. He and John discuss exposures and white balance and the way light falls on steel struts and how, sometimes, you have to wait a time for the picture and be there when it shows. Ian came here in 2003 and has never known the place like it once was, full of smoke and smog. For him railways have always been history. But he's laid on a van and is intent on showing us all that remains.

Trains still work here, he tells us. But only a small number get this far south. A few a month. If you're lucky. They bring in steel, never coal[3]. We drive south of the vast area of reclaimed land known as the

Prairie. Here were once the holding sidings for the anthracite that came on trains, one every thirty minutes, all day, every day, rattle and shake, down the Roath Branch. The five miles of lost line John and I have just walked. Nothing left. When the tracks were lifted the dust and gravel revealed was used for a time as the final stage of the Network Q Rally. Today it's full of diggers preparing the ground for use as steel storage. South, where Beach Sidings once ran, stand the tanks of the Texaco depot. South Wales' fuel supply. On Clipper Road we reach a point where tracks still enter. Rail, steel, rust. They sit there, embedded in the tarmac, shine lost, full of dirt and overgrowth. Ghosts. Little evidence that anything has used them for quite some time.

It's the same story throughout the Port. Small stretches of corroded rail then swathes of empty land. In the distance, north of Roath Dock, where the iron ore sidings once were, we spot a wagon. The only piece of rolling stock in the entire place. Belong to anyone, I ask? No-one answers. Broken and forgotten. The *Beware Loco* signs and their antique pictures of engines with smoke rising from their stacks stand at junctions, superfluous, ignored. The lines of track cross roads that never close, run under locked gates that never open.

Just off Cold Stores Road are the gantries of the ABP Container Terminal. A 15,000-ton tanker, *The Pembroke Fisher*, is tied up nearby, water flushing from its bow. Containers are big port business. They ship in, are loaded onto lorries, and driven on over the remains of the old railtracks. Ironically they are then taken by road to a container freight depot at Wentloog or Birmingham. There they are

loaded onto wagons and carried on to their final destinations by rail. Twenty-first century economics. They bring us goods we probably don't need from countries that really can't afford to make them. They ship them across countryside that gets damaged by the transit. Who wins? Some guy somewhere with a big car, an accountant and a mansion. Why should we worry? It's always been like this, hasn't it?

We stop on the swing bridge on Compass Road, the much repainted steel lattice that lets traffic cross from the Prairie to the south of the Roath Basin. Trucks are going past us like this was Newport Road. We get 30,000 a month, says Ian. Spotting us they slow. They think we're using a hand-held speed camera, says Ian. That we're traffic cops. I look over my shoulder to see John, orange hi-vis and, Mamiya round his neck, Pentax in hand, reducing great petrol artics from zoom to crawl. Take care down there, Ian tells me as, equally bright orange and sternly booted, I peer over the dock edge into deep dark water. To do that you should be wearing a life vest. In the b&w pre-war photos of this place the dockers are wearing badly ironed suits and waistcoats, felt hats some of them, ordinary shoes. They are dressed like they were going to the pub or out to watch the football. No more. Today it's a new and endlessly regulated world.

The shore south of the Queen Alexandra Dock is an acreage of hardcore, mud and river boulder. This whole place is land reclaimed from the estuary. If the docks were still extending that's where they'd go next. In the bright sun the foreshore gleams. We get fishermen here, Ian tells us. They claim that it's their right to cast from the coast anywhere they like, common law, European statute, right of man, but ABP ownership extends hundreds of yards into the water. We send them on their way, protesting as they go.

ABP are keen to be seen as a socially responsible, community focused operation. They have a sustainable development policy to ameliorate the environmental impact of the company's industrial growth. Their carbon footprint is of some concern. They work with the RSPB. They put money into the arts, including the opera and have commissioned Welsh artist Mike Briscoe to fill their new office with bright paintings of gulls, beaches, holidaymakers and kites.

The Port itself is certainly tidy, far cleaner than I remember from my previous visit in 2001. The new walkway running from the east end of the Barrage to the Norwegian Church is now in place. Leisure creeps closer. The Spillers Mill has gone. Demolished with high regret. The pontoons and jetties have been cleared of wreckage. The Sand Wharf north of Roath Dock is about to be developed. Recession allowing more housing, new techniums, endless gleam.

And of the long-lost and seemingly mythical railway – still barely anything. No signals, no gantries, no platelayers huts, no engine sheds, no buffers, no water towers, no coal stacks, no coal dumps, no coal yards, no coal in lumps or pressed blocks or dust, no coal anywhere. Nothing. But surreally, in the car park, where Majid, the van driver, drops us, is the dinky Bay Road Train. It's parked for the winter, Porthcawl white smoke stack, Barry Island carriages, rubber wheels. Nearest we're going to get. And even that's not moving. We leave slowly. Pass the Missions to Seamen – Cold Beer, Pool, Darts. Pass Adventurers Quay, high life living. Pass the guard hut and the barrier, radio, security cameras, phones. Back into the city. The old Roath finished. Coal exhausted. Memory lost. Existence almost gone.

What did they do when they lived here when this place was booming full of work and dirt and dust?

coal tipper clerk rigger engineer cab driver marine engineer refiner board of trade officer seaman manager fitter boatsman pilot builder shipwright foreman pilot's helper mariner dock labourer ship steward dyer labourer engineer baker sailmaker seaman mason mariner boiler-maker mariner seaman manager joiner dockgate man water clerk water clerk marine engineer scripture reader pilot builder manager commission agent ship carpenter painter coal trimmer ship steward storekeeper mariner dyer distiller clerk

---

OCEAN PARK

From its name this should be funland. Ferris wheel, dodgems, figure of eight. Rock. Candyfloss. Del Shannon singing *Runaway* to shriek-ing girls moving ever-faster as the waltzer spins. But it's not. Ocean Park is Cardiff's inner city industrial estate. Former site of the East Moors steelworks. Now a sprawling wind of red-brick new build enter-prise. Arc roofs. Glass. Grass and car park. Ocean Way, the entrance highway, spins in past Pierre Vivant's magic roundabout[4], a Cardiff

landmark of stacked and mangled roadsigns, making art out of how drivers feel about the Highways Agency and their proscriptive traffic commands. The road is a slowly curving, vehicle-filled southern distributor. It takes commerce east along Rover Way to cross the Rhymney on the East Moors Viaduct reaching Eastern Avenue and the motorway out of Wales. In this space once stood a part of Cardiff's heavy industrial heritage. The steelworks (see p.13). The street names take us back. East Moors Road. Keen Road. Dowlais Road. Nettleford Road. Seawall. Tidal Sidings.

In the glory days these places were so full of dirt and darkness that no roadside flower grew and the sun rarely penetrated the murk. Men as black as coal miners would sit in the lower Splott pubs and try to drink the tiredness out of their systems. Industrial pubs. Workingmen's pubs with men-only bars. Places where they still put sawdust on the floor and where the seats were hard benches. You drank dark beer and you smoked. Hancocks. Brains. Ely. Crosswells. Park Drive. Woodbine. Gold Leaf. Capstan. Pipes. An occasional roller of their own. The Rhymney Hotel. The Splottlands. The Adamsdown. The Canadian. The Tredegar Hotel. The Cottage. The Vulcan. No bandits, no jukeboxes. Just beer.

Today the estate boasts a single drinkery – The Ocean Park on Keen Road. A Brains tavern. It's next door to the signposted Ocean Park Hotel, a Travel Inn. The Ocean Park is new build, anonymous. Fitted out from the standard Brewers Fayre design manual of polished wood and chintz. The Revered Baz's review on *beerintheevening.com* sums it up: 'Does its owners no credit whatsoever… the food is poor – tasteless and badly prepared. My "well done" steak was bloody in the middle and my wife's pasta was welded to the plate it was microwaved on. At the next table a customer was complaining about the lack of meat in his cottage pie. The Brewers Fayre website has a banner that reads "Can't be bothered to cook?". Looks like they followed their own advice.'

The estate mixes light engineering, car part and scrap merchant of the kind that cluster at the edges of seaports with shining bases for charities, office furniture suppliers and finance companies. Leapfrog Day Nurseries. Jewson building supplies. ASD Metal Services. E&B Air Compressors. Lamby Engineering. St Johns. BHK flooring. Yes Loans. RNIB. IT Skills Wales. Barlow Handling Ltd. The Welsh National Tennis Centre. The Bayside Fish and Chip Café *Open All Day (closed)*. Clean air. Zoned. No housing.

On the Sunday when I visit the district was almost entirely deserted. An African slumbering in the security gatehouse to the Castle Works at the end of East Moors Road. A Chinese delivering a packed lunch for someone deep inside Cardiff Windows. The car parks empty. To work here you need to travel. The nearest walking suburb is lower Splott around Moorland Park or the low density social housing off Sanquahar Street. The nearest new housing single-occupancy apartments are on the site of the old Moorlands pub, miles off in Carlisle Street. Corner shops zero. Nourishment via burger van. We should be keeping our cities alive by letting us again live right next to where we earn. Not in this ocean of ghosts.

When Ocean Park was East Moors it was as much a part of Dockland as the docks were. The industrial sprawl merged in a haze of rail track and waterway. Today Ocean Park is as separate from the Bay as Soviet East Germany once was from the West. The north-south verticals of the preserved East Dock and the vehicles-only elevated Central Link Road see to that. Uncrossable barriers. Only the lost and the new ever walk them. Women in robes bearing packages. Fishermen with rods and baskets. A ragged drunk. Man on a broken push bike. Once a smart suited crisp shirt with briefcase strolling the wrong way north from the Future Hotel. Travelling west is not possible. Ocean Park is an island. Artics who miss the turning vanish with their eight wheel trailers in the gloss and smile of Bayside's Mermaid Quay. Ocean Park? Never heard of it, mate.

SENEDD

Hurricane Myfanwy is coming across the Bay in a mounting roar. There are white-tops out there and churning boats. Storm is a permanent condition this time of year. Autumn. Rain and rain.

Pewter skies. The new Assembly Building website shows that the architects have done plenty of work on wind analysis, designing in shelters and lots of screening along the entrance steps. Doesn't stop doors shaking, though, as hair gets ripped back from faces and plastic carriers spiral like weather balloons high into the air.

I've walked round from the airport check-in that is the Millennium Centre entrance foyer where Dafydd El has been introducing the poet Grahame Davies as a sort-of washing machine for the ideas of our nation. Grahame was launching his new Barddas book *Achos* (in English that's *Because*). The Assembly's Presiding Officer lent presence, illumination and gravitas. He'd also come with his resident instantaneous-translation service – two women with microphones and a stack of headphones for the non-Welsh or those not yet able, all sited behind a table fronted by bottles of wine and complimentary crisps. Grahame had done brilliantly banging out half a dozen incisive poems and looking as much as he could like the ten years younger photo of himself inside the book. Dafydd – Yr Arglwydd Dafydd Elis Thomas, former leader of Plaid Cymru and now the Presiding Officer for Wales – just by being there had shown that politicians in this small country value culture just that little bit more than they do elsewhere.

Dafydd is with us again on the other side of the Assembly's security machine. Put your keys in the basket, sir, and your coat and your phone. If there's a positive threat they also check who you rang up last, what's among the lint in the bottom of your pockets and have a look at the soles of your shoes. We, the Millennium Centre Arts Community, are there to check the site prior to the Royal Opening. In the presence of HMQ our National Poet, Gwyneth Lewis, will read a poem to mark the occasion. Gwyneth is taller, of course. Most people are. But by use of clever camera angles the public will never know. Diversions will Dance. The National Youth Symphonic Brass will play.

Dafydd has fixed the problem of anthems. Sending her victorious inside the new home of our burgeoning Welsh democracy could not possibly make the right historical mark. We'll sing it on the steps. Military bands. Fanfares. The Welsh Regiment in red coats. The Navy in the Bay. Taffy the Goat. But once inside we'll do *Hen Wlad Fy Nhadau Yn Annwyl I Mi* although I hate those words. We need new ones. Can I quote you on that? Of course you can.

The Senedd is being built for the Assembly Government but once it is complete it will be handed over to the Parliament. The government will use it but the building will belong to the people rather than the politicians. This fine distinction in ownership is important and one that means much to the Presiding Officer. It is an important component of the democratic process. "We would not be a proper country without a proper Parliament," he tells me. "The world has to see that."

The Richard Rogers designed building has been a long time coming. On the earliest maps the area of future build is shown as sea. Tidal flats. When Bute got round to building his first dock at Cardiff in 1839 the debating chamber's site was sunk in salt marsh, south of the town's fragile sea wall. When that West Dock was joined by the still extant East in 1855, and the complex connected to the sea by a series of basins and locks, the Assembly's land, reclaimed by drainage and infill, became the site of the Rumney Railway's coal sidings. Steam and dust. Dolphins and coal staithes. Black gold.

But a twentieth century of stagger and decline put paid to all that. The docks dimmed and the railways went. Basins were filled, locks removed. By the 1990s, under plans for redevelopment, the site was shown as a luxury hotel. Near it was the Roald Dahl Centre for Children's Literature, a spinnaker tower at the end of a spiralling jetty, a leisure flag for an as yet unreborn Wales.

The 1997 referendum changed everything. Wales would be like Scotland, deciding its own destiny, with its own government and its own parliament. But reined in, just that little bit. No powers of primary legislation. No powers to tax. Downgraded so as not to frighten the urban middle classes, parliament avoided, called an assembly. But by a combination of stealth and forthright rebranding we are hard on the way to changing all that. Already the Assembly is a government and its principle building a Senedd. There's a new act with new powers in the offing. We have Ministers, a Cabinet, and a Presiding Officer.

In 1998 Ron Davies, First Minister Elect, rejected the claims of Carmarthen, Swansea, Aberystwyth, Wrexham, Llanystumdwy and Merthyr as site for our new government and chose the fifty-year old capital. Not the City Hall (wrong image, too cranky, too difficult to police and upgrade), not Callaghan Square (wrong shape, too noisy, inglorious) and chose the heart of the Bay – full of water, space, and light. Crickhowell House on Pierhead Street – at the time housing NHS staff – was selected to house support staff and a temporary debating chamber while the site next door was earmarked for the real thing. The Richard Rogers Partnership won the bid process with their vision in sustainable wood and stone. Their house would be of air and glass with a torrent of grey steps moving ghat-like into the south-west waters of Cardiff Bay. Their edifice was topped with an enormous and louvered wind cowl in stainless-steel, largest in Western Europe, bent like an oast house, pushing out waste air into the prevailing winds.

Compared to most rival European debating chambers the Senedd is cheap. Almost £67 million for a national landmark which will demonstrate further to a reluctant Wales the pre-eminence of Capital Cardiff. The Senedd steps up from the water on slate, throws itself skywards in glass, and then bends back in a huge roof soffit made from western red-cedar, to plummet into the building's centre and the circular mother nest that is the debating chamber itself. Chapel, Star Wars cruiser, concert hall. The space is full of rounded air and plunging light.

Our group cross the steps from the south to hide from the wind in the large slate-floored neuadd. "This is the Neuadd," Gwen Parry, the Assembly's Head of Communications, tells us. "Neuadd. That name won't be translated." Security working for the builders, Taylor Woodrow, are not keen on me taking photos. I might see something I should not. Although I can't imagine what. Gun emplacements. Bomb shelters. Drinks cabinets. A workman padded tight inside a yellow-green security vest goes by. He is carrying a motorised stone-cutter and has his hard-hat ear pads swivelled up reminiscent of Mickey Mouse. Keith from Music Centre Wales reckons that the building, which he'd christened a filling station when we were outside looks more like a crematorium now we're in. Totally unfair.

The giant slatted-wood ceiling high above us undulates as if the sea had come here and left its waves behind. The views of the Bay and Penarth Head beyond are huge. The Debating Chamber itself is surrounded by a 125 seat gallery, made from local oak and installed by a wood-turner from Bridgend. You can peer down and watch AMs click their keyboards, check their notes, scratch their heads. There are glass screens to stop you chucking things or throwing yourself off. Like CJ from *The West Wing*, Gwen shepherds us on to view the committee rooms and the glass fronted elevators. The Monarch doesn't do lifts, she tells us. The world would end if HMQ got stuck. Her Majesty will climb the stairs.

The building is significantly green. Ventilation will be natural Cardiff Bay prevailing, the boilers will burn wood chip, wind will be harnessed to generate some of the Senedd's electricity. Tokenism is the scale of things but significant in the signal these things send.

Outside again we walk back across the yard where a multi-storey may someday be built. Or maybe not. Car transport and the Bay do not mix well. The Roath Dock to the south of us berthed the rebuilt *Sir Galahad* last time I looked. The week before it was a nuclear sub. Today there is only the Helwick lightship A red painted water-borne outpost of multi denominational Christianity, sandwiches and tea in cups. Lloyd Robson did a poetry reading on deck once, said there was little swell but a whole lot of roaring from the ships generators. He reached a new audience. A small one but growing. Like the Senedd's. And at £67m for five thousand new built square meters that's not a bad investment at all.

In the event it snows. An inch or so. March 1st, St David's Day 2006 is white for the first time in decades. School trips to witness the historic opening are cancelled. In most places outside Cardiff the Welsh world slows and stops. Children watch us on TV, stamping around in the slush. The Army is here, red dress uniforms. *HMS Westminster*, a type 23 frigate and about the best the Navy can do these days sits, guns ready, in Roath Dock. There's a flypast from four Hawk trainers. Dafydd El is inadvertently

broadcast from the Senedd Chamber, adjusting the height of a seat and referring to the monarch as a short arse. Later he says that, of course, he was referring not to HMQ but himself. No one cares. In the Neuadd Gwyneth Lewis reads her official verse. A challenge resolved to perfection. Over the road at the WMC Simon Mundy gives an alternative view. There is cheering. Mike Jenkins reads a short story with strong republican leanings. The front row of his audience walk out.

Outside the local police (yellow jackets) stand and shuffle, the specials (wearing red) stride, test doors and ask people who they are. There are a couple of bomb threats and a few low key protests *Colonial Governor Out Of Welsh Democracy* and *People's Rights Not Royal Prerogatives* are seen on banners tied to the Dock railings. There are cameras on cranes and podiums, hand-helds, in floating studios, atop buildings, on stalks and sticks. More media than visitors. More visitors than locals. The locals are back there in The Packet and The White Hart and The Bute Dock. This isn't for them.

At tea time Charles and Camilla meet the crachach before taking in an opera. Their audience is thick with Brigadiers wearing medals and dignitaries from the greater Commonwealth. Robes, hats, turbans, ceremonial headgear of kinds I've never seen. When he speaks, in Welsh first, rather like Churchill once used French, the Prince is surprisingly entertaining. A dozen camera phones take snaps. Then on the Millennium Centre stage it's Bryn Terfel's Dutchman. But I go home. Outside someone skateboards along the edge of vehicle barrier. Snow's gone. Everything is different now. Is it?

LINE OF THE FAULT

Almost everyone knows that there's a fault in the space time continuum which runs right through Cardiff. My mother used to tell me about it when I was a kid. Watch you don't fall down it, she'd say. Be careful where you put your feet. The fault runs in where the leys used to be, when we had leys, but this is the hard contemporary future, so we don't. The fault is the Cardiff Rift, a wormhole in space and time. What happens on this rift is the subject of enormous international speculation. There are mags, websites, and mass internet discussion. The past is seen through it. The present gets sucked back. Fragments of the future appear and disappear like they were ghosts.

The guys who police this fracture in the air we breathe have a hub right in the middle of Cardiff Bay. A secret base for operations built into the white brick-lined tunnels which run below what was the Bute West Dock Basin but is now Roald Dahl Plass. Access is via a lift shaft secreted under the basin's stone kerb right next to the silver water tower[5], the celebrated focus for Cardiff's north-south grand boulevard – Lloyd George Avenue. You see the tourists there, having their photos snapped. Japanese pressing the place where Captain Jack stomps his foot to make the lift open up. Emos with their arms held wide. Goths dancing. Hoodies recording the scene on their phones. Non-Cardiffians here to pick up the fame of *Torchwood* by osmosis.

Torchwood – the word is an anagram of *Doctor Who* devised to disguise the true identity of early rushes. It is part of BBC Wales's new millennium revival as science fiction television producers par excellence. A genuine fulfilment of Cardiff's media pretensions. Right on the button in the way it mixes space opera with youth fantasy; sex and streetlife with alien technology; and gore, darkness and death with camp humour and magic. Out there in promoland the Council have spent £45,000 designing a new symbol for our international city. Cardiff & Co, the city's marketeers, have given us the name of the capital set bilingually and surrounded by a half-disc of coloured Smarties. In the real world of blogs and notice boards more than one commentator has suggested that the city needn't have bothered. The logo of the Torchwood Institute, a honeycomb of hexagonal Ts, has already done the job. Among the young *Torchwood's* Cardiff is recognised world-wide much more readily than the actual one.

The new second and terrestrial network series of *Torchwood* launches at the Wales Millennium Centre. The BBC have lit Gwyneth Lewis's now world-famous *In These Stones Horizons Sing* inscription with coloured lights. There's crime scene tape on the access handrails.

The cast is here, all bar Jack, and the production team, unaccountably less Russell T[6] whose idea the whole thing was. We get drink and risotto in little bowls and then an upbeat, we have conquered the world speech from Controller Menna Richards. She wears hot shoes and a haute couture suit. The episode about the survivors of some time fracture accident being housed in an underground hospital on Flat Holm is shown in high def on a regular cinema screen. Full of colour and places Cardiffians know or half-know, and rich with emotion. *Torchwood* has depth beyond its camp, post-pub, Channel Three surface.

The Hub is below us. The dissection room, the computer relays, the board room, the morgue with its cryo-chambers, Captain Jack's office, the curved and tiled tunnels looking like part Underground station, part junction basin set in a complex of Victorian sewers. There are manholes, and brick arches, guard-rail protected walkways, a dungeon basement with glass doors, Jacks' bedroom below a submarine hatch, the chill-out room, the Torchwood diner, and the great circular door like the cap of an atomic furnace. William Pye's silver fountain, the stainless steel tower, focus for the Bay, runs right into it. But of course, it doesn't, and it isn't. It's not here. Below the Basin are the immovable walls of ancient dry docks, drainage shafts and filled-in Victorian excavation. The Hub, or rather the studio in which this part of future Cardiff, along with its fellow space-time rift tracker, Dr Who's Tardis, actually sits, is at Upper Boat, Glamorgan.

Leave the Bay and the silver tower, head north up the A470, enter Rhondda Cynon Taff and there it is again, built of card and silver plastic and papier-maché. The studios are as hard to access as GCHQ and as secret. An unmarked complex at the back of a trading estate, surrounded on three sides by river, rail and road and the fourth by a warehouse recycling plastic. The BBC have been here three years, rebuilding the city outside the city, keeping the fans at a distance and the paparazzi here to snap Kylie or Catherine Tate at arms length.

Inside the two story shed-like complex the sets of the three BBC successes, *Dr Who*, *Torchwood*, and *Sarah Jane*, nestle against each other for warmth. The level and quality of build is amazing. The arrival of HD has seen a need for fine detail and *Torchwood* delivers this in volume. These are not pale painted two-dimensional backdrops but believable artefacts. When you touch the tiles of the

Hub's underground walls reveal themselves not to be cold and porcelain as expected but warm and hardboard instead. Beth Britton, Branding Assistant, who shows me round, sits me on the bench under the Torchwood sign and, using my Ixus, takes a picture. I've signed a release saying that not only won't I breathe a word about what I've seen but I won't surreptitiously photograph it either. But this tourist snap is what everyone gets. Do you get many visitors here, I ask? Loads. A writer brought his kids once and one of them locked his brother in the morgue's body tray. Couldn't find him until he started shouting. We are standing in the dissection room, a Flash Gordon mix of past and post-modern. The equipment is all genuine, salvaged from an east European hospital. There are trays and lights and surgeons' requisites and operating tables. The past and the present colliding. But then this is a temporal rift, so I shouldn't be surprised.

Out of the window of Torchwood Gwen's vast and Ikea-styled Cardiff flat you can see the roofs of Cardiff streets, Cardiff lights, Cardiff terraces, Cardiff trees. Open the window and reach out and they'll turn out to be life-size photographs assembled on scenery flats. The wall at the edge of Jim Carrey's world in *The Truman Show*. Push at it and it'll shake. *Dr Who* and *Torchwood* both track the same space-time rift. They share characters. They mix their preposterous pasts. A dalek sits inside the *Torchwood* hub. Captain Jack's Office is a wreck of spilled papers, broken furniture and crumbled brick. There's been an explosion. The tourist office through which visitors to the on-screen Torchwood hub gain access is empty. Between scenes. Undressed. In the real real world it would sit on the edge of Roald Dahl Plass near Pizza Express. Daleks rove the basin. The Tardis lands outside the Millennium Centre. The film crews cluster. When the show broadcasts you can see yourself sometimes crossing in the background.

Torchwood goes out in two flavours. Pre and post watershed. The one for the vulnerable is cut. What's lost, I ask? The gay hugs and the same-sex snogging? Nope. Series creator Russell T is determined that *Torchwood*, fantasy though it is, should reflect the real world. Gay stays in. Swearing gets dropped. The world of the young stays protected. Sometimes the world is a sensitive flower.

In *Torchwood* the streets of real Cardiff flicker into constant view. The Barrage, Mary Ann Street, Queen Street, St Mary Street, the city's nightlife in full swing, the roofs of multi-story car parks, the headland at Penarth, the inner harbour, Jack standing proud on the top of Altolusso, Gwen rushing through the darkness of Crockherbtown Lane. The accents of the actors sway around yet rarely hit the Cardiff adenoidal drone. No ice scraping extended vowels. No Arms Paark. Instead Cardiff is depicted as a sort of modernist Pontypridd with soft Welsh valley accents mixed in from most of the south and much of the west. Gwen's a Cardiff girl but crossing the city she never meets anyone she knows. Cardiff bends and turns. And it is the city. An ambassador for the Welsh capital that never knowingly mentions rugby, never shows a choir or a daffodil or a miners lamp or a leek. Thank Russell T for that.

THE RED HOUSE

Stan and Arthur would have come here in the early nineteen seventies. That would be before the brewery upgraded the place. Smallest pub in the Welsh Brewers empire[7]. They changed it, said Stan. The peace and quite went. We didn't go there much after that.

The Red House, like the Ferry Road peninsula on which it was built, was on the edge of decline. Stan Williams, who had been Port Engineer at the time they closed the tunnel, told me that in the hard winter of 63 the big water tanks froze at Penarth and the hydraulics cracked. Bust. That finished it. Too costly to fix. They closed the dock, shut down the subway. Nothing doing after that.

But it was good while it lasted. The Red House was a dockers pub. Few locals. No houses nearby for there to be locals. Instead scrap metal merchants and car dismantlers. Rail track outside taking coal to the two operating staithes, oil to the storage tanks. Ferry Road that slipped down, dirty as it could be, to the peninsula's end. Down there by the Penarth Dock subway was a piggery and next to that a battered yacht club. Sylvia Tudor kept them, the pigs. She lived in a cottage on site, played the piano at the Red House in her spare time. Hit you in the face, the smell, as you unfurled your sails.

Arthur Gummer, Master Mariner, was Master for the whole of Cardiff Docks as well as the tidal harbour at Ely. Before that he'd been in charge of channel dredging with nineteen ports to manage. He and Stan had put the navigation lamp up on the seaward corner of the Red House. White light. Lined it up with a buoy out there in the dock channel. Gone out in a row boat to do it and then got caught by the changing tides. Tides at Cardiff changed so bloody fast. The boat had bottomed and they'd sat, stranded on the mud for several hours, cursing. The channels needed to be scoured and when you'd done that you had to mark them. This one was for oil tankers, big ones, coming into the Ely Harbour terminal. The

Red House, only pub in Britain to double as a navigation light.

For most of Stan and Arthur's time there the Docks had been waning. The West closed because it had been too small for modern ships. The East went the same way. At the Roath they looked for new things to do. Imported timber, took on passenger traffic to St Helena, began to bring in oranges and set up a packaging plant to service the demand of supermarkets. Cardiffians loved oranges, always had. But it was never enough. Before Maggie Thatcher broke them the dockers would send sixty men to do the work of three unloading grain for Spillers. Arthur was appalled. We drank tea while he told me this. Pale sun through his Taffs Well windows. He'd always lived up here on the fringes of the city. Blaengarw, Nantgarw, Taffs Well. Married the daughter of the farmer at Ynys Gau, Gwaelod y Garth. Stan Williams lived in Cathays. Nearer his target. They'd go down fiery Bute Road to work and there'd never be any trouble, none at all. There's more trouble now there's no docks, much more. Same story all over, the moral panics of the old, and the harking back, harking back. It never used to be this bad. Never did.

Down Ferry Road it is quiet. When I visit in 2006 The Red House is a flat space of broken brick and fragmented mortar. Wire fence protecting. The outline of the walls make this such a tiny place. There are still bits of red painted render and some black. The wall footings were that colour. A crushed lager can. Airbrick. Some wire. A damp, furled paperback, cover gone, pages yellowing: *Eroticon Voyeur* by Anonymous. Delta Books. 'Robyn shivered as his calloused hands slid up the backs of her thighs. I shall be an anchor and a refuge to you in the months ahead, he averred. Her plump white buttocks bulged delightfully.' Anonymous certainly knew how to write. The security guard, Bluetooth, waterproofs, docs, tells me they might be building a casino here[8]. Be a good thing. It'd bring work. All he can remember about the pub was it being closed.

Stan and Arthur are in their eighties. Stan's been back to see the changes but Arthur[9] hasn't. Not in an age.

Susan Tanti's father, Ashley Young[10], was the last long-term landlord of The Red House. Him and his father before him. It was The Penarth Railway Hotel then although everyone knew it as The Red House. It had been painted that colour in the early days but for much of the twentieth century the outside walls had been beige. Ted Young, Susan's grandfather, retired in 1972. His son took on the tenancy for £300. This bought him a bar, a smoke room and a lounge, a fixed counter with a Formica top, a length of wooden horsing, fixed upholstered seating along two walls, one fire extinguisher, one Bass Pale Keg dispensing unit and a load of laid lino. There were eight rooms upstairs for rent, each big enough for a bed and a chair and a night stand. But no one ever stayed, not in Susan's memory. The family had lived there since the early 1930s and for them the place was like a Tardis. Four wooden casks on wooden horses along the bar. Sawdust on the floor. Women in the lounge and the smoke room, men only in the bar. No rule, just a practice. The pig keeper played the piano on Saturdays. Ron Jones played drums. Roll out the barrel. Nellie Dean. It's a long way to Tipperary. No rock and roll.

Who was there before that? Jonathan Thomas Heard in 1882. J.P. Deslandes, Master Mariner, 1889. Charles Came and his son Richard from 1901 to 1917. Elizabeth Williams after that. John Morgan in 1929. Gareth Allsopp came later. Steve French and David Dalton were there at the end.

Ashley Young's customers were the dock workers, those the docks still engaged, regulars from the Esso Refinery, from Crow Oil and the Gas Works, Daf Trucks, Uniroyal Tyres, Plumrose Warehouses, Stan Ford Scrap Metal, Haydn Lane Car Dismantlers. Locals driving in from Grangetown. Did they have lock-ins? No, never, well maybe, yes. Tommy Gallagher lived in the cottages next door but they were demolished in the sixties. The space revealed became the pub car park. People didn't want to walk anywhere. In the great drought of 1975 they ran out of beer. Had permission to buy Party Sevens from the cash and carry and resell their contents across the bar. Snowed up in 1981, Ferry Road impassable. Almost lost. Watched the QE2 dock at Cardiff, white and huge. Workmen smiling, beer and woodbines, dockers with heavy hands.

Did they advertise? No need. As Kingsley Amis once remarked, all you ever need to say is that beer makes you drunk.

In 1976 Welsh Brewers refurbished. Changed the name officially from the Penarth Railway Hotel to The Red House, knocked the bar into the lounge, put the barrels downstairs, stopped using sawdust, Stan and Arthur stopped coming. Trade hours 11.30 to 3.00 and then 6.00 to 10.30. In 1981 Ashley Young died. Susan, 19 and with her own family on the way, tried to take on the tenancy but the Brewery turned her down.

Susan tells me this in her dining room in Corporation Road. She went back on 23 May 2005 when the demolition finally happened, saw a machine slice right through her old life, half a world hanging in the air, it was a wrench, heart in mouth, the past becoming palpable dust. But the world doesn't stop. Got to move on.

The pub is a hole in the ground now. Susan shows me a water-colour, done post-war, a fawn coloured Red House with cottages alongside it and a Hancocks horse-drawn dray delivering. The early nineteen fifties were all like that, pale, cream and khaki, grey.

The pub name flickers and changes. *The Penarth Railway Hotel* in 1871. *The Red House* in 1913. *The Hotel* again in 1924. *The Red House* in 1932. *The Penarth Railway Hotel* in 1934. *The Red House* in 1976. *The Red House* in 2005. Space in the air then flats after that.

After Ashley died the place gradually declined. Drink and music hung on but by the millennium the pub was taking little more than four pounds a day. Didn't open till six. No custom. Why bother. Steve French and David Dalton had the pub in its final year. Took it on a whim. It would be a botel. A place you could sail into for a drink, sleep upstairs, pie and chips. Verandah on the bay front. Pontoons. Free house. Bass. Real ale. David Dalton, otherwise known as Mr Natural[11] and who'd made leather belts and fixed rips in skin jackets since the 70s, told me he and his partner had ended up losing thousands. Cleaned the foreshore themselves. Collected litter. Hoped. Watched construction roar up around them and their takings sink through the floor. Dalton went back to belts and cases. French behind the bar at taverns in town.

Opened in 1871 with a licence to 'serve tea, coffee and intoxicating liquor to the working classes' the Red House was never regarded by CADW to be of sufficient historical interest to be listed. Die was cast. Pub was lost.

Despite a much publicised campaign to save it which included emotional support from councillors, former regulars, local inhabitants, passers-by, construction workers, real ale buffs, bird spotters, and both the BBC and the *South Wales Echo*, the bulldozers moved. The plans to turn the by now boarded and abandoned tavern into a local history museum were never realistic. Could you generate as much money from such an enterprise as you could from the build and sale of sixty apartments of blonde wood, aluminium and acres of glass? If it were 2009, post-crash, things might have been different. But it was 2005, height of the boom. The Red House was lost.

Red House Myths

IRA plotters drank here
Race riots
Red Navigation light on the roof
Tom Jones
Tunnel from here to the Pier Head
Room service
Most southerly pub in Cardiff
Billy the Seal
Grangetown Whale
Local
Lipstick
Book
Dress
Stripe
Face
Communist
Open always
Never closed

THE SUBWAY

The Yardbirds are in my ears. Needle cord jacket, hush puppies, collar buttoned down. It's a long cycle ride from Roath to the Ferry Road peninsula. Even more to roll along it to its distant southern tip. Road dirt, coal smoke. Gasometers. Engine repairs. Recycled car parts. Rust, wreckage, scrap. I'm on a bike, pushing the peddles, sit-up handlebars taken out and put back in upside down. I've got five lights on the front, fixed with Halford's brackets. They are powered by Eveready batteries and a dynamo that worked by rubbing a small, furled wheel against the turning, white-walled tyre. Free light in exchange for small roaring and just that little bit of slowing you down.

Down here at the far reaches of Cardiff, where the docks still clang and the mud stretches out all the way to America, the new world has just begun. Grangetown kids are on the streets popping benzedrine and purple hearts. The Docks boys are selling. The Who are on the players. *My Generation.* Graham Bond. Sugar Pie Desanto. Tommy Tucker. *Hi Heel Sneakers.* Fingers snapping. *Put your wig hat on your head.* My Raleigh is no Lambretta. But it's all I've got.

The tunnel goes right under the water. Takes off from the Ferry Road tip and dives, changing direction once, under the whole of the Ely tidal harbour. It emerges near the Master's Office at Penarth Dock basin. Hundreds of yards of total darkness, water running, curved from start to finish with no flat sections, a challenge to pass along alive. This subway, large enough to get a horse through in one direction, two could never pass, was built in 1899[12] to take workers from the walking suburbs of Grangetown to the coal loading staithes of the impossibly booming Penarth Dock[13]. It replaced the earlier ferry from which the Road and, indeed the whole peninsula, took its name. From 1865 when the docks at Penarth were dug the crossing was managed at first by a few row boats and then later by a cable-drawn covered raft operated by two men turning a windlass. There's a famous grainy photo of it in the histories looking like an early hovercraft. Penarth had thirteen staithes and shifted coal at an increasingly prodigious rate. Hands were needed and in they poured. When the subway opened at the turn of the century the hand-cranked ferry disappeared. A couple of open boats hung on hoping for the tunnel to falter. But it did not.

When I first came here in the late 50s there was a hut where the

turnstile keeper sat and a sign that listed charges. 1d to cross, more if you had a cart. Yet there was no one there to take the cash. An old unshaven shambling by in a flat cap and wearing a mack tied with rope tried it on once. That'll be a penny, son. But I didn't stop. Inside the tunnel lights once shone but they've all been smashed. I rev my bike, dreaming of scooters. At the bottom would be water. A dribble or total, who knew. You got enough speed up on the down run to take you at least half way back out again. It was a claustrophobic, fearful rush. Despite their number the lamps on the bike show almost nothing. Cast tunnel ring linings, scarred concrete, rusted wires from wrecked lamp housings, and then the black of the water. Here the world might end. But it's only six inches, a slash of spray and loads of air. Now I'm on the rise again. Breathing once more.

Penarth is a holiday. Beyond the Docks, up, out and through the rising headland terraces, lies the pebble beach, the famous pier, and the ubiquitous sea. Victoriana alive and kicking. A place of perambulating long dresses, cigarettes and tea and men in blazers. I circle and amble. Stop and stare. Cycle the worker's streets. Watch the Penarth world. On my return I can't find the subway entrance. Left in a rush of fear and exhilaration. Have to ask.

Ferry Road slides back up across what were once the West Moors and into industrial south Cardiff, turns at Holmesdale and heads for Lower Grangetown. My bike is roaring. Fur on my hood. Parka trailing the back mudguard. *Da doo ron ron. Da doo ron ron. Night Train.* Downliners. You remember them. Such Pretty Things.

The Dock's Master

Things you do: ensure the safe movement of shipping, deal with ship's agents, pick up the pilot at Breaksea, get the gangs in place, deal with the lockgatemen, roster the tugs, talk to the pilots, listen to the complaints from Masters, get the owners in early so they can catch their trains, check the charts, accept the hydrographics, fix the inside boatmen and the outside boatmen and the lockgatemen who do not speak to each other or ever do each other's work, never do that, get the watcher's timesheets to the maingate, read them, sign them, assist the vessels docking, talk to the tugboatmen, get the ropes put around the right bollards, read the charts again, prevent damage to Dock's property, manage the Board, know the blockage factor and how long that takes, and the ebb and the flow and the space under ships for the water to escape, how long this takes, during the day, at night, at dusk, when things are steaming hot and when they freeze You can see your breath then and everyone's watching and you keep a change of under-clothes in the office just in case

---

NELSON AND LOUDOUN

Cardiff is awash with deregulated historians. Tiger Bay fixators, glory of the port recallers, dockland visionaries, coal fanatics, ship spotters, tattooed drunks. All admirers of the battered and difficult past this area once held as its own. Neil Sinclair[14], who has written two histories of Butetown's core, reckons the place to be as close a community as you can get and massively misunderstood. It has a reputation as a wild land that is totally undeserved. It's a point of view. We're standing on the wide flat roof of Loudoun House observing it all. Jonathan and I. Loudoun House, flats for singles and couples, and next-door Nelson, apartments for the elderly. You see them sitting in the entrance porch in their dressing gowns. Sticks and wheeled-walkers. Talking away the day.

These are the twin blocks which John Williams celebrates in his *Cardiff Trilogy* as a base for a pirate radio (could have been) and a centre for drug abuse (certainly was/still is). Jonathan can remembers the lift shafts so full of trash in the seventies when he first came that you couldn't move through them. They are clear now. Sort of. The twin entrance porches upgraded and rebuilt in the late nineties into one architectural plinth of light and space. Keypad entrance doors. Serviced notice boards. Staffed concierge counters. Cleaned floor areas. The architect Oscar Newman's defensible space[15]. First proposed in the late seventies. Delivered now and as a deterrent to anti-social behaviour clearly working. Took twenty years for that message to get through.

The gardenless nineteen-sixties replacement for Butetown's once jumbled core runs north and is full of taxis. I count thirteen. Mainly driven by Somalis who make up a high percentage of the locals. Yemeni, Somali, afro-Caribbean, some whites, no Asian. It's the only work a lot of them can get, says Shahida. One car, multiple drivers. You get a return on your capital that way. To the north is the Noor El Islam Somali Mosque on Maria Street. It's next to Islamic Court where letters have been trashed from the name plate. It read *Lamic* when I passed. South is the Yemeni Mosque on Alice Street. Shahida Ali-iqbal who has brought us here talks about her family. Her father used Alice Street despite being Punjabi from over the river in Grangetown. He died in prayer in the mosque in 1989. Why is Paki such a derogatory term, Shahida asks. 'Stan' means land and 'Paki' means pure. My son uses it as his internet tag. He doesn't care. In 1905 Fred Fischer had a hit with a song called *If the Man In The Moon Were A Coon*. I tell her. Wouldn't get released now.

These flats, at sixteen stories and built in 1964, were pretty early

examples of Welsh highrise. Put up when the planners imagined that highways in the sky would solve all our social ills. The community of Butetown was bulldozed and these bland apartments installed at it's heart in Loudoun Square. The great pubs of the district went too. Replaced by the Paddle Steamer. Featureless housing estate brick. Closed for the same reasons that the Dusty Forge in Ely went to the wall. Couldn't be controlled. Violence, drugs, prostitution, anti-social everything. Now a café. Tea and buns. Anti-social behaviour hums in the air.

We've come up in a decent and largely smell-free lift and accessed the roof by the now expected method of pull-down ladder and ceiling flap. This ladder has a neat and padlocked shutter which completely covers it. When we climb (and Shahida does this in black and very pointed fashion shoes which I would never have tried it in – "it's alright I've done this in heels") she takes the padlock with her. "Left it behind once, someone locked the ladder up and I was stranded here for hours." She smiles.

She knew Lynette White, the victim of the now famous Cardiff dockland murder. Went to school with her. Scene of the crime in nearby James Street. We're looking out at the new development. The armadillo Millennium Centre. The Ikea-styled multi story car park. Lloyd George. Orange new build everywhere. Before she took over management of the two tower blocks she worked as a council asylum officer, got to know the way everything worked. The northern Somalis claiming to be from then lawless south. You could tell they weren't by their accents. The Sudanese hated by the Somalis and spending much of their time in hiding. The local whites so integrated that they refused to be rehoused in white-only districts.

The social sprawl of the whole area is shrinking. There's a space where the health centre once stood at the edge of Bute Street. Site for a new community facility and improved shops. To the north west the Angelina Street redevelopment looks like something done by the private sector. Beyond is the wall of the east-west rail link and the new centre high rise beyond. Altolusso. Meridian Gate. Ty Pont Haearn. The new central library with its brass-coloured southern facing. Wouldn't have been that colour if it hadn't been for the steel roof of the Wales Millennium Centre, says Jonathan. The Library has an installed sedum roof. Brown when its was first affixed but now turning green. The same sedum is underfoot here at Loudoun. But seeded by birds rather than installed as green design. And covered with a scattering of chicken bones from scavenging gulls.

Shahida is talking about her novel. The one she's writing. A book full of honour killings. She's has experience of at least eight, she says. Wants to use the material, expound on it, do with this terrible activity what any good writer would. Expose it, take it beyond. There'd be a market, I tell her. Finish fast.

Is this Tiger Bay, I ask? Or is that just a name loved by the tourist marketeers and the nostalgic. We're down now in the foyer looking at the black and white framed shots of the world as it used to be. Long lost schools and streets. The Hamadryad hospital ship beached on the mud. Coal Staithes. Working men smiling. Ships unloading. If you live here then these are the docks, says Shahida. Still.

Outside Jonathan's car is unmarked, pays to drive something ancient, the sun shines. *She'll Either Go Sleep Hungry or Full. This Ramadan You Decide* reads an Islamic Relief Charity poster on the end of the bus shelter. Men in Arabic dress drift by. Women shrouded in black. Kids playing ball. There's no smog, little dust. No loading cranes moving. Work vanished in the Loudoun[16] ground. Quietest dockland in the world.

THE BALLAST BANK

Cardiff is forever looking for itself. For the places of its origin. For the spots where history launched. For the locus of just what made it. Is there some epicentre of Cardiffness out there, in the long grey days? Can we stand somewhere and have our feet in four counties and two countries simultaneously? Hop from foot to foot changing dimension? Not a chance. Cardiff is a city that floods us with its contemporary ordinariness. Little left of what made it great.

I thought I'd found this place, where all the power lines crossed. Where Bute sat on his horse, smoked his pipe. Where Rawlins White preached the unadorned. Where Robert Fitzhamon put down his iron-clad boot. Where Jack Brooks thought about Baltimore. Where Dannie Abse saw the spark of *Ash*[17]. Where Peerless Jim first made a fist of his small hand. Somewhere east of the Castle, north of the North Gate, on Kingsway, near the once canal's once weighbridge. There.

But now I'm here, where James Street meets Clarence Road and I'm not so sure.

In the days when Penarth was famous for its harbour and Cardiff for its Sea Lock this was one end of Penarth Harbour Road. A snake across the mudflats and river estuaries from booming Saltmead Grangetown to the workers suburb of Lower Penarth. The slice of land I'm standing on, between the canal and the Taff was Rat Island.

Water on all sides. Swamp of the river bends and the Timber Float to the north, Taff estuary to the west, the Glamorgan Canal on the east, Severn to the south. An island.

In the days before Bute mechanised the whole coal loading process with his Ship Canal wooden boats would come in here empty. Two-hundred tonners weighted in the water with a ballast of rock taken from whichever land they'd originally sailed. They'd tie up at the Ely coal staithes, or enter the Canal Basin and dump their ballast in a sliding heap that stretched out the length of the island. The ballast bank. Almost half a mile long at its greatest extent. This was ultimately the source of the foundations for half of lower Bute Town, ballast hardcore sunk into endless meters of native alluvial mud.

In 1893 when the rails came running from Cardiff Riverside Station, south of Cardiff General, they built a passenger platform alongside Harrowby Lane. This was the Glamorgan Canal Railway's[18] Clarence Road station. Opened to connect the canal to the expanding UK rail system, it brought in workers from Barry and Pontypridd. It was well patronised right up to closure in the 1960s. The platform was nothing: stubby planks and ill-cast concrete. The trains had reversible wooded seats. Men spat on the floor. The goods line carried on south. It went over the road using a level crossing to service the Corporation Yard and the reclaimed metals business of J. Ford alongside the Canal Sea Lock. That line closed in 1963.

The crossing of the Taff to the west was once a wooden shambles of a toll swing bridge managed by the Taff Vale Company. It ran from Eleanor Street and across the top of the Sea Lock. In 1890 it was superseded by a new crossing. The Meccano-like lattice of the new Clarence Road Bridge, named after His Royal Highness, the Duke of Clarence and Avondale[19], who opened it, was a Cardiff landmark until it, too, was replaced with the present river crossing in 1975. A road bridge that you only recognise as a bridge because of the lack of houses climbing its sides.

There's an historical flux here. A place in space-time through which men move and around which history circulates. In 1886 workers rioted against the Taff Vale Company toll charges, threw the toll gates into the river, attacked the toll house. Nearby, opening the new bridge in 1975, James Callaghan made a speech about the resurgence of Cardiff. All around him the Cardiff world was falling down.

In 1963 the old Bute Town Police Station[20] was demolished as part of the Tiger Bay slum clearance. A new police station opened on the corner of Dumballs and Clarence Road. Its vehicle yard spread across the railway goods link. That police station closed in 2007. A new structure, bulk bent inside unstealable lead roofing, is going up as I pass. This is the new 2009 South Wales Police HQ. Hard determination and clear authority clothed in smooth orange brick. Muscle like a weightlifters' arm inside a short-sleeved shirt.

I stand outside, where the artwork will go, and experience the flux. It all flows through here. Did once.

The artwork is the creation of Renn and Thacker, public artists. Builders of the *Green Man Walking* at Bromsgrove and a horse in the air outside Cork airport. They are putting the ballast bank back and installing a light on top of it. Visible as you approach from Grangetown, light flickering across the David Jones frontage of the WMC beyond. I'm working on the text. More words that'll flow from the ballast sides and into the Police station behind. Softeners for a hard projection of power.

I love this idea of rebuilding that which has been lost. The land artist Mags Harries, with whom I once worked on the *Demon Trap*[21] at Swansea, had a plan to rebuild the now drowned Cardiff Bay mud flats along the sides of present day Bute Street. Didn't catch on.

Behind me the past just about lingers. Walters Building, 1915. Temporary police station hiding on the first floor. The embellished Bath stone frontage of the London Salvage Association rebranded as the Lottery-aided Wales Resource Centre for Women, Science and Technology. The distinctive and conically towered Avondale Hotel, corner of Hunter Street, replaced the pale imitation of Avondale Court.

But mostly the past and all of Rat Island with it has been sunk. Anonymous and silent brick and glass where once industrial workers housing jostled for space with industry itself. No smoke, no smog. No grit in your face. The flux here has at last ended. Bent in under the earth's surface on a sinking tectonic plate. Recession bound.

SOUTH AND THE MOORS

Before the industrial age, Cardiff was a tiny place. A stagnant backwater of eighteen hundred. The size of the audience for *Chitty*

Chitty Bang Bang at the WMC. Back then the moors that stretched from the Taff to the Rumney were the ones raiders would cross when they came. Vikings pillaging by sea. Marauding Irish in their currachs. Men in boats made from daub and leather, arriving in search of wealth, women, copper and tin. Anything to grab, to take by sword and broken bone. These Cardiff flatlands were saltmoors, tidefields, lands riddled with small creeks and shifting pools. They were covered at high tide by the fast-rising Severn. You crossed them by causeway[22], navigated the floodwaters by coracle, or never did. Welsh badlands. Cocks Tower in the eastern town walls guarded Cardiff against what they might contain.

Eventually sea walls begun by the Romans were extended eastwards to hold back the encroaching tides. And, saving the occasional breach by tsunami[23], they began to work. Drainage reens reclaimed the once lost and even the never had. Sea receded. Mud beach became land. Over centuries these wetlands became dry. They were used first as farmland. At Pengam, Adamsdown, at Splot Isaf and Splot Uchaf – ancient names from the early records. They turned to streets as Cardiff expanded.

Adamsdown Farm was demolished, rebuilt as the Kames Place Gospel Hall. The farm at Splot Uchaf, *Upper Splot,* became the Great Eastern Hotel. It's just about there, still, on Metal Street. Only I wouldn't try to stay. Splot Isaf, *Lower Splot*, became St Saviour's vicarage. Built in 1915, at Courtenay Road. Its watery fields never again to be green.

Metal workers came. The Thaisis Copper Works opened in 1873. There was tin-stamping. Enamelling. Brass. In 1888 the Dowlais Iron, Steel and Coal Company needing ores from Spain moved to East Moors from Merthyr. In 1900 they amalgamated with Keen's of Birmingham. In 1902 with Nettlefolds of Shropshire. Guest, Keen and Nettlefolds, primary steel makers[24], the heart of Cardiff's dark, heavy, industrial past.

Housing expanded west towards the Rumney River. Splot became Tremorfa, (lit. *Marshtown).* Terraces, ever more of them, clustered under a constant fall of ash.

Between them steel and coal made Cardiff a grimy, estuarine place. You wouldn't sit down unprotected on its few public benches. There was little light in its tight and scruffy terraces. The people coughed and spat. There was smog in the air.

In 1905, renting a damp field from William Williams at Splot Isaf on East Moors, Ernest Willows, Cardiff air pioneer, flew his first airship. The Alexandra-Willows I. 70 foot long and looking like a fat banana. His dream was that great dirigibles with screw propellers and steerable vanes would replace the iron-clad ocean liners that dominated long-distance transport. He would build Cardiff's Hindenburg. He would fill the Cardiff skies with shapes like ships from Mars. The brains behind the enterprise belonged to organ builder William Beedle who had made and flown airships in London. The abundant enthusiasm came from Willows. The finance came from his dentist father. Beedle and Willows lasted for four years before parting in 1909 just before the Willows II appeared. The following year Willows flew in it from Cardiff to London. In the November he launched Willows III and flew that on to Paris. Christened *City of Cardiff,* his dirigible made the city famous. There are period photos of airships over Roath Park Lake and sailing serenely in front of the dragon-topped dome of City Hall. Captain Willows, contracted to the War Office. Zeppelin maker. In the vanguard of the rush towards a Flash Gordon future. But he never quite got it right. Things came down. Things refused to take off. He died in a balloon disaster at a flower show in 1926. The Hindenburg Willows might have been chasing caught fire in New Jersey ten years later. All that's left of his airships is the V8 engine used on Willows II, kept in a museum in Bedfordshire[25]. Airship adventure over.

I'm south of Willows High School, on Willows Avenue. The great man's name, if not his undignified end, remembered. It's 2008 and all that remains of Cardiff's heavy industry stands before me. I turn into Seawall Road, pass the Pengam Moors Social Club and then a renegade cluster of car breakers, part fixers, car menders, compressor renters, wire rollers, metal turners and light engineers. This stuff once filled half the city. Ahead is not the sea but Celsa, last remnant of Cardiff steel making, today sanitised, sky blue roof, clean white steam escaping. The enterprise is a quarter the size of the GKN East Moors works which, until they closed in 1978, filled this area.

Allied Steel and Wire grew from those GKN ashes and struggled on as a minor metal player until it too collapsed in 2002. More than 1600 men redundant. Huge fuss about the failed pension fund. Dark industry leaving Cardiff at a rate of dirty knots. Encouraged by the Welsh government Spanish Celsa rode in to the rescue. They had new ideas, made new investment, took back 450 men plus another 450 contractors. They rode the green metal wave of endless recycling. Celsa installed a new 33,000-volt arc furnace melt shop in the Tremorfa Works next to Rover Way. They reactivated the long, blue-roofed sheds of the Castle Works Rolling Mill alongside the East Dock link road. Took safety seriously. Thought about

where they were. Kept their ash from the line-hung sheets of the Splott housewives.

Tim, who is showing me round, is a computer man. He maintains Celsa's networks. White-collar job, I thought. White would last about five seconds, as it turns out. On the surface what Celsa does here is simple enough. Nothing with ore. Nothing made from scratch. They take scrap from all quarters and sort it. They fill great hoppers. Bashed shiny metal like a heap of giant unravelled cans. Using a hoist the size of a terraced house they load scrap into an arc furnace. 33,000-volts and a cloud of furious spark and body-shaking roar turn this shredded metal into white-hot sludge. Lime and fluorspar are added to help filter the impurities. Steel emerges in a yellow-red river. Turned into rod. Cooled into bars. Made into billets.

South of Rover Way on the Tremorfa foreshore I can see the scrap dealers. Cranes and dozers pushing cubed cars and desiccated metal waste into pyramid piles. Sorted by type. Prices in China are edging up but for now the stuff is still sold to Celsa. In the yard we enter are tractors with chain wheels. As big as double-decker bendy-buses. Bigger. There are also fields of water and then dust in quantities I've not encountered since seeing a sand-storm in the Sahara. Flue ash. Rises in clouds as your boots move through it. Fills yours clothes. Your nose. Your ears. Your eyes.

The real action is in the meltshop. I've been driven in past the weigh bridge and the detectors that look for radioactivity. Imagine what would happen if we got some isotope into the mix. Have to close the whole place down. I've been kitted with helmet, safety goggles, ear

protectors, metal boots, and a flame-proof suit. I try four of these on before I get one that fits. Must look smart. Temperature out in the sun is 25°. Inside my suit it's over 30°. We go up the ash covered stairs and through the ash-covered double-door air lock. The far side is a place beyond my experience. Yes, I've seen all this on TV. The hugeness. The fear-filled might. The yellow sparks, the gouts of fire, the men in helmets and face visors stalking the furnaces like armoured transformers. The molten metal running in streams. Man-made magmatic eruption. Steam and Strombolian shower. Screech and screaming power.

When you experience it in person it's something else. The heat and noise come in under your skin. The temperature rips upwards pulling sweat from everywhere you have. Breath shakes. Chest vibrates. Eyes stream. Like Cape Canaveral when Apollo blasts. Darkness with great streaks of violent, crackling light.

The three electrodes of the arc furnace, rods the shape and size of telegraph poles withdraw, white hot, and then return, crackling with the sound the sun makes if you could get close enough to hear. Tim's talking but between ear protector and roar I don't hear a word. I take a photo and watch the screen on the back of the camera white out with the light. The lens fills with blowing dust. Despite safety glasses, and with my own varifocals on under those, so do my eyes.

Outside the silence is palpable. There's a sense of the fresh air being something you haven't breathed in an age. Even if it's still largely full of dust. We drive across the works and out through the amazingly silent Splott streets to reach the nearby Castle Works. This is the rod and bar mill. Here Celsa's still warm re-cycled billets are reheated and sent on a half-mile run through a series of enormous mangle-like rollers. Each successive machine reduces the size of the cross section. The results extrude at ever increasing rates. By the time we get to the top end of the plant one-inch wire is coming off in red hot spirals at the speed you'd throw a lasso. What do they use this stuff for? Concrete reinforcing. Mesh. Fasteners. Screws. Nails. Production is up. Celsa are rebuying land they once sold as surplus for new storage and processing. A white butterfly flutters over the moving metal. Crusted red outside, still molten in the centre. Men stand inside air-conditioned refuges, drinking cans. Heavy boots. Helmets. Earphones like the military. Safety first.

There's an 'It's Against the Law To Smoke In These Premises' Assembly-provided notice affixed to a pillar. We are technically indoors, after all. Does anyone? Course not.

That evening, by complete coincidence, I find myself in the not yet demolished Vulcan[26]. Behind the prison on Adamsdown. Hanging on as one of the last unreconstructed working men's pubs in the city. Wood floors, sawdust, splendid toilets. Just over the rail line from where East Moors used to be. A place that once filled with dry steelmen slaking their thirsts. It's now isolated in a sea of car park with the imminent threat that it'll be replaced by apartment blocks associated with the St David's 2 mall development. I have a few beers with the writers who gather here now and again. There's talk of fiction and biography. Free sausages from Liz Smart, the landlady. Bunch of students in the corner speaking in German. Retirees, unemployed standing at the bar, chucking darts, eating crisps. Anyone wearing protective footwear? That hasn't happened here for a long time.

WALKING OUT ALONG THE BARRAGE

Cardiff is feeling the slump. Too much silence. *Coming Soon 18 Luxury Apartments*, on the corner of West Bute Street, metal frame rusting. High rise glory, Oval basin, crane dismantled, site vacant. Beyond the magic roundabout where Ocean Way hits Windsor Road the rise of the new bristling offices have slowed to a crawl. The Meccano mesh of abandoned tower cranes fill with birds. There's

been rain for ten days. Every crack in the entire city is sprouting green. Science fiction novels begin like this. Man gives up. Nature returns.

Routes across Cardiff east to west all involve river crossings. They are at the heart of why the city is where it is. The ford at Llandaff. The Taff crossing the Romans made near their fort. The bridge the Normans built near their castle. To the south where the rivers delta and the tide fields fan the old toll road to Penarth has been replaced with the elevated Butetown link flying up from its tunnel below Stuart Street to arc on stilts over the yachts of the Bay.

To the south is the barrage. The once highly-controversial blocker of the Ely and the Taff. A 1.1 kilometre, £220 million concrete and rock drowner of mud flats. A flooder of basements and a displacer of wading birds. Now a gem in Cardiff's crown. In just over twenty minutes you can cross from the Bay's Norwegian Church to Martinez's La Marina restaurant opened in the 1865 Custom House at the edge of Penarth. Fastest direct crossing ever. The nineteenth century ferry from Cardiff Pier Head to Penarth took longer[27]. I've got as far as the Bay. Fifty minutes down from Southminster, crossing the Mason-Dixon that is Newport Road, skirt Broadway, slip through Splott then Adamsdown, over the Black Bridge at Kames Place, onto the cycleway along Tyndall Street, under the Central Link massif and then leaping walls and driving between apartmentised warehouses, stroll down the west side of the weed-filled East Dock to emerge below County Hall. Bay water in sight.

The way out along the Barrage, the Cardiff Bay Barrage Coast Path, was finally opened as a through route in July 2008 – thirteen years after Balfour Beatty and Costain began their joint construction. Setting off on it today is like heading for Checkpoint Charlie. There's an ultrasafe double-sided high-railed new bridge over the entrance to the Roath Basin. Warning notices festoon across it like flags. Beyond here the four-metre wide pathway over Cardiff Port

Authority land is surrounded by vandal-proof wire mesh. *CCTV Images Are Being Monitored For The Purpose of Crime Prevention and Public Safety. Danger Deep Water. Path Closes at 8.00 pm. Restricted Area. Emergency Telephone Number.* We are a nation of the mindless who need constant chiding. Care for us, control us, corral us, o Fun Police. If your eye ever stops watching we'll be there smashing our heads on picnic tables, breaking our arms on rocks and throwing ourselves in the slimy sea. As I walk I am passed by joggers, kids on bikes, and men with dogs. Our bright blue funland imitation, the Cardiff Bay Land Train, toots along Locks Road. Packed full. Don't want to walk but still want to have the experience. Much like going up Snowdon on the rack and pinion.

Beyond the Port with its interpretation boards, picnic tables and views of the water-filled Channel Dry Dock and the broken windows of the Cargo Road warehouses, is the Barrage proper. A half-mile long rock and sand armoured bund. South the salt sea, the dollies and the lock gate into what remains of Cardiff's once great coal docks, the Queen Alexandra and the Roath. North, the fresh water of the peaceful and tideless Bay.

Just past the Barrage Offices and lifeboat station is the Barrage leisure centrepiece. A bunting-strung children's playpark made to look like a pirate's galleon. Just before it is a festooning of history of which the old Barry Island fun-fair in its cheaper, plaster of Paris days would have been proud. *The Age of Coal.* An outdoor mass of bilingual signboarding, pit drays (apparently called Alan and Yank), a miniature pit wheel, plastic coated lumps of coal, an interpretative disc that tells the story of energy, a resin-bound pavement dragon and a dispiriting set of sea grass growing from slate-filled beds constructed from bits of rail track. You can catch the water taxi from here. Barrage North. I am severely tempted.

Boat owners are warned that the Bay now contains Zebra mussels which can block water intakes and sever ropes. Parents are warned that the water is still deep and are given the phone number of the nearest A&E. The wind has an edge to it which tells you that you are in an exposed place. The views across the immensity of the impounded waters to St David's Hotel and the gleaming Millennium Centre roof put the pirate boat in its place.

The fish pass, sea locks and associated gate lifting machinery that form the most visible part of the Barrage sit at the Penarth end.

From the Cardiff distance the mechanisms look like oil-well nodding donkeys. Here the ever-present written cautions are supplemented by warning sirens, guards with walkie-talkies and fencing in abundance. But there's a flash of freedom. Something that makes me think that all might not yet be lost in a future of padded gloves, head protectors and are you okay my love sit down here's a cup of tea made with warmish water. The Swiss landscape artist Felice Varini has been allowed to paint his bright yellow *3 Ellipses for 3 Locks*[28] across the whole metal and concrete development yellow arcs concentrically swirl, turning the complex into the impossible, making flat structures appear to bend. When viewed from the eastern end the circles enormously float.

Where the Barrage ends, beyond the bascule bridges, so too officially does Cardiff. The car park and the almost always closed Barrage Café, blend into what's left of Penarth Docks. The Custom House, the still boarded-up1865 Marine Buildings, the Marina apartment development, the marina itself, full of boats. I walk on, Vale of Glamorgan territory now, over the edge and round the headland, bound for the pier. There are plans to build an elevated walkway here, the Headland Link, currently on hold. The beach is a bomb site of broken rock, concrete groynes, and bladderwrack. Rusted ferro emerging from the shattered remains of the World War 2 searchlight emplacement that was once here. The headland erodes constantly. Evidence of rock fall everywhere, sea-washed beds of red mudstone splattered with new accretion, small sections of cliff collapse in a rattling shower as I pass.

Over the long decades attempts have been made to halt this erosion. The pier end of the headland is potched with a mass of concrete infill. Rivers of poured hardcore have been cemented to the seaward face of the land. Holes plugged. Patches fixed. And as those patches fail they have been concreted over again. Sea fishermen pass. A middle-aged man, fully clothed and with a rucksack on his back, stands on a rock performing calisthenics at tai chi speeds. The clamber across a final but fallen and fractured concrete walkway to reach Penarth landfall on the Esplanade requires some agility and determination. This is the old world, the one we had before the glitter of development arrived. Mangled slightly, and certainly down at heel, but free. There is not one Health and Safety warning notice on any part of this territory, not that I can see. No fences keeping citizens out. No barriers preventing access. No apparent need for helmets nor protective glasses, ear pieces, or gloves. No need to turn back. Got beyond the barrage and am alive and unharmed. Got to Penarth without a scratch.

CARDIFF BY THE SEA

In America one of the many new Cardiffs of that new country sits on the coast between Los Angles and San Diego. Cardiff by the Sea. Pop 12000. Zip 92007. Seafront, rock, beach, reef, palm. That's something we do not see in this Cardiff. The sea made us but actually it's hard to find. Down at Mermaid Quay the front faces fresh water. Beyond the barrage is mud. The Port is inaccessible. The most Cardiffians get is the long view south from Penhill or Penylan – the sea a distant smudge of grey channel. Wave action zero. River estuary. Delta accretion. Clevedon and Somerset beyond.

But a last Cardiff beach does exist. Lost between the Port and the Rumney. A place where Rawlins White once fixed his fishing henges. Where reens drain across the Cardiff Flats to the Orchard Ledges. Once fenced by industrial railways. Now barriered by industrial roads. I walk there. It takes half an hour. A civilised stroll. I pass down Roath's not so broad Broadway with its line of failing pubs. The New Dock Tavern shakily holding, the Bertram in trouble, the Locomotive, home for decades of Cardiff's finger-in-your-ear folk club, now boarded and the inn sign gone.

I take a left into Piercefield Place, Victorian wrought iron embellishments over the door porches, Sikhs in their front gardens playing radios, Metal Street, Star Street, Iron Street, Copper Street, Silver Street, Sun. This is the place where Adamsdown rubs against Splott. Saint Germans of Auxerre[29], Church in Wales, built in 1884, big enough for 700, rises like a gothic implant. God, buttresses, bulk.

Singled out for love and praise, a masterpiece, by Simon Jenkins[30]. In the Church Hall on Star Street rooms are rented to the Adamsdown Day Centre (meal for the aged in progress as I pass), a rehearsing pianist, and the artist Brendan Burns.

Brendan actually lives round the corner with his artist wife Ruth Harris on Metal Street. His studio, small enough for a double bed and wardrobe, desk and chairs, is packed with paintings, boards, bubblewrap, frames, boxes, bags, wood strips, paper and rolled canvas. Mounds of paint harden on a tabletop. A CD system totters precariously above a wooden filing cabinet. Against the long window stand a board covered with dozens of photographs of the beach at Druidstone. The west, where the world ends. Light floods. There's loads of light.

Brendan has typical Cardiffian credentials. Irish father, Welsh mother. Catholic upbringing, St Josephs, Lady Mary, joined in then let it drift. His art, when he studied at the Slade in the mid-1980s, was essentially politically motivated. Those were Thatcher years. The time of Toxteth, the Gibraltar killings, and the violence of the Protestant marching season. An uncomfortable age in which to be decorative. A difficult period in which to be detached. Brendan was neither. He drew, he made sculptures, casts of soldiers, paintings of the streets of Belfast. Reacted. Was involved.

He visited New York with Peter Prendergast. Had his eyes opened, saw the size of the world and what was possible. Visited the Matisse retrospective and was in awe. Didn't look up as most NYC visitors do. He looked down. Onto the streets, onto the cracked and crazed urban detail below. Beauty is so simple, he tells me. You just need to know where it is.

Back home he discovered the Pembrokeshire west. The Pembrokeshire paths, the Pembrokeshire coves, the Pembrokeshire light. Was seduced by what he found.

He came upon Druidstone. A lost beach in a place so hard to get to. Small hotel, cluster of cottages, cliffs, rock and pool, sea and sky. His

work became this beach, the
shifting space between low tide
and high. The place where
bladderwrack bent over rock
and pools slipped and slid like
Duchamp's *Standard Stoppages*,
in between the wave marks
across the wrinkled sand.

A Brendan Burns painting is
as much a sculpture as it is a
daub. Oil in clotted totters,
colour like a light-filled sky. Sea
dust, fragments of shell, sea
creature, and shifting rock. As the sea changes so too does a Burns
painting. He walks the beach sketching, taking photographs. He
knows the entire place. Could draw a map of its rockscape. Walks and
rewalks it. It's like visiting old friends, he tells me. Will you do this
forever, I ask. Yes, he says. It's my life.

The works are named after map references. SM862594. Go there
to see the original rockscape. The wash of dampness. The lodestone
of sand. SM861171 – *Liquid Light Series, 2006. Spindrift.* Find Burns'
inspiration on Landranger 157. Like Mark Boyle firing his arrow into
the arbitrary map. Visit the spot.

The latest stuff is in the process of being packed for a forthcoming show with the Ysbryd/Spirit[31] Group at Newport Museum and
Art Galley. On the wall is a large-scale work of white empty bounded
by bitumen black. The lines run like tide races. The sea is
omnipresent in Star Street. A version.

But Druidstone Haven, the Burns sea, is two and half hours away
in a fast car. Does Brendan know of the local tidescape? Twenty
minutes south of where he lives? Never been there. Looked once on
Google Earth. Industrial mess not worth investigating. Satellite shot
taken while the tide was in. Fuzz. We decide to go. An easy walk.

We stroll south, past the boarded and abandoned Great Eastern
Hotel (full of illegals – Iranians mainly – Brendan watched them
emerge to shriek in the street at Iran's success during the 2006 World
Cup), on through hard-core Splott. We cross the railway on Splott
Bridge, pass the fixed and extended Star Centre. On the northside is
Joe's Imperial Café next door to a closed florist and a boarded green-

grocers. Past and present. Sign of the times.

Carlisle Street gets us to Tyndall Street. Road humped. More life on these streets than in Rhiwbina. A million times more. We pass gaggles of kids in hoods and uniform white trainers. A boy on a tiny pushbike with a flattened Coke can fixed to rub on the rear wheel and sound like a motor. Beyond the once bonded brewery warehouse now used for records storage, the Maltings, Victorian housing gives way to post-industrial social apartments and light industrial prefabs. The near riotous hurley of Splott market has moved to a shed south of the Cardiff Bay Business Centre on Titan Road. There are burger vans and the sound of Dizzee Rascal in the air.

The beach we are heading for, Cardiff's last beach, sits in an inlet to the east of the docks. Access is by walking the roundabouts of Ocean Way, avoiding the artics, and finally climbing the fence below a giant hoarding which reads *Who Cares? Explore The Meaning of Life with the Alpha Course.* There's an outfall here – worked sewage, drain water, damp from the tidefields that once ran north all the way to Newport Road. The beach is genuine. Has sand, in tiny quantity, but sand nonetheless. Has green rocks on the tideline. Lines of dry, black bladderwrack. Fragments of shell. The outfall trickles. And there's copious mud.

The top end is riddled with dumped hardcore. Brick, block, steel-work waste, hunks of red-rusted iron, plates, pebble, boulder. In the outfall someone has abandoned a Toyota Hilux. Next to it are complete sections of brick wall, thrown down like pieces from a giant jigsaw, mortar still in place.

The sea is out about as far as it goes. The beach is huge. In the distance gulls. A tideline of wave action merges with the estuary, with the cloud scape beyond. The light is the best we've seen all day. Like Mondrian, says Brendan. Colour in horizontal bands. Gradations of grey turning to gradations of blue. Birds giving scale.

Behind us there's the thrum of Celsa's blast furnace. You couldn't sit here in the heat in a deck chair. Could you? Ignore what's behind you, just look to the front. Ignore the bricks, think of rocks. The beach coast goes south round the Heliport to bend west and run on towards the Port. Wire fence and warning notices. Keep outs. Do nots. Keep offs. We pick a way across the boulderfield. Big steps, difficult steps, noisy steps. Not like Pembroke, not like Druidstone. Like Cardiff.

The sea fishermen casting from the point, tattoos, old faces, catch flounder, conger. They get here on bikes using the coast path which runs all the way back to Rover Way. A flattened mud track through the undergrowth. Bends and dips, rolls and climbs. Could be the path up out of Broadhaven towards Nolton. If you half close your eyes.

Getting back is quicker. You've seen the sights once already. At Brendan's studio there's tea. As good as Druidstone? No need even to pose that question. But a beach nonetheless.

notes:

1. Council Chief Executive Byron Davies announced plans in 2007 to sell on the Heliport, Cardiff Bus, County Hall and anything else that moves (or indeed stands still). A hunt for efficiency improvements is the official line. The hunt for liquidity is the reality.
2. He did at the time we visited but in late 2008 invested in a fully-featured digital SLR.
3. Welsh coal is not over. The open casts at the heads of the valleys are now producing enough for it once again to be exported. In small quantity maybe but still going out rather than in. Where does it leave from? Newport.
4. Pierre Vivant, *Landmark*, Windsor Road Roundabout, Cardiff. 1992.
5. Cardiff Bay's Water Tower, designed in 2000 by Nicholas Hare Architects, in collaboration with the sculptor William Pye.
6. Russell T Davies, born 1963. Reviver of *Dr Who*, saviour of BBC Wales production, creator of *Torchwood* and the *Sarah Jane Adventures*. The Swansea Jack who made Cardiff world-famous again.
7. Welsh Brewers absorbed Hancocks in 1976.
8. Didn't.
9. Won't now. Sadly Arthur Gummer died in 2008.
10. Edward Ashley Young had been a merchant seaman in his early days, a mason, a carpet salesman, night shift loading on the jetties, then a stand-in bar man. Did the three jobs simultaneously to keep his family, body and soul together.
11. Mr Natural operated first from Albany Road, moving to James Street in the 1990s and more recently to West Bute Street. You want a pouch to fix to your belt or leather satchel or a hard-topped travel case? Come here.
12. The public subway from Ferry Road to Penarth Docks was built by the Taff Vale Railway Company. It was of tubular design and lined with six cylindrical ten foot external diameter caste iron sections bolted together. The walls were 18 inches thick. Work began in 1897 at Ferry Road with the digging of a trench and the lowering in of tunnel sections by steam crane. The Penarth side was also created by the digging of a trench. Only in the middle did tunnelling have to occur. The tube sections were covered with brickwork. At its lowest the tunnel was eleven foot below river bottom. It opened on Monday 14th May 1900 and closed on 30th September, 1963.
13. Penarth Docks opened in 1865. In 1885 three million tons of coal went through them. By 1912 the total had topped four million. The Docks closed in 1963.
14. Sinclair, Neil – *The Tiger Bay Story* (1993) and *Endangered Tiger – A Community Under Threat* (2003) both published by Butetown History and Arts Association.
15. The architect Oscar Newman (1935-2004) created the concept of 'Defensible Space' in

New York in 1972. He proposed that crime and anti-social acts would decrease in areas where the community felt a high sense of ownership and where community spaces were not only observable but became extensions of the community's own private domains.

16. Loudoun – pronounced 'Lowdon' locally – was named after Loudoun Castle near Kilmarnock, once owned by the Marquis of Bute.

17. *Ash On A Young Man's Sleeve* – Abse's 1954 novel of growing up in south Wales.

18. When Cardiff Corporation took over the Glamorgan Canal, such as it was, in 1944 it also acquired this railway. It bought a new battery electric loco and ran the line for the next eighteen years. Profits ranged from poor to non-existent. For a fuller account check the excellent *The Glamorganshire and Aberdare Canals* (Vol 2) by Stephen Rowson and Ian L. Wright (Black Dwarf Publications, 2004).

19. His connection with Cardiff? Slight. Prince Albert Victor was the first child of Albert Edward, Prince of Wales and Alexandra, Princess of Wales. He was styled His Royal Highness Prince Albert Victor of Wales from birth.

20. In the heart of Tiger Bay on the corner of Bute and Maria Streets.

21. *The Demon Trap*, 1995, a temporary installation for the Swansea Year of Literature.

22. Causeways were lines of stones, raised banks, pathways across damp ground made from fallen trees, boulder, piles of dirt, and layers of trampled branches. When it wasn't designated the Roman Portway, Newport Road east of the Crockerton was the Causeway – a path across bogland made from stone and impacted earth.

23. January, 1607. The sky was blue. The tide was high. The Severn floodwaters came. According to *Lamentable newes out of Monmouthshire in Wales*, a 12 page pamphlet printed in London the same year, all along the estuary and especially at Cardiff there were 'huge and mighty hilles of water, tumbling one ouer another, in such sort, as of the greatest mountains in the world had over-whelmed the lowe valeyes or marshy grounds.' The waters arrived at 25 mph and flooded four miles inland across the Wentlooge Levels. Hundreds of lives were lost. A plaque on the wall of Peterstone Church shows the high water mark at 1.9 meters.

24. And that might have been at the heart of the problem – primary production. As a city enterprise Cardiff consistently failed to diversify. The city made heavy steel, in quantity. East Moors ended up as uncompetitive and overmanned. The world was now making its own steel and much more economically. Why should they want product from Wales?

25. The Shuttleworth Trust, Old Warden, Bedfordshire.

26. Included as one of only four Welsh pubs in the all-UK *CAMRA Rough Pub Guide* (2008). The others are The Plough and Harrow at Monknash in the Vale, The Dyffryn Arms, at Pontfaen, near Fishguard and Tafarn Sinc, at Maenclochog in the Preselis.

27. The subway (see page 131) took around four minutes by bike. But half an hour at least to reach from the Norwegian Church (in a different place at the time of the subway's closure. The original Norwegian Church stood at the south eastern end of the now filled in West Dock. The present reconstruction at the end of Harbour Drive opened in 1992.

28. The art work, the result of a Public Art Wales/Cardiff Harbour Authority commission, was opened by Councillor Nigel Howells in 2007. Varini continues, in ever increasing number, to paint his site-specific works that never resemble the Mona Lisa on buildings elsewhere around the world.

29. The Church began in 1857 as a converted barn, Splott Chapel, where Metal Street now runs. Replaced in 1874 with a second-hand iron building from Dudley. Replaced with G F Bodley's present structure in 1884. Renewed, extended. Clergy House next door opened in 1894. Church Hall destroyed by bombing, replaced post war by the present structure. 50s educational building style. St Germans given Heritage Lottery money for extensive renewals in recent years. Congregation active. Father Roy Doxsey a powerhouse.

30. *Wales: Churches, Houses, Castles* (Allen Lane) 2008.

31. Iwan Bala, Sue Williams, Martyn Jones, Glyn Jones, Peter Spriggs and others.

WEST

ALTERNATIVE CANTON

The Believers are explaining to us what it's like to drive on the wrong side of the road. All the way down here from Gloucester, forgetting themselves, finding their hire car back on the American right. They've been hit with the hillbilly stick, they tell us that too. Craig Aspen and Cynthia Frazzini out of Nashville and now loose in the south Wales rains. They sound for all the world like Emmylou and Gram, like the Everlys might have been in another age, those back of the neck shivering harmonies, those keening southern state voices, those acoustic guitars driving the music on. Craig's got a pork pie covering fading grey. Cynthia's got a flower print dress, boots, hoop earrings and tied back hair. Two guitars. Cynthia's is bigger. She puts one leg behind the other and sways. This is alt cardiff. Our take on alt country. Blind River Scare were the warm up, Gene Clark and the Byrds flying again, not a rhinestone or western shirt or big hat in sight.

We're old, most of us, smoking in this bar is banned now, but we do have real ale in our hands. Country music is the last bolt hole of the middle-aged. That hankering for Dolly Parton and for Hank Williams, for Glen Campbell and Charley Pride only comes when the rest of your life has run out of innovative steam. Country music with its fiddles and electric steels offers few challenges. Like rock & roll it's a mature music with nowhere further to progress. But this is not that. This is the alternative. No one here wears M&S lycra or an Evan Roberts blazer with a badge on the pocket. No shined black day shoes. Nothing pressed. Scruff tees, jeans and worn out sweats. Handsome Family territory. The south's daddle with the dangerous. Punk-upped four pieces, new gen rock grapplers, root guitars hunting for what we might have lost.

Night before I'd been next door at Market House, Chapter's extension, a mess of artists' studios, work rooms, offices for small arts companies, designers, publishers, dancers. I'd been *Real Cardiff Live*, talking up the city, giving the assembled my take on what makes this great place tick, how it shines and shimmers, how it had been in its dirty past, what its strengths were (always knowable), and its weaknesses (endlessly uncertain), how did its Welshness work, how did it fit into Wales, post-industrial coal valley capital, growing ever larger over the hills that stand behind it, recovering land from the mass of tidal bog to its south.

I bought your book when I first came to Cardiff, says the Turkish girl, smiling. I thought it might tell me where I was. I tell them about the lost wells of Penylan and at one the shape of Christ's knee on the rim and how I'd seen the two imprints of Mohammed's footprint in a glass case in the museum at the Topkapi Palace, Istanbul. The imprints were different sizes. One taken when he was much younger the guide there had said. They smile, they don't laugh, should they laugh? They don't know. I tell them about the Butes being like Bill Gates and buying out anything that sprang up in opposition. The austere second Marquis with his docks and his visions. The Catholic third with his Victorian Disneyworld at Cardiff's heart. I talk about the rivers, the Tan, the Whitebrook, the Canna, the Wedal, which we no longer have. We sup Cabernet Sauvignon and abjectly nibble at the crisps brought by the organiser, Renée Lertzman. Some of the listeners buy books.

For many years I came here to the *New Welsh Review* offices, presided over, then, by the late Robin Reeves. Robin was a green-leaning nationalist socialist. Voice of understanding. Knew the world's shape. He ploughed a liberal furrow with his literary magazine. *NWR*. You got a free mug if you subscribed. Idris Davies or R.S. plus poem. Mug collectors signed up and then threw the magazine away. Robin would have been an alt country follower if he'd lived long enough. Would have enjoyed the way the rules got broken with the music somehow still staying on board. Robin's vision was a walking route all the way from here to St David's. A path those offering penitence would once have travelled when two pilgrimages to the far west of Pembrokeshire were worth one to Rome[1]. But the magazine itself has now moved west and its former offices are occupied by men with drawing boards and computers and tubes of paint. Out of the window I can see early evening Market Road revellers, hair pulled to the back of their heads in severe ponies, tattoos, white trackies, setting off for the pubs of Cowbridge Road – the Corporation, the Ivor Davies, the Kings Castle, the Admiral Napier. Places full of shine and light.

It has always been like this in West Cardiff. Before the Arts Centre came to Chapter in 1971 the buildings were Cantonian High School (opened 1907) and before they were built the space was used by the monthly Canton cattle market. 1859. Ran from the Police Station to Carmarthen Street. Sheep and cattle pens, stables, slaughter house, meat market, manure, dust. Pubs that opened all day for the traders.

Drinking, shouting, falling down. Men in shoes that leaked. Women in shawls. Gin. Small beer. Rum. Pints in thick glasses. Pots. Tumblers. Jugglers, fire-eaters and story tellers. Men selling miracles. Soap makers boiling fat at the end of Grey Street. Goats and chickens. Cockle girls. Butcher's boys hawking joints from wooden trays.

The Believers do five encores. One singing gospel acapella. One on a solid body Gibson. One like the Louvin brothers but with a blazing female lead. "The shoes on my feet will be a-shining when I arrive at the top…"

We buy CDs and if we've already got them then we wish the Believers had recorded more. Night outside is full of silence. Sky as ever full of rain.

COCK HILL

Up beyond the ancient bridge at Leckwith the road rises and the sky comes into view. We're nearer the sun. This is the wedge of wooded hillside that separates the sink of Ely from the double garages of Michaelston le Pit[2] and the fairways of Dinas. Where Cardiff aspires but hasn't got to yet. Temperature is in single figures, warmest it has been all week. I'm hunting for the rumoured Bryn Ceiliog vineyard, dark red grape flourishing on the dismal south Wales hills.

Although it is hard to believe Welsh vineyards are nothing new. They arrived with the wine-drinking Romans and when those invaders left were kept on by the monasteries. The well-to-do and the holy drank white, red and rosé. The rest of the population stuck to mead. Henry VIII did the practice considerable damage when he dissolved monastic lands in the sixteenth century. The seventeenth's Thames- and Taff-freezing downturn in temperature finished it off.

By the time the third Marquis of Bute had become a feature on the Welsh landscape and had bought up the medieval wreck of Castell Coch wine had virtually vanished from these lands. Too cold, too wet. A place of mists and barbarians. A country where you took weak ale for breakfast and were glad. But Bute, always the romantic innovator, was a man with money and one with lavish flamboyant ideas. He employed the great William Burges to rebuild the castle as a place of fairies and magic mushrooms and then, along with a number of other early hippie innovations, planted the lower slopes with vines. This was

1875 and three acres were filled with French Gamay Noir and Le Miel Blanc. Two years later these vines had cropped well enough to produce, using a wine press at Cardiff Castle, 240 bottles. By 1893 annual production had risen to 12,000. This was an expensive, exclusive product which, to the Bute's dismay, was never as sought after as he'd imagined it would be. *Punch* magazine had it that it took four men to drink a bottle of Bute wine. One to imbibe, two to hold him down and the fourth to pour the stuff down his throat. Production hung on until the time of the Great War when sugar shortages and further failures of temperature called the whole thing off.

Ian Symonds resembles a tall version of Bill Oddie and has a similar affinity with birds. A renegade from Caernarfon, he once owned a construction company employing three hundred people but sold out to the French. He now farms West Hill and the slopes further up Leckwith, Bryn Ceiliog, Cock Hill. We meet him in the village from where, aboard a mud-splattered Land Rover Defender, we bounce up fieldtracks and through managed woodland to emerge on a patch of south-west facing, gently sloping acres. Here, against all the odds, Ian has planted two thousand vines. He talks at high speed, spraying out facts about his achievements like an industrial grass cutter. Land is well drained, faces south west, vine roots go down forty feet into the limestone, first planted in 1998, coped with the slugs. Took two years to mature which got him three quarters of a tonne. Beaten, then, by mildew, output was reduced to a quarter. Yet undeterred grew on. The last few years have been bad but all the signs are that the next will be better. Ian gets advice from Peter Andrews at Llanerch and his grapes pressed by Three Choirs Vineyards in Newent, Gloucester. It's on sale in a few places only. The Village Stores in Dinas Powys. With your food at Le Gallois, the Olive Tree, Manor House Hotel, Penarth. Ian has completed his seventy-six pages of forms and has won approval from the UKVA (United Kingdom Vineyards Association) to sell his stuff as a 'Welsh Regional Wine'. *Bryn Ceiliog* that's Cock Hill in English. As a marketing tool that'll stand up to Jacob's Creek. And Jacob's Creek, remember, won over the world.

We're standing amid the leafless stalks, this is March, and there are the remains of plastic bags flapping on poles. Bird scarers. This is Ian's biggest problem. Marauding mistle thrushes who attack in flocks of over fifty. Over the years he's tried a hundred methods. Bags on poles, strips of aluminium foil, CDs on string, man-shaped scare-crows, flags, sheets, streamers. Sometimes these acres have more prayer flags on them than Tibet, he tells me. The trick is to keep changing before the birds catch up. They are up there now, in the leafless trees, chirping. Asking me to be fed, says Ian. He takes a handful of seed from a gillet pocket and leaves them atop one of the vine frames. They're nuthatches, great tits, blue tits, jays, chaffinches, magpies. I spend a long time out here in the open air, he says. Hard, hand labour, few machines. You get to know what's around.

The grapes are Phoenix, Orion, Reichsteiner, Bacchus, Kernling, Findling, Rondo, Dornfelder, Regents. German, French. They harvest in September and October. You walk down the endless rows and pull them off by hand.

Ian got interested in vineyards when he married Maria Fernanda, an au pair from Spain, whose father grew wine on the slopes of the very Welsh sounding Mount Teide[3] in Tenerife. They all thought Welsh wine would be a joke, he says, but I've proved them wrong. You keep the mildew back by spraying but you don't do that for several weeks before picking. Keep the flavour pure.

British vineyards are on the increase. There are more than three hundred and fifty in the uk now, with at least nineteen in Wales. Global warming is making all this possible. The French are buying acres in England's south east to expand their own production. There's even a vineyard in Scotland although that one is under plastic. Ian thinks this is cheating. His faces real Welsh rain.

We slither along the tracks to Ian's sister's farm, Beggan, where

some of the Cock Hill output is stored. I don't keep it all in one place, says Ian, I spread it around. A hundred bottles here, fifty somewhere else. Who hunts for it? Fourteen year olds from Ely, light fingers from Barry, rough-necks from the Bay. I make sure they don't get much. Beggan has shire horses and Welsh Black cattle and a long barn full of dust and carts and ancient machinery, a thirties Riley, a steam engine called Nellie, an Idwal Symonds Fferm y Felin hay cart, chopped wood, fence posts, wire, water pipes, gates, boxes, cans. A farm like we imagine all farms to be. The past hanging on.

The business at Beggan is Welsh Black beef sold via the internet[4]. Organic, desirable. The future. Ian yanks a case of six, unlabeled bottles of white for me to try. Plastered the Welsh way on Cock Hill. Singing then dancing then arguing then falling down. Next year there'll be some of this in the specialist stores and on the wine lists of a few decent restaurants. Year after in the stores and wine bars. That's the plan.

On the way back we look out over rebuilt Caerdydd spread before us. Millennium Stadium, Millennium Centre, Barrage, roads, glass, apartments, water. Plural city. Multiple city. Drinkers everywhere. Still growing.

LECKWITH BRIDGE

Near here in 1928, at the old pre-barrage tidal reaches of the Ely, the magnificently named Jockenhovel O'Connor discovered a hoard of bronze-age armaments. 600 BC. One rib and pellet socketed axe, one socketed axe fragment, four leatherworking knives, two socketed sickles, two razors and a chariot pole cap. Buried three feet down in the Ely flood plain. Deliberately placed there. Hidden away but never collected. Rotted. Dug up two and a half thousand years later, washed and cleaned, given to the National Museum. They were heading west, those bronze-agers, Brythons sliding home.

The bridge I'm standing on was in its day a main route west. It's still busy enough with a smog and slap of vehicles heading for Barry and the Glamorgan Vale. It was built by Norwest of Liverpool and deemed important enough to have the then Minister of Transport, Leslie Hore-Belisha, open it in 1935. Hore-Belisha of the beacons.

He made drivers take tests and erected globe yellow flashing lights on poles at all pedestrian crossings. Saved a lot of post-Brythonic lives. A six axel artic roars passed me through the icy air. No such crossing here.

Looking down from the new bridge, parapet soaring over the placid Ely, the old one, sixteenth century and replete with triangular recesses, three gentle arches and period narrow width, can be seen still there. Dark shadowed by its mighty and so much younger replacement. Stone marvellously unfaded, pointing intact. It once took carriers' carts from the salt marsh of Leckwith moors, up the long incline of the Pen-y-Turnpike, through Leckwith village (pop, in 1871, 169) and on to Cadoxton, Barry, and the sea. When the new bridge opened the old was left in place giving access to the ancient farm, Leckwith Bridge House, which stood at the foot of the rising woods.

Today the old road is gated. The scrap of flatland on the river's west bank completely industrialised. Autogas, Concrete Products, Vehicle Storage, Police pound, American Burger van parking, Stone Flair Paving, portacabins, shacks, garden with a well in it, tarmac, mud and damp.

This is the place where Cardiff ends and the Vale begins. The twinned towns of Nantes, Hordaland, Stuttgart, Lugansk and Xiamen give way to Fécamp, Mouscron and Rheinfelden. Hands up those who've been to Rheinfelden. A mud-decked runner goes past, mp3, woolcap, pulse-monitor wristwatch. Not him.

The path in through Plymouth Woods sags with running damp. Under a thick mix of oak, hazel and alder the churned cream of the Leckwith incline slops over boot-tops and mortar-like jams the cleats. These woods are ancient, what's left of the great deciduous woodlands that had stood here at the flank of Cardiff for hundreds of years. The path slides at more or less ground level, paralleling first the silent Ely and then the roaring link road. Birds drowned out. Couldn't hear any above the four by fours and town shoppers. This is Sunday. High blue somewhere above the leafless branch canopy. Ice cold.

In the ivy choked undergrowth are half-emerged root structures, oak clinging where the rain has washed the cover, empty cans of Carlsberg, evidence of sink penetration, tree trunks showing attempts to burn (failed), trolley detritus, wrecked Cortina rusted almost back to base metal, fragments of stolen Kawasaki, tyre high in the branches, Victorian hard-core dumped and mashed into the bog of the now rising pathway. Grasp and grapple. Up past an ancient clay pit, excavated and filled with Russian vine escaped from suburban horticulture, got here by bird, or wind.

The path turns east towards the still thundering link road, a dual carriage way cutting north on concrete pedestals. The Ely river has snaked far east and is now out of view. The writhe of tyre tracks increases. My large-scale Cardiff 1980 OS map has the explanatory key printed over where this place would be. Land not worth much then, less now. Would the Ramblers come through here in their elderly gangs of a frosty morning? Where does the track take us? Through a concrete underpass thick with green moss and water, graffiti and branch backlog; over bent and rusted 70s fence and abandoned stile and gateway to emerge at the top end of the long green stretch that was once Ely Racecourse but is now Trelai Park. Prams. Push bikes. Footballers. Dogs. City Hall on the eastern skyline with Capital Tower to its right. The rest of Wales rising ever so slowly straight ahead.

So this is it. The bent ley between the Brythons' abandoned sword and sorcery and a twentieth century green-lung for one of the vastest of Wales' social housing estates. They came along here on their small horses, bearskins, sweat and grease we wouldn't recognise. Threshed the earth, made their marks, tried also to burn a tree or two. Probably.

ELY RACECOURSE

Cardiff is not full of horses. Unless you count the crowd control police or the equestrian statue of Lord Tredegar[5]. There is a riding school at Pontcanna Fields and the gypsy horses loose atop the capped dump at Lamby Way. But the sport is not an urban thing. Racing occurs at BetFred and William Hill. Men in doorways desperately smoking. Copies of the *Racing Post* under their arms. The nags go round the track in glorious technicolour. None of the men following form who

watch with bates in their breath have ever been near enough to smell them. Their tiny riders perched up top like toys. Money in the wind.

It wasn't always like this, here in this pedestrianised, motorcar city. I'm sitting in my car, parked on Aintree Drive. Up beyond where the paperworks were, at the vast estate's southern end. Aintree Drive – that ought to signal something. Between 1855 and 1939 the Ely Racecourse was here. Home of the Welsh Grand National. Waterjumps. Stand. Owners enclosure. Place for the sport of kings. In the old photos you can see the great and the good and the enormously well to do taking their places on the stand. Top hats, spats, high collars, fur stoles, shiny boots. The owners and their cohorts. The trainers. The masters of the turf.

Ely was a vale village. You came by shooting brake or arrived, as the horses did, at Ely station by train. The Cardiff racecourse was no place for the sons of toil. The predecessor of the track at Ely was the track on the Heath. That one appears like a sort of iron age earthwork ring on the ancient maps. The Horse Racecourse on Cardiff's Mynydd Bychan, the open lands, the common lands, the great heath. the Heath track ran horses from the early 1760s to around 1840. A two-mile lozenge between the Wedal and Llanishen Brooks.

At Ely I've got Brian Lee with me. Racing correspondent, turf historian, master of old Cardiff, author of the column on the local past which appears weekly in the city's freepaper, the *Cardiff Post*. Brian worked here after the war when horses no longer ran and a fire in the stand had seen the facilities off. The Ely estate housing had recently been constructed and the council was turning the redundant track into one of Wales' largest leisure provisions. Soccer pitches, courts, changing rooms. Facilities for the people. Trelai Park. The hoi polloi had moved on.

Brian is full of talk of horses and trainers. The Welsh Grand National and its winners. Father O'Flynn in 1892 and the legendary Cloisters in 1893. The jockeys took drink between races in those days. A shot of whiskey to keep them going. Fell off at the water jump, half cut. One of them lost his false teeth and when the racing was finished the all the jockeys, still in their silks, trawled through the water to help him get them back. The stand was over there. He points towards a row of red brick houses on Epsom Close with more behind them on Ascot. And the track here. He points again. We gaze at a waterlogged expanse of empty green. Light bouncing off the surface. Not a horse in sight. In fact we don't see one all day, in our hunt for the traces of Cardiff's equestrian heritage. Here at Ely the only connection that remains are the race track street names. There was a newsagents called The Racecourse round here somewhere, says Brian. We stop a passing local exercising his golden retriever to ask. Long gone. There was a pub too, called the Anthonys, after the three great trainers[6]. No sign of that one either. Keith Piggott, the father of Lester, rode the final winner, Grasshopper. After that it all went. Racing has been completely cleaned away. All that's left are books and bits of memory. Even those blurring like evening shadow.

I did groundsman work here, says Brian. Painted in the white lines. We mixed used engine oil with the whitewash to make it stick. Wouldn't be allowed to do that now. I've even painted pitches with two halfway lines by mistake. Didn't go down too well.

Brian fronted Cardiff Council's Manpower Services Commission-funded depression buster, the Historic Record Project, during the last great recession in the 1980s. Job creation gave the city funds to spend on organising their mouldering documents. A sort of rerun of the work carried out by Hobson Matthews at the time of Victoria's jubilee. Letters from Captain Scott, Bute memorabilia, menus to the Mayor's dinners, plans for what had come to pass as well as plans for what might have been. Open the cupboards, list what you find. For Brian this was a dream job. He found a document from 1953 describing a plan to open a racecourse in Sophia Gardens. They didn't build that. In the City Hall's silver safe room amid the cups and plate he discovered a signed print of the film *All Quiet on the Western Front*, a maquette of the equestrian Lord Tredegar, and a set of ceremonial swords. He had to stop his youth workers fencing with those. There were full sets of Matthews' *Cardiff Records*, signed, and still in their wrappers. Might they still be there, I ask? Rare as hen's teeth now. Who knows? The Project produced a dozen booklets on aspects of Cardiff's history – *The Market, The*

Mayor, The Mansion House and the often reprinted *Cardiff Notebook,* copies of which can still be readily found.

Brian got into writing by sending letters to *Tit Bits* and *Reveille* and soon discovered that if you were deliberately controversial they printed what you had to say. He wrote in complaining about Shirley Bassey miming at the London Palladium. Wrote again

suggesting that he would never allow his wife to open his mail. Got paid a guinea and received a deluge of complaints from readers. Just what the publisher ordered. His interest in the city into which he had been born along with a taste for the turf grew. He began writing on local history for the *Cardiff Post.* His reports on point to point and other race meetings still appear in the *Western Mail.*

We drive on to the Heath via the end of Sloper Road where Brian is sure Cardiff's White City once stood. The White City was a dog track used for speedway and athletics. Taken over by GKN as their sports facility but did long public service before that. It's here somewhere, says Brian, stopping a passing taxi driver to ask if he knows. Doesn't. The White City raced greyhounds back in 1928. At the first meeting 9000 people turned out to see a bunch of dogs fighting rather than running around the 470 yard turf track. Things improved after that. Mick the Miller won the 1930 Welsh Greyhound Derby here in record time. We check the City Gardens housing development for street names that might chime. But they don't. The past no more than a drift of dust. When I check later I find that the City Gardens has been built right on top of where the White City stadium once stood. Port Office sorting office on Penarth Road to the south, Sevenoaks school and Virgil Street to the east.

On the Heath in the sloping winter sun there is about as much to see as there was at Ely. The track went along the line of King George V Drive East turning across the ends of St Anthony Road and St Benedict Crescent and eventually following Maes-y-Coed Road to return to its starting point via Heath Halt Low Level[7]. On Yates' *Map* of 1799 it looks as big as the town of Cardiff itself. Joe the Crwys[8] was famous here in the early 1800s. More than a life away now. We park the car and enter the Heath from Heath Park Avenue. The starter's box, known as the Chair, stood here. Now nothing but trees. Couple of walkers. Women with pushchairs. Air.

You don't make money at this, Brian tells me. Not writing about horses nor putting money on their heads. Two pound is about the most I ever bet and that only if I am actually at the meeting. That was it. A Cardiff day chasing nags. Didn't see one. Couldn't find the greyhound track. Went home with Brian's copies of *The Welsh Grand National* in a plastic bag. Read about them instead.

THE PENARTH CON CLUB

The arms of Cardiff reach out ever stronger. Already Penarth's marina, where the dock once was, has been encircled by Cardiff Bay's empounding. The Cogan Spur, the elevated A4055, rises from Grangetown's giant Asda to rush past the crumbling Billy Banks and into the old town's heart. If they ever find the money there may soon be an elevated walkway running right round the headland. The foot and cycle path through Harbour Drive, past the re-sited and so-white Norwegian Church, to cross the Barrage is already a reality. There'll be a bridge soon, Pont y Werin[9], for foot traffic and cyclists across the leaking Ely. The marina's Marconi Avenue seems as much City of Cardiff as it does Penarth Vale-village. It runs past the Tesco off Terra Nova Way and into the heartland of the classy small-town waterside apartments of Penarth Haven. The soft air of this Victorian and still leafy suburb is changing. Still not the city, certainly. You can tell by simply standing on Windsor Road and looking at the make of the shops, big business not pressing, multiples mostly absent, locals still trading. Or the colour of the architecture: stone grey, older. No recladding. Few amended frontages. Slow change. The Washington on Stanwell Road restored to its thirties glory. White and art deco. Residential housing still mixed with commerce. Dog walkers. Parking possible. The difference between town and city.

The Conservative Club stands beyond the railway where Westwood Court turns off Stanwell Road. Earlier, when the Conservatives met in Windsor Road, this was the Westwood College

Private Boarding School. Eton of the Vale. Double-fronted. Gabled. Rambling. Flag poles. Covered porches housing ancient municipal slatted benches. Notices for weight watching and line dancing. Stern signs warning that entrance is only possible on production of membership card. Or being signed in. Or being David Cameron. Officially supported and approved. Background checked. No slatternly socialists here. You press a buzzer. I press the buzzer. A ten-second wait then, unchallenged, the door opens. The hallway beyond is full of portraits of the Conservative past. John Major. William Hague. Iain Duncan Smith. Margaret Thatcher. The half-glass doored downstairs bar has a hand-made sign attached by cellotape. Men Only. You can see what looks like a poodle modelled out of old Woodbine packets on a shelf beyond. But we're upstairs.

I'm here chasing shadows. The Shadows. The three, solid-body electric guitars and one set of drums that were the centre of British pop after Bill Haley's American rock and roll and before the beat boom of the British Beatles. The Shadows. They were ostensibly Cliff Richard's backing band but developed a vibrant life of their own. They started out as The Drifters. They changed when the Clyde McPhatter-led American Drifters took out an injunction to prevent them using that name in the States. They played guitar instrumentals. Twangy things with three minute tunes. Fast leads following a throbbing bass. A lost form in the new millennium. The original Shadows were Hank Marvin on Fender Stratocaster who, in thick black-rimmed spectacles, reminded you of Buddy Holly. Reliable boy-next-door rhythm guitar Bruce Welch. Steve McQueen crew-cut drummer Tony Meehan. And red-head, Teddy-quiffed renegade, Jet Harris, describing himself as leader in contemporary publicity, on electric bass. *FBI, Apache, Man of Mystery*, you remember. No, you don't, you're too young.

The South Wales Shadows Club spent five years meeting in Malpas, Newport, but since most of their members live in the Cardiff area they've moved here. They meet upstairs in the Prince William Suite. It says 180 Persons Max over the door but inside there are only twenty. Virtually everyone present is over sixty. I say virtually because bucking the trend the club secretary is a thirty-seven-year-old university administrator, Steve Burnett. Steve likes everything from Metallica to Mingus, he says, but for him the Shadows have a special resonance. He owns a Dansette. A rare thing. In his thick-soled blue suede shoes he's up front by the ancient stage working the sound deck. The members, eighteen men and two women look as if they've recently stepped from an Isle of Wight cruise ship. Grey haired if haired at all, M&S scruff, old men's trousers, check shirts, v-necks, pints of dark. They take the stage in sequence, genuine flat-bodied Fender Strats[10] in

hand. The club owns a valve Vox AC15 amp just like the ones the original Shadows used. A Squier Precision Bass. A Burns Marquee Deluxe. A Burns Marvin Guitar. Past and present, real and replica, mixing. Looking real is a consideration. Getting near the original sound is vital. How loud do you play, I ask Richard Rudd, a post-sixty long grey-haired former chartered surveyor who acts as the club's chairman. Never so loud you still can't talk. He's married to Jackie, the only woman guitarist present.

Steve keys up the backing tracks for members to replicate Hank B. Marvin's thwung on top. *Walk Don't Run. The Breeze and I. Foot Tapper. Nivram. Shotgun. Sleepwalk. Wonderful Land.* No one does the Shadow's *FBI* walk. That youthful and arrogant footstep[11]. Mostly, as all good retirees should, and John Lee Hooker certainly did in his recording eighties, they sit. Jackie has her shoe on a guitarist's foot-rest. Beyond, on the floor, a couple slowly line dance. Two of them, in perfect step, at a speed so slow you wonder if they are on mogadon. From his mp3 player Steve keys up another backing track for Keith Twine, the club treasurer, who fingers his way through *Nivram*, from the Shads first album. *Nivram* is *Marvin* backwards. Schoolboy delight when I discovered that.

In another era these guys would be jazzers listening to ancient New Orleans numbers and identifying the names of every session musician and every take. Or folksingers dredging up farming songs from Gower or hay-binding chants from Suffolk, finger in ear, thumb behind brass-buckled belts. George, who plays bass on a genuine replica, awash with the irony of remaking the past in a post-modern present, tells me that the Sunsets, Shakin' Stevens's rocking band rehearse here on Thursdays. Occasionally they show up on Shadows' evenings and throw in a few bits of roll and rock to leaven the twangy mix. Not tonight.

In the second half backing tapes are abandoned in favour of the live. A quartet of club members take the stage together. They'll play music of the Shadows era, Richard tells me. George is on bass. Steve on lead. The excellent Lawrence Williams playing a great white Gretsch on rhythm. They do *Peace Pipe*. *True Love Ways*. *Runaway*. They rock so slowly. Most of them do it sitting down.

But things do brighten when a singer called Butch clad in wrinkled khaki denim takes the stage. We get a full-on leg twitching *Move It* and then *Long Tall Sally* with head flicks and arm gestures. Elvis as sung by your builder. The most lively the Con Club has been all night.

Weeks earlier, in a car, hitching a lift to a blues gig by Zoot Money and Maggie Bell at, of all places, Abertillery, I admit to owning a CD which consists entirely of versions of the Shadows' *Apache*[14], the Jerry Lordan hit of 1960 which put the Shadows on the map. Here I have the Indian drums and deep guitar lead done by everyone from the Ventures to The Spacemen, The Jet Blacks, The Surfaris, The Arrows and even the much-maligned Bert Weedon. Two versions by the Shadows. The original plus a retake from 1975. You can only listen to this set a half at a time. It's like Groundhog Day. The melody loses what meaning it had as *Apache* comes round, each time slightly altered but still essentially the same, again and again. We play *Apache* at the Shadows Club[15], says Steve. Every time. He's in the same car.

But on the night I visit, of course, no one does.

CHANCE

In the back room, my study, Henri Chopin and I have the full apparatus before us. The stacks of papers and the dictionaries, the prints of microfiched newsprint drawn from the library, the cards, the maps, the histories. These things have accumulated over time like dirt at the sides of churchyards. Graves sinking, the land rising like a sponge. Accumulations of flotsam and jetsam, things lost, things found, drifted behind doors, fallen into corners, coming loose in great showers when you pull the desk out from the wall. Their colour is not white. It is grey and brown and nicotine yellow. Mildewed, foxed and spotted. Ripped and bent. Rust stapled. Grey. Touched with death and ash. Surfaces dulled from being hidden from the sun. The pores of their paper surfaces chock with microbe and mote. Marked by time, they call it. Marked by time before time had even begun to spin. The paper stock was always weak and full of acid. The data banged down in thin inks that was always grey not black and turned ever paler as the years got among their atoms.

The Cardiff maps are blotched like the faces of aged men. They have been acquired from a dealer who rips them from atlases, pulls them from the backs of great works on the city that would shimmer on their own but can make three times as much cash in their separated parts. He droops them in bowls, seven parts water, three Parazone Bleach bought from the corner shop. Hauls them out, clean and white, ink barely smudged. Dries on pegs. Flat ironed, low temperature. Hand coloured using Pentel markers and pencils sourced from Smiths. Glass and frame. *Map of the Towne of Cardiffe. In alle her glorious partes.*

Chopin, maps in hand, has been up on the Common looking at the shape of the land. Why is it flat here? Shouldn't it fall away slowly, westwards, towards the river? Has there been intervention by agriculture or industry? He's put his head near the green sward and looked for lines and revelatory bumps. Chopin, his name forever addled by pianistic association. He's chased his genealogy. Tracked the Chopins of Switzerland, the Chopins of Northumberland. The Poles. The French. The ones from Kent. In the Cardiff phone book there are no Chopins Not a single one. A Chop, a Chopper, two Chopings. A Copner, rumoured but not found. One Chopin in Bridgend, but that's too far out. Your name has no Welsh connection, I tell him. No children left in this landscape. No Irish ties, nothing from the West Country, no Polish immigrants. No Frenchmen. Cardiff for you is virgin territory. He smiles.

Chopin is the forgotten master of the French avant-garde. Poet. Publisher of the review *Ou*. Discoverer of language's microparticle. Run out of France in 1968 for the artistic freedom of England and settled in Ingatestone, Essex. Never came to terms with the accent. Made dactylopoèmes, audio-poèmes, poesie sonore extraordinaire by swallowing the microphone, moving it across his intimate body, recording the sounds his pipes and organs made. He fragmented the results by tape manipulation. Broadcast them to stunned audiences who had come to hear the linguistic brilliance of France but got words in dazzling micro-fragments, shower on reverberating shower, instead. It is 1970. May. Chopin has been in the Welsh capital for *A Sound Event* mounted by *second aeon* at the Reardon Smith. Film and verbivocovisual poetry. Tickets 5/- (students 2/6). Film mostly absent. There have been slides showing swirls of letters and typewriters on fire instead. Chopin has come on stage after Bob Cobbing, Peter Mayer, and Andrew Lloyd have beaten the Welsh audience to a sonic pulp. Appeared with a microphone and a slowly spinning Grundig tape deck to make of his body a great acoustic piano. He smiles, exuding Gallic charm. With roars and stutters his concerto wins them over. He's slept with us on the orange sofa. The avant garde has never paid enough money for anything else.

The morning after, before Henri leaves, we delve into the world of change. Permutation. Chopin's verbivocovisual eyes, his sound poetry hands and his typewriter voice making new from old, mashing ancient documents around us. Let them flicker. Let them twist and turn. Poems emerge. Ils démontrent comment un homme rassemble toute ses resources interieures pour analyser et combattre sa propre peur – des destructions, de la vie, de l'acte de mourir – et finalement la vaincre[14]. Then Henri takes the train back. London first. Then on to Essex. We got him a Welsh Arts Council cheque. Enough, just, to keep the wolf from the door.

It's 2009 and I am sitting on the waterfront with Herve-Armand Bechy and Jean-Bernard Metais. We are at Café Rouge, French enough for Cardiff although the waiters are a mix of Italians and Poles. Same the world over. Metais is building *Alliance*, an installation of spike and circle, to be sited in Hayes Place, in the square where the new Cardiff Library faces down the warship prow of John Lewis, heart of Cardiff's St David's 2 development. Metais's vision is four-story liquid filled ring. The liquid rises and falls in line with Cardiff's giant tides. The spike houses great daylight-able projectors called gobos that paint poetry onto the surrounding streets. The square itself is etched with a permutation based on the names the city has been called and how those names have been spelled down the centuries:

Cardiviae
Cardiffe Kerdif Kairdif
Keyrdif Cardyffe Kerdyf
Caerdyf Cayrdif
Gaerdydd Kerdif
Cardiff

The letters are half a meter tall and cast into the paved surface. They bend and turn. They fragment as Chopin would have had them fragment. A Finch creation in the European tradition of poesie concrete. I explain this to the site engineer. Concrete: is what it is, doesn't mean something else. Poetry: liguistic, concise. Concrete poetry. He thinks it's a joke for construction workers.

Up on the gobos the poetry tells the history of the place. Blends what has been on this spot down the centuries. Tide fields, Roman armies, Irish raiders, Norman conquerors, town walls, town ditches, defences against the roaring high tide sea, medieval watch towers, ancient prisons, the Glamorgan Canal, the tow path, bridges (three), alluvial deposits, lost leys, Bridge Street, the Greyhound, Huxley's Surgical Goods, the Asian Spice Box, Rawlins White, the *Dr Who* time capsule, fish henges, John Freeman's great groaning second hand bookshop, god, gouts of fire, the Bible, the flood.

Walk this place at night and the words will be projected across your skin. Jean-Bernard in his slick tweed and great D.H. Lawrence moustache drinks a cappuccino. Herve, the academic and the trans-lator, tells me about Jean-Bernard's prowess in the cities of Western Europe. Illuminated metal towers at the Vannes Palais des Arts. Enormous sky spikes at the Place d'Armes, Valenciennes. Spirals in the landscape at Fort Lambert, Ville de Luxembourg. Plans for a river mounted ring in London's docklands and a *Une structure Anthropologique de l'Imaginaire* at Strasbourg[15]. Jean-Bernard smiles indulgently. We open my layout plan for the names of Kairdif. The grid will be visible from the upper floors of the library, walked through by shoppers and diners bound for Gourmet Burger, crossed by panhandlers, seagulls and skateboarders. Cardiff reduced to microparticles, bent through time and space. Henri Chopin[16], who died in 2008, would have loved it all.

notes:

1. In the Twelfth Century Pope Calixtus II announced that two pilgrimages to St. David's would be equal to one to Rome, and that three pilgrimages to St. David's would equal one to Jerusalem. The importance the Pope gave to distant west Wales brought pilgrims in their thousands.
2. Llanfihangel Yn Y Gwaelod. Population in 1801 – 68. Today more than 700. Still small.
3. Mount Teide is an inactive volcano. You pronounce it Mount Tidy.
4. www.graigfarm.co.uk
5. Godfrey, First Viscount Tredegar, who took part in the charge of the light brigade, sitting astride his horse Sir Briggs. Sculpture by Sir William Goscombe John unveiled in 1909 in the presence of the aging Lord. Located in Cathays Park, Cardiff.
6. Ivor Anthony, trainer of Welsh Grand National winners Boomlet and Pebble Ridge, rider of the 1911 winner Razorbill; Owen Anthony trainer of Golden Miller which won the 1936 Gold Cup; Jack Anthony won the Grand National three times on Glenside (1911), Ally Sloper (1915) and Troytown (1920).
7. A full route along with copies of Corporation plans can be found in Gareth Williams' truly excellent *Life On The Heath*, Merton Priory Press, 2001.
8. Joseph Butler Jones, son of Thomas Jones who had a bakery in St Jones Square. Farmed at Crwys Farm, now the site of Maindee Barracks.
9. Pont y Werin will run from the Oystercatcher and Tesco in Penarth into the Ferry Road peninsula Sports Village. It will be built with £1.15 million achieved by the cycling charity Sustrans winning the Big Lottery Fund's Living Landmarks: The People's Millions Programme.
10. The world of the Fender Stratocaster is arcane, to say the least. Genuine Strats from the period cost and arm and leg. Mexican-made standard Strats are cheaper than their USA-made equivalents. Replicas and fakes abound.
11. I tried it out this morning in the bathroom. No longer a youth. Couldn't remember it.
12. *Apache Mania* on the French Magic Label. The French are far more fanatical than we are when it comes to instrumental guitar music. Le Fan Club de les Shadows is in the safe hands of one Bernard Broche. Magic have identified dozens more bands who feature *Apache* in their repertoires. Watch out for *Apache Mania* volume two.
13. In the Bristol branch, apparently, they once managed to play *Apache* seventeen times. Five short of the record.
14. *Henri Chopin on Henri Chopin – Poesie Sonore Internationale*, Jean-Michel Place Éditeur, 1979
15. http://www.jbmetais.com/
16. Henri Chopin, poet and artist, born June 18 1922; died January 3 2008.

NORTH

THE LESSER GARTH

Mario is convinced he knows just where it is, the cave, the one I've climbed vertical slopes, mud slid, and cracked my ribs for, but never found. On the maps it looks so simple. *Lesser Garth Cave* printed in that quaint Ordnance Survey cod Germanic script which is supposed to indicate something ancient. It's there, just behind the Ty Nant Inn, Morganstown (1815, beer garden, Sunday roast, quiz night), next to the Ty Nant Quarry (dis). In the beech forest. Up higher than I've ever been.

The Lesser Garth is the Greater Garth's southern neighbour, a hill that rises to 590 feet, western side of the Taff Gorge, the gap through which everything travels, rail, road, river, on the way to the technicolour south. The Greater Garth, the big one, with its three burial chambers (one fake but two real) on top and its starring film role[1] is the place all Cardiffians know. The Lesser, wood-clad and with few roads leading to it, is much more of a mystery.

Mario Fiorillo is half-Italian, half-Portuguese. He's a one-time sailor with the Italian Navy who, when declared to be no longer of a militaristic state of mind, was demobbed and somehow ended up in evergreen and jobless south Wales. Mario, raconteur, painter, cyclist, chain smoker, round, bronze-skinned and stocky like a Merthyr Welshman, was once a garrulous poet with manuscripts in every pocket. Stopping him was always the problem. Give him a platform and he'd take it. Poetry to defy and delight. An immigrant Dylan Thomas cracking out verse in a new and challenging language. He does less of this today.

Astride his tough terrain bike with its fat tyres and strengthened frame he's cycled over everywhere there is to cycle within a sixty miles radius of his Grangetown home. Merthyr Mawr, Southerndown, Chepstow, Aberdare, Beacons. Bike that climbs mountains. He took it to the top of Corn Du and then struggled on to the peak of Pen y Fan. When he sees a route he follows it. Where does this path go? And this gap in the trees, this lane between buildings, this hole in the ground. The Lesser Garth is easy, done it many times.

We go straight up, following a path from the end of the Ty Nant Inn's car park, a steep climb. Mario has locked his bike to the pub railings rather than try to carry it with him. He scrambles hard then he stops. Wrong route. We come back down. The slope is precipitous, thick with beech leaves on soft mud, made worse by recent rain. It's here, he shouts. We climb. It's not. Are we looking for a path? Yes. No. We go up a gully, find abandoned nineteenth century quarry workings. The hill is carboniferous limestone, porous, immensely valuable. Mario is like a mountain goat, ascending vertical inclines with breathless ease. We haul ourselves up between the tree trunks and masses of new sapling. Fifty feet from the top is a platform, hard to see among the topgrowth. The hill rises on from it like the Antarctic plateau. Mario has reached he lip and is signalling. Yes, it's the cave, the Lesser Garth of legend, a four foot by ten foot slot in the rock face, today firmly barred and padlocked by Cemex Materials Limited, owners of the Taffs Well Quarry[2] beyond. You want access you ring the Quarry manager. His number's there but as this is Sunday he's not in.

The Lesser Garth Caves are famous among the fraternity. Humans once lived here. The damp rocks have yielded up shards from the Bronze age, Romano-British pots, dark age metalwork, rings, broaches, flint artefacts, human bones[3]. Deep within have been found animal remains, bones of mice and bats, of feral cats that wandered in the cold and dark and never found their ways back. As recently as 2004 cavers reported overhead passages, narrow rifts, stal flows and glorious rock curtains. The system sinks, bends, squeezes and turns to emerge into the much larger Ogof Ffynnon Taff. Here can be seen evidence of vandalism committed by quarry men who have smashed their way in through the limestone from the Walnut Tree side. Daylight, chambers and curtain walls hidden for millennia now gone. The rock at this spot is incredibly thin. The great slopes of the Lesser Garth, viewed from the pub car park to the south, are actually only feet thick. Push them and they might fall. Behind, the enormous Taffs Well Quarry has been blasted down to river level. Make a mistake now and the Taff will drain in.

We reach the ridge top above the cave and in one glance have our breath removed. Beyond is the singularity that is now Cemex. The multiple layered Grand Canyon from which all rock has been removed and crushed or slabbed and sold on. They make aggregate here. For use in water and chemical filtration. And as roadstone. The Lesser Garth is entirely hollow, a drilled back tooth of vacant air. The quarry benches, there are at least seven of them, descend six hundred feet to

a distant orange pond at the far bottom. Rock layers syncline and anticline. Geology bare. The entrances to cave systems undiscovered or known-about and now ruined can be seen on the face. Ogof Tynant Fechan, Ogof Pen-y-Graig, Ogof Ffynnon Taff. While there is financial return to be obtained the quarrymen will eat on through the mountain. To the east, deep down, a tunnel exit for trucks is being blasted through the limestones to emerge near Pughs Garden Centre and the Morganstown roundabout. Cemex will not yet bring down the Lesser Garth's eastern face and destroy the now wooded and abandoned Ty Nant Quarry which faces Castell Coch. The famous Taffs Well Gorge will remain. But for how long.

As we slip back down Mario keeps up a scatter-gun of reported facts and local discoveries. Paths he's investigated, buildings he's seen, wells he's drunk from. We move west to access the gated entrance to the tunnel through which the Barry Railway carrying coal and iron from further north once came. Its tracks sliced right through the mountain. The tunnel exit, barred by two giant metal doors, topped with a tag put there by someone called Canabal, is rich with evidence of drug use, of urban human wreckage, detritus, rust, and smash. Trains through here crossed the gorge on the Taffs Well viaduct, the pillars of which still stand. They are visible daily to drivers on the A470. Blue and yellow brick pillars, one embellished with a good luck message to HMQ on the occasion of her 1977 Silver Jubilee. Good Luck Your Maj. There were letters in the *Echo* about that. Waste of money, declared a few of our city's lesser informed ratepayers, imagining the whole edifice had been erected in honour of the Queen.

The quarry itself is topped by a complex of site buildings, rock crushers, conveyor belts and parking space for yellow Cat trucks bigger than double-decker buses. Cemex make breeze blocks from their excavations – there's a yard here bigger than Wal-Mart containing hundreds of stacks. I try to roughly estimate the number of blocks on the inventory. I get somewhere up above 100,000, miscount and give up.

The Garth Wood beyond is a *Site of Special Scientific Interest*, bats, 590 species of British spider, Solomon's Seal, Peregrine Falcons, Old Man's Beard. This is where Cemex have not yet cut but where they'd love to. In these protected beech forests are ancient coal measures, mined where they surfaced, iron diggings and abandoned tram levels. The Lesser Garth was rich, is rich, has a whole long history of being cut up and sliced, powdered, melted down, and sold. The sounds of Kawasaki sliding bang through the trees. On a ridge sits a valley girl, short skirt, white handbag, fag in hand, weekend warrior boyfriend in helmet on a blue and yellow KX250 coming up the wet slopes in a cloud of mud. Contemporary cowboys. You get this anywhere and everywhere north of the M4. Don't walk, hammer through in a crash of burning fuel oil, much more fun.

250 feet below us is a vast underground lake, 200 feet deep, known as the Blue Waters. Once used by the Taffs Well quarry as a water source for its washery, then abandoned, drained, stuffed with rock waste and allowed to fill with water again. Access is through a ground level passage cut into the north side of Garth Wood. Barred, naturally. This was originally an 1840s tunnel dug in the hunt for iron ore to be smelted in the valley below[4]. Mad ideas have emerged to turn this whole place into a tourist attraction. Visit Victorian Iron workings, see the stalactites, view the underground lake. Take a peep at the great orange quarry. Dust and damp. Industrial paradise. Nothing has happened yet.

Mario takes us to an ancient well. On the OS this is Ffynnon Gruffydd. Limewater. He's hidden a cup made from half a plastic bottle in the undergrowth. Try it. Clean, cool, pure. Tastes of nothing at all.

The tram level we are following drops us east of the string of houses known as Georgetown, above the green in Gwaelod y Garth. Bottom of the Garth. Upmarket Welsh Wales now subsumed into the big city but still desperately clinging to its otherness. Mario rolls up. Garth encircled, mysteries uncovered. Entering Morganstown again near the offices of Real Radio (no welcome just a sign announcing the district's twinning with St Philbert De Grand Lieu) we stare down at the Forge Dyke, the return into the Taff of water taken out further north to power the Pentyrch Furnaces. At this spot the dyke, a giant mill race, is kept back from the river by a wall no more than a yard or two thick. Beyond the roundabout are the remains of ancient lime kilns. Enough industrial relics in a few square miles to start a revolution. Up ahead the Ty Nant and its post-industrial Sunday drinking. Mario's bike still locked to the railings.

RIDGE

Right across the north of the city runs the ridge. Cibwr, Cefn Onn, Graig yr Allt, Thorn Hill, Garth, Senghenydd, Caerphilly Mountain. It has many names. A ruck of limestone. A coalfield edge. A cliff of enormous antiquity. A barrier. A protecting arm. A defendable line. A path has run along its top as far back as history goes. Used by the neolithics, the palaeolithics, the mesolithics, the silures, the druids. East to god, west to the sun. The sea was there, almost touchable, below. Today it is more distant. Moved south towards the Atlantic salt. Pushed by the rivers. The Taff, the Rumney, the Ely. Deltaic depositors. Builders of the Cardiff alluvial fan.

Cardiff hates and loves this escarpment in equal measure It's the fence that imprisons us. Holds us back from national domination. It's the thing that preserves us. Protects us from the wilds of Wales. This is the ridge that has made us, in Welsh terms, unique. We've never been hill farmers, men of the peat uplands. We've never revelled in greenness. Never felt the mountains to be places which deserve our allegiance. Instead we've spent industrial centuries finding ways to bleed Wales of what it has. The ridge today is the barrier that stops the rest of the country from loving us. Cardiff's curtain, Cardiff's cloak. In 1955 Cardiff was made the country's capital. The country booed. In 1998 Cardiff opened its glorious Assembly. In Caernarfon nobody watched. In 2005 Cardiff was not elected to be the next European Capital of Culture. The city, the judges said, does not connect with its hinterland. It is as if it floats in its bubble like one of Mekon's city states on boiling Venus. It holds hard its spoils. Its valleys, it thinks, remain populated with jerry-builders, drug users, men waiting for their operations, fat women lolling outside supermarkets cigarettes in hand, leadless dogs, tattooed youth wearing tee-shirts against the prevailing, permanent, coal-tip eroding rain.

I'm up here with Morgan Francis, fellow traveller, poet, talker, carpenter, photographer of flowers, a man who knows south Wales intimately but who still finds walking it a voyage of discovery. We are following the Cardiff ridgeway. We've accessed the twenty-first century path near the front of a cottage, Hafod y Milgi, opposite the thatched Traveller's Rest. The pub is stuffed solid with Sunday lunchers. Everyone arrived by

car. Trainers and running pants now rather than three piece suits. Aftershave. Kids in tow. Hafod y Milgi was itself once a pub. The Greyhound – Milgi in Welsh – opened 1846 although there was almost certainly a pair of cottages on the same site before that. The Cardiff/Caerphilly border snakes past here. Milgi is Cardiff. The Travellers Rest is Caerphilly. The cottage garden could be either. The path itself falls into the hands of a dysfunctional consortium of local authorities, sometimes Cardiff, often Caerphilly, touching Blaenau Gwent and Newport, yearning for RCT. No one is quite sure how the route should be maintained or promoted. Is this a resource of which council tax payers should be proud? Or an irritation on the borders still carrying worrying hordes? It crosses three OS maps[5] and no one seems to have produced a guide since Taff Ely did in 1979. It no longer runs along the ridge top either. Field borders and centuries of farming have let it slide to run as a mud-sludged slog around twenty meters to the south. Morgan is talking about meat pies as we climb the fence at the back of the car park. Not the ridge path yet but a diversion before we begin. I've nothing against meat, declares Morgan, but you are never sure what they put in pies. Clarks have never crossed his lips. Do they ever reach this far in the Cardiff north? Can you get them down there in warm Caerphilly? Probably not.

What we are looking for are the remains of the mystical, lost and enormously uncared for Castell Morgraig. Last castle of the Welsh. Home of Ifor Bach or Llewelyn ap Gruffydd, ein llyw olaf[6]. A defence on the borderland between Welsh Senghenydd and Norman Glamorgan. Or maybe slung-up and never finished properly by the Norman Richard de Clare. Built as a stop-gap before his world-beating castle at Caerphilly came on stream.

What's here isn't much. Stones overgrown with moss, tangled with bramble, beech trees growing in their midst. Given the site's antiquity and the dominance of CADW in the affairs of the owners of listed buildings wishing to put in new windows it is amazing that such a place should, in the western world's green twenty-first century, be in such an appalling mess. You can pick out the towers, round ones at each corner. The Welsh didn't go in for these. No surrounding ditch either. A Welsh must. And the castle walls are made from Sutton Stone, quarried near Southerndown, Norman heartland. Further out along the ridge to the east are collapsed defensive towers. Not yet excavated. Welsh lookouts perhaps. Or Norman guard posts abandoned when Caerphilly was built.

Rumour persists of a great defeat here in 1315 when Llewelyn Bren's rebellion came to nothing. Bren, buried at Greyfriars, coffin dug up and thrown away in 1967 when the Pearl Tower was built[7]. That Bren. Maybe Morgraig was never finished[8]. There is no evidence of internal courtyard buildings nor roof. Abandoned then, still abandoned now. We scramble back across the beech mast and walk a hundred meters along the A469, past Morgraig Cottage, to the mud and slush of the repositioned ridge path. This is a bridleway, hand-made 'take care' notices everywhere. Don't frighten the animals, hold hard your dogs, beware of zooming vehicles, no fires.

Heading east the path grinds through trees to emerge, skirting abandoned Cefn Onn limestone quarry, high up on Graig Llanishen. Are we in Cardiff or Caerphilly? Caerphilly, Cardiff dormitory, where the house prices are affordable and the pubs are full of karaoke, destined to join the city soon or forever use its mountain to stay apart. Morgan, six coats on as a weapon against the cold when we started, has spent the past mile or so systematically disrobing. I tell him he could bury his jackets in the bushes and retrieve them on our return. Or, like Morgan's alter-ego Katz, Bill Bryson's companion in his *A Walk In The Woods*, just throw them away. He opts instead for carrying them in a great bundle tied together with a pashmina scarf which he then wraps around his hat. He sways through the trees like an Afghan. Mujahadeen from Onllwyn. If I'd called him that to his face he would have argued with me. Not Onllwyn, boy, Pant y Ffordd.

We are now above the Caerphilly rail tunnel. On nationalisation this

was the pride of British Rail Western Region. Now it's just the Arriva Trains line from Cardiff to Rhymney. The vent shafts, like Norman defensive towers, emerge among the trees. These twelve-foot high brick constructs are topped with metal fence to prevent ingress by tree, animal or yob. High enough and hard enough to stop anything being thrown down them. Shafts up which once poured the smoke and steam from the Rhymney Valley Railway's iron and coal trains. Dis now. Says so on the map. Morgan's plan to photograph the shaft is for us to stand either side of it and toss across a digital camera with the self-timer set to a ten-second delay. I settle for a shot of the writing on the structure's side. Shaft 2 6.67 Car. The other four vents are elsewhere.

When it was built the Caerphilly tunnel was a triumph. A shaft, right through a mountain. To the Victorian Welsh such things were marvels. It was opened by the Rhymney Railway Company in 1869 when the battle for transport to Bute's Cardiff docks was white hot. Labour, as for most everything else in south Wales, was mainly Irish. Fenians suspected local Cardiffians. The work camp at Llanishen was guarded by police for fear of attack. Half way through blasting the mile-long (1.76k) two-track tunnel engineers struck an unexpected and enormous spring which delayed completion of the tunnel by three months. There were Irish deaths and water everywhere. The spring was eventually tamed to provide an amazing 60 million gallons of water a year, a gift to a steam railway. Put it in your tank. Boil it. Make it work.

Above us the sky is darkening. You can't explore on a winter day, just glimpse. Caerphilly rolls out below us. Caerphilly – in the world of food up there with Pembroke potatoes, Lincoln sausage, Kendal mint cake, Gorgonzola cheese, Frankfurters, and Bombay duck. Despite an annual Big Cheese festival (fireworks, face painting, bouncy castle, rock, beer in plastic glasses) do they make much of the stuff in the town today? Probably not[9].

Back where we started, taking breath, watching well-dressed idlers chase balls across the former chicken farm that is now Ridgeway Golf Club, we speculate again on the significance of this place, where Wales bangs hard against the Norman Empire. Morgraig was a Welsh Castle, declares Morgan. As good, any day, as Dinas Bran. We stand within its psychic range. The source of the Nant Cwmnofydd, the stream of deluxe Rhiwbina, is up there beyond it. Things in this place are not ruined by graffiti: too high up, too much climbing from the cut-price wastelands of Caerphilly. The Sunday lunchers are as numerous as they ever were at the Traveller's Rest. No future in beer. Food is the new drinking. We head home for ham and chips.

THE HOLLYBUSH AND THE HOSPITAL FOR THE MAD

I'm sitting in the Hollybush having a beer with Norman. There's been a pub here for centuries. Merthyr Road, the main horse route south from the iron at Dowlais to the quay at Cardiff. Today there's also a sizzling steak restaurant, awnings, outside umbrellas under which cluster a dozen smokers, and a couple of working-class bars tight with locals. On quiz night they come from miles away. A bandit blinks in the corner. The extractor whirs and fails. A giant screen, which no one watches, shows men with a ball running across a great green field.

This is Coryton. North Whitchurch. Squashed between the older village and the just as ancient Castell Coch at Tongwynlais. John Cory built a mansion here[10]. His plans were for a garden village like that at Rhiwbina but the Great War intervened and the development never happened. As a separate entity officially the district doesn't exist. But on the old Rhymney Valley Railway line which passes just to the south of the pub, the suburban stop is called Coryton. Could have been Asylum Halt if the early twentieth century developers had been given their head. Over the bridge and in the Elysium fields beyond stands Whitchurch Mental Hospital. Norman has just come from there.

He's big, Norman. An ungainly lump. Austin Reed cord trousers, a tweed jacket from Howells. He has five of his paintings with him. Oils, large, portraits, all done front-on and showing madmen with faces like balloons. Puffed brows, cheeks full of air, otherness in their eyes. Norman's portrait work involves therapy, he tells me. Could be his own. Who can tell. The paintings won't sell. He's hung them at a city gallery and along the railings on the front at Penarth. No takers. No passer-by even slowing down.

The paintings are all of patients, or the idea of patients, the lost souls, the ghosts in the underbelly, the raging in the air. Norman turns out these things with captivating dexterity. They hang on the asylum walls. To illuminate, he tells me. Lights in the endless corridors. His favourite painters are Edvard Munch, Vincent van Gogh, Jackson Pollack and Ralph Albert Blakelock. All, to varying degrees, were off their trolleys.

The hospital, back over the road bridge which crosses the railway, was opened in 1908 as the Cardiff City Mental Hospital. Greenfield site. Well outside the city boundaries. Spread over 120 acres of farmland between the Taff Vale Railway and the Glamorgan Canal it was a masterpiece of Edwardian Lego build[11]. Red brick, copper covered water tower, theatres, wards, restraining rooms, workshops for tailors, upholsterers, carpenters and brushmakers, recreation hall, stage, admin block, outbuildings. A standard Victorian-era lock-up as found in endless out-of-town locations right across England and Wales.

The farms – Ty Clyd for flower and veg, and Llwyn Mallt for cattle – were kept on as an exercise not so much in therapy as self-suffi-ciency[12]. Trouble no-one, grow your own. Cae John Hent, Cae'r Ywen, Nine Acres, Six Acres, Cae yr Gubin Ddegum, Sunny Bank Field, Five Acres, Cae Yr Gubin, Ten Acres Cross Road, Velindre Field, The Lawn. Field names, gone now. To make space the mansion at Velindre, home of successive proprietors of the now declining Melingriffith Tinplate Works next door, was pulled down.

In the grounds was an 800-seater neo-gothic church, playing fields, bowling green, and endless gardens each with its own weave of paths, benches and green-painted octagonal gazebos. The immediate perime-ter fence sat in a ditch, concealed from inmates' view. The wards ran in two enormous horseshoes. There were 750 patients.

The regime: cleanliness, clarity, fresh space, cool air, real

air, pure air, comfort. Exercise, breath, arms out, arms back. Knees bend, knees straight. Vests. Indian clubs. Medicine balls. Hats. Moustaches. Liberal supplies of all sorts of objects which can interest and amuse.[13] Brilliantly coloured woollen rugs. Gramophones. Board games. Cards. Sunlight. Space. Sky. Cloud. Carbolic. Water. Soaped-up skin.

Victorian care for the mad – which is where this hospital had its origins – hardly changed until the nineteen sixties. Until then lunatic meant the deranged, the unhinged and the depressed, the poor who were strange, and after that the criminally inexplicable, the ones for whom there were no ready slots. In the public mind poverty, promiscuity and insanity were all linked. The mentally ill were removed from society and locked up, corralled with their fellows, in places far beyond the booming ant-heap cities. The nineteenth century's failure of asylum therapy to change absolutely anything had convinced many in the general population that insanity was actually incurable. The prevalent fear was of racial degeneracy[14], that a submerged tenth of the population, damaged or congenitally marked, promiscuous and unhinged, would begin to outbreed the rest. We would be weakened then swamped. The land would go down and madness would stalk the earth. To prevent this idiots and imbeciles who could not be treated would be removed from society. The morally harmful would join them. Defectives would be separated from the nation's burgeoning gene pool and locked away. The clean, pure world of industrial Britain would stay that way.

This penitentiary-like solution had, of course, a long pre-history. Society has never found managing the mentally ill easy. In early days if you were unstable then you were possessed of demons. Heads full of smoke and serpents. Skulls were rent to let the devils back out. In the Roman era the mad were made to suffer starvation, fetters and flogging and anything 'which thoroughly agitated the spirit'. Make it shout. In the dark ages they let your blood, they burned stones and sat you on them, they sought the black bile within you and tried to pull it out. In 1290 England if you were a natural fool then *de praerogativa regis* the King took your land. In the fourteenth century mental instability made you a witch and got you burned at the stake or drowned. If you were a woman who stirred men's passions or a deviant or loose with your morals then you had the devil in you and you were damned. Madness and profligacy became intertwined.

The early madhouses were private places where the insane who roared like beasts were treated like animals. Harried. Bound. Spat on. Gagged. Purges were applied and the organs of dead creatures smeared up the unfortunate's shaven skin. In the eighteenth the insane were locked in asylums – 'dark holes, less comfortable than cow houses' – restrained, barred, chained. If you were a pauper lunatic, mad with no money, then you had no rights. If you were a lunatic of resource then you paid for your own medical certificate and then they sent you down. Treatment was by bloodletting, ducking, cold water therapy, isolation. If you were not unstable to begin with then after this treatment you certainly became so. In the minds of the public guardians deviancy, sexual profligacy, and criminal obsession merged with psychological uncertainty, psychosis and paranoia. Fit the norm or be cast out. Everyone must be the same.

By the nineteenth century the asylum was as much a prison as a house of cure. In the early years of that century there was hope of improvement but by its end, and especially after Darwin's *On the Origin of Species* (1859) had appeared, the prevailing opinion was that madness was hereditary and that the possessed should be removed from our midst and locked permanently up. Doctors hunted for a cause, dissected brains, pulled out nerves, examined the blood, measured spinal columns, weighed glands, scraped, scratched and stumbled. Mental disease could be nothing more than an infection. Find it. Burn it down. Their patients languished. Their patients screamed. Their patients aged and greyed and failed. The rest of the world pretended nothing was going on.

Were social cures possible? Could therapy assist? Could the institutionalised be helped and through a mix of open door and half way house get a foothold back in normal society, whatever that was? No one seemed prepared to try to find out.

The Whitchurch enterprise was developed at considerable

cost. It took ten years to plan and build and when it was done the bills topped £350,000. Its self-sufficiency was paramount. Its distance from the top end of Cathays, the then northern extremity of the new city, was at least five miles. Green was everywhere. Here the cures went on forever.

DEALT WITH

Acute stress disorder Adjustment disorder Agoraphobia alcohol and substance abuse alcohol and substance dependence Amnesia Anxiety disorder Anorexia nervosa Antisocial personality disorder Asperger's syndrome Attention deficit disorder Attention deficit/hyperactivity disorder Autism Avoidant personality disorder Bereavement Bibliomania Binge eating disorder Bipolar disorder Body dysmorphic disorder Borderline personality disorder Brief psychotic disorder Bulimia nervosa Circadian rhythm sleep disorder Conduct disorder Conversion disorder Cyclothymia Delusional disorder Dependent personality disorder Depersonalization disorder Depression Disorder of written expression Dissociative fugue Dissociative identity disorder Dyspareunia Dysthymic disorder Encopresis Enuresis Exhibitionism Expressive language disorder Female and male orgasmic disorders Female sexual arousal disorder Fetishism Folie à deux Frotteurism Ganser syndrome Gender identity disorder Generalized anxiety disorder General adaptation syndrome Histrionic personality disorder Hyperactivity disorder Primary hypersomnia Hypoactive sexual desire disorder Hypochondriasis Hyperkinetic syndrome Hysteria Intermittent explosive disorder Joubert syndrome Kleptomania Down syndrome Mania Male erectile disorder Munchausen syndrome Mathematics disorder Narcissistic personality disorder Narcolepsy Nightmare disorder Obsessive-compulsive disorder Obsessive-compulsive personality disorder Oneirophrenia Oppositional defiant disorder Pain disorder Panic attacks Panic disorder Paranoid personality disorder Pathological gambling Pervasive Developmental Disorder Pica Post-traumatic stress disorder Premature ejaculation Primary insomnia Psychotic disorder Pyromania Reading disorder Retts disorder Rumination disorder Schizoaffective disorder Schizoid personality disorder Schizophrenia Schizophreniform disorder Schizotypal personality disorder Seasonal affective disorder Separation anxiety disorder Sexual Masochism and Sadism Shared psychotic disorder Sleep disorder Sleep terror disorder Sleepwalking disorder Social phobia Somatization disorder Specific phobias Stuttering Tourette syndrome Transient tic disorder Transvestic Fetishism

THE ASYLUM FUTURE

At Whitchurch today, a hundred years from the hospital's founding, parts of the grounds have already been sold on for residential development. At the brand new Clos Coed Hir there's upmarket housing on the field that used to be known as nine acres; the northern meadows will have two hundred new town houses, and on the westerly reaches, where the hospital touches the Glamorgan Canal, are late twentieth century day centres: the George Thomas Hospice, Tegfan and Hafan. But the greenness is still overwhelming. You turn from busy Park Road and enter a wash of sylvan meadow. Poetry after tabloid prose. Emmylou after Metallica. There's a gatehouse[15] but no keepers. Then fields and space and a red-brick, domed water tower, vacant faces for clocks on its sides[16], watching all from eight stories up. Ian Wile, Senior Nurse Manager, who meets me, reckons that early arrivals must have found the place a Shangri-La. Lyonesse, Middle Earth, Narnia. How could this be the real world?

Gary Rix, the Hospital Manager, has that slightly grey look of a bureaucrat dealing with change. Harassed but winning. He hands me a copy of Hilary M. Thomas's 1983 hospital history. The only official publication to use the word 'shag' as its logo, he tells me. And there it is on the pamphlet's corner. *SHAG* – the initials of the old South Glamorgan Health Authority placed in a circle, spelling out a word their creator had not intended. The Hospital is now in the hands of Cardiff and Vale NHS Trust. Change, the driver of contemporary society, is happening again.

The sub-text to all this is that regime shift is about to create us another new world. The present, vast, and slowly falling apart complex is an anachronism. Elsewhere in the UK they've pulled them down. At Bexley in London, 2002, there was a ceremony when they demolished their red brick water tower, that Victorian asylum addition which had come to symbolise madness. Lots were drawn and a former nurse got to push the plunger blowing the tower, and, to huge cheers, brought the red bricks down. At Cardiff most of the complex will be sold to a developer, hospital listing notwithstanding. A new 100-patient unit will be constructed on ground near the former Glamorgan Canal. No extra cost to the NHS. Smaller because, although there may be more of us in the population today, we are no longer as mad. We have as much pain but we dribble less.

We come as day visitors. We are controlled by psychotropics. We are talked to, not tied up. Unbelted, rehinged. We live in flats and bedsits and wallpapered rooms. We visit facilities not asylums. When we are ill hospitals help us. Arms open. Smiles. Stethoscopes. Gowns. We mix. We mingle. We emulsify into the community. Out there amid the roaring. We *are* the community. Unbolted. Unlocked. Lost. Found.

From Gary's office window above the Baroque entrance can be seen the pristine bowling green with its scoreboard and the vandalised, brick, lancet-style chapel. Windows smashed. Lead loose and twisted. Bath stone fractured. But the bell not yet gone. Beyond them the vastness of almost empty playing fields. Three teenagers on the bench smoking when I went by, another on a small Kawasaki doing slow wheelies across the pitch.

Songs sung at Whitchurch before the Great War:

My Little Chimney Sweep – Miss Jessie Ewart
daisies in the Grass – Miss Paull
Selection on Tambourine with Bones – F. Harries
Two Little Sausages – Miss Mary Mander
A Bovine Barcarolle – Fred Wilshire
Ring Out, O Bells – Patients
Dear Little Sunbonnet Lady – Mr Frederick Mantell
English Hearts of Oak – Mr Geo Goodwin
Aderyn Pur – Miss Hilda Morgan

Then arrived the physically fractured, the ripped open and the blown apart. In 1915 the Hospital was taken over by military and became the Welsh Metropolitan War Hospital. In 1919 it was given back. The bandaged war wounded went home. But many, those whose minds had been shattered by shells and bombs, they stayed on.

Ian keeps up a commentary as we walk, disorientated (me anyway), along the main horse-shoe shaped corridor. An electric-wheeled tug passes us towing a train of trolleys holding food waste in scratched aluminium trays. Alan Davies, Project Coordinator for Mental Health Service Development, and John Briggs, the photographer, are with us. John never likes to miss an opportunity to record some slipping part of Cardiff's past. He gets Alan and Ian to hold open the flapping green doors between units and smile back at us as if in welcome. Takes the photo. The gates of hell.

In the yards at the back the red brick has hardly aged. The sun burns it. Before us is the water tower, green cupola on top surmounted by a further, junior version of itself, reaching for heaven. A lighthouse, a Tardis. Hard-hatted we climb through the floors on a mix of built wooden step and metal runged ladder. Bob Bosley, Estate Engineer, talks us through pipes, pumps, valves,  insulation, ventilation, boilers, water pressure. With its huge main tanks this tower still functions yet each floor we pass through is empty. Abandoned valves, sheared bolts and debris litter the corners. Detritus. Dust. The limewashed walls are like those of an early church. If I scrape the surface will I find images of the ancient mad beneath? At the top we emerge onto a balconied platform ineffectually netted against marauding birds. In the middle are cell phone repeaters from Orange. White doves sit along their tops. The world is green again, fields rolling always in an unmolested stream. Castell Coch in the northern distance, the high rises of the city centre to the south. What you don't expect is the silence. The world as it once was still there. As we are handing back our hard hats on the ground floor I spot a stairwell leading down to a space below. Where does that go? Inspection chamber, pipe distributor, fan complex, service duct. Passageways running under the wards and outbuildings. Across the courtyards. Under the roads. Another complete hospital down there right under this one. Dark and full of muck? Bob Bosley nods.

The main hall and theatre have largely been abandoned as places for concerts or dances. League of Friends jumble sales, patients five-a-side, training facility for managing the violent and the aggressive, exam hall, place of dusty silence. Church-like windows bear coats of arms; gold painted heraldics carry words of inspiration: Deffro Maen Ddydd Y Ddraig Goch Ddyry Gychwyn. The slumbering world as it once was.

Ian is strong on explaining the philosophy of the care system, putting the battered building into its historical context, describing

how shifts in attitude and
changes in technique have all
contributed to this institution's
demise. How can disabled
people and Muslim women
manage in a mixed ward of
thirty patients, all crammed
into the same day room?
Through the windows the
gazebos rot slowly, roofs
sliding off, wood still painted
Edwardian green. One with the
word *FART* on it, in huge

letters. Here are the wards, tall-backed chairs, abandoned wheeled-
zimmers, silvered trolleys, clamps, flower arm-chairs with the stuffing
loose, mobile toilets, fractured tables. Everything scuffed and
buggered. Locked. On one of the wards there is a sign which reads
Most Patients Are Here Voluntary And Are Free To Leave If They Wish.
Should You Wish To Leave Please Contact The Nurse In Charge. The
word 'Please' has been scratched flat, all its paint removed. The
names on the ward doors read *Gwynedd, Enfys, Dewis.* Like the
houses we had in school.

Can we visit a ward? We do. On Gwynedd Cerian Evans, the
manager, tells me this ward should be called Dewis. Names are
wrong. Doesn't matter. She's got seventeen patients in a ward that
used to hold forty. They're here, the patients, because they have to be.
Sectioned, mostly. You're an in-patient when there's little hope. In the
hospital entrance a framed script carefully explains that 'People with
mental illness are admitted into hospital only at times of severe need
as one would expect for any other form of illness.' These are those.
These are their times. The seventeen are mostly managed by drugs.
When we come through they are lying about the dayroom. Trainers,
tees, miss-match trackie bottoms. Lethargic desultory conversations.
No television. That plays, quietly to itself, in an empty yet sun-filled
room further on. In a dismal side-chamber containing four chairs, a
low table and a number of foil trays filled to busting with butt and ash
a young man, rough shaven and grimacing with fear, pulls smoke
deep into himself. They've voted, Cerian tells me. The patients.
They've decided unanimously to ban cigarettes from all communal

areas. Unexpected and rather dramatically they've taken the healthy option. I ask how many actually smoke. All of them, she says.

Bed numbers have been falling steadily since Enoch Powell, then Minister of Health, made his famous Water Tower speech in 1966. That was the one which ushered in care in the community. Erving Goffman had written his masterwork, *Asylums,* in 1961 which questioned the whole basis of custodial keeping. Suddenly more than a hundred years of asylum as prison began to be swept away. Patients in bedrobes were found wandering the stores of Whitchurch village. Dressing gowns appeared on the buses. A man in pyjamas ordered a pint at the bar of The Plough. Not like that that now. Cardiff has community health teams out there today to support those who need help to live in their own homes. So how many staff have you here, I ask? 1100. And how many patients? 244. Good numbers.

Yet I've got this feeling that I'm missing something. *One Flew Over The Cuckoo's Nest* runs across the back of my mind. Images of straight jackets, trolleys full of drugs, people screaming, cells with padding on the walls. Do you have these things? There might have been a padded cell here once but that would have been a long time ago. Cold water immersion? Abandoned. Lobotomies? In the whole of Britain there may be one carried out annually, but not here. Restraints? Maybe. Drugs? Yes. Endemic, like in prison. Illicit substances flow in and out. Best we can do is to manage. Bans. Sniffer dogs. Searches. You can't control everything that moves. You can't be the person you manage. We have to help them somehow.

In the back of the pre-First World War cuttings book I've been loaned I find tables showing the number of cures that Whitchurch achieved. Lunatics made normal and returned to society. Great victory. Doctors deserve pay award. (applause).

Ian returns to his ward duties. Pleased to help. A Welsh learner. Easier to do that over a pint, I tell him. Un peint, dau beint, tri pheint[17]. In the concert hall we'd both tried to translate the Welsh heraldic slogans. Looking back we'd both got it wrong. We don't do this as our day job, says Gary. Walking people like you around. For us this is fun.

GNOME

Travelling the turnpike south from Caerphilly to Cardiff was never easy. Hills behind, hills in front. A rutted road of rock and mud. A turnpike thick with mule trains. Horses laden with panniers. Horses dragging sleds. Horses pulling wagons. All full of soft black rock that got in your skin and your ears. That seeped behind your eyes. That bent your frame. That burned your heart and turned your legs to water. The dark trade that obscured everything in life beyond the blast of drink you wiped it out with at days end. Before the canal opened in 1796 there was no other way.

The turnpike today is the A469. Following it back it runs through Birchgrove and Heath, up Thornhill and the outer suburbs, past the Cardiff Crem, before climbing to the golf clubs on the Cardiff ridge. Caerphilly is beyond. Where the Cardiff disenfranchised live, an outer suburb with a different name. No one on this road now carries coal, or anything much come to that. Industry has gone to the winds. I've come along it to what was once the heart of the Great Heath looking for milestones. Remnants of the past.

In the eighteenth century this entire road was marked by mileposts. Each section was maintained by a local trust which imposed tolls to pay for maintenance. Such milestones dotted main roads right across the country. They told travellers how far it was on to the next town and how far it was back. At this one it's three miles to Cardiff, four and half to Caerphilly, three and a quarter to Roath. If you hunt you can find other examples across the city. There's one outside number 243 on Albany Road[18], another near the Angel Hotel. More at Canton and Ely Bridge and out along the A48. Most of them are eighteenth century cast-iron with sloping sides which could more easily be read by passing horse-drawn coaches. Some numbers have been chipped off by early vandals but most survive. Their predecessors were flat-sided, often round-topped stones. They are worn now to virtual illegibility by centuries of rain. There's one on the patch of grass that once grew elm trees outside Roath Library on Newport Road. And there's another milestone near the junction with Maes-y-Coed Road. You can still just about make out the word *CARDIF* on its side. It sits in its purpose-built niche, next to its white-painted metal successor, in the wall outside that new play-palace of the pennyminder, Lidl.

The milestones are not where they were originally sited. 1999 road widening had them moved a few meters east. Their present-day, purpose-built brick surrounds and, indeed, their actual on-site survival, are unusual in a city that normally wipes away the past as if it were industrial dirt.

The Great Heath ran north here right up to the mountain. One of its earliest enclosures created the farm at Mynydd Bychan, later known as Ton-yr-Ywen. This survived until the 1940s when post-war light industrial development along Maes-y-Coed Road led to the building of the Gnome factory. A Cardiff landmark by its name alone. Private enterprise re-badging cameras and manufacturing slide projectors. Sought after now by collectors. Gnome lasted until the dawning of the digital 1990s.

The new Gnome, a north Cardiff example of the ubiquitous Lidl, looks like any other branch of the German chain. And that's the idea. Lidl (say *Leedl* rather than *Liddle* to get closer to its German origins) began as a partnership between grocer Ludwig Lidl and trader Joseph Schwarz. Their enterprise sold discount food. They almost called it Schwarz Markt (which translated as *Black Market*) but thought Lidl Markt a safer bet.

The store with its emphasis on fast throughput of customer, till operators who knew all the PLU[19]s and didn't have to scrabble for missing bar codes, no credit cards (until recently, anyway), limited choice, no free bags, coin-deposit trolleys, low pricing and a standard layout for every store brought immediate rewards. The chain's arrival in the UK (alongside rival Aldi) ten years ago saw off Kwik Save and rolled magnificently into our recession-enveloped future.

Lidl's joy is that you almost never recognize a single brand and everything is always in the same place. Fizzy drinks at the entrance, chillers along the back, alcohol next to checkout. Asti Allini, Rachmaninoff Vodka, Ben Bracken Whiskey. Route 66 Marmite, Feshona Peppers, Lord Nelson Tea. Their own-brands are like 1960s cover versions of pop songs – cheap and delivered with spirit but never quite the same. They've a reputation for getting you back out into the car park with a week's shopping for two and change from £20.

How do they do it? Staff are few and always seem to be on the run. Clearing packaging from the remains of customer-emptied pallets of cans at ferocious speed. Why shelf-stack when you don't need to. Banging items through the check-out scanner at a rate unequalled anywhere else in the supermarket world. Lidl operators are supposed to be able to hit a thousand items an hour. If they don't they get a conversation wit their line manager. Staff are young. They need the stamina. Sides of heads shaved, body enhancements, tribal markings, lilac hair. *The Black Book on Lidl*[20] reputedly exposes staff maltreatments. Spy cameras, no toilet breaks, management recording of staff conversations to weed out trouble makers. But there's no popular movement to close Lidl down.

In the Maes-y-Coed Road branch they demonstrate their other specialty. Utterly unlikely items on sale in the middle of the food aisles. Crispbread one minute, zipper jackets, exercise equipment, divans and replacement sinks then next. On my visit I spotted an all-in-one single bed (mattress, pillows and built-in sheets – open the box and go to sleep), a curved TV lounger (makes sitting on the floor a dream), Herbst-Rasenmischung Autumn Lawn Seed, and plastic bottles of Maribel Summer Blossom Honey all for sale in the same run. I try to back-track to the fizzy drinks but can't. That's another thing. Lidl shelf runs roll seamlessly. Start at the beginning and, rather like Ikea, you've got to keep going until you reach the end. Near check out there's a sign that reads *Lle Ceir Ansawdd Am Bris Rhatach!* Lidl's nominal attempt to win our Welsh hearts and Welsh minds. I buy a giant bag of biscuits for 40p, enough to keep me going for months.

Outside, next door, they are demolishing the factory that once made Signor Rossi ice cream. Beyond are the flags that mark Barretts' increasingly desperate attempts to sell their new orange brick homes. These are tough times. Although not at Lidl. Round there business booms.

TREODA CASTLE

Treoda is an ancient name. The *Brut y Tywysogion* records that the hated Saxons roared through Cardiff in 831 burning everything they saw. They wrecked the monastery, the huts of the farmers, their barns and sties, and then the castle at Treoda. Treoda, the place of the great house of Yorath Mawr, of Edward ap Richard Gwynn, of the Stradlings, and of the waste lands of the Manor of Album Monasterium. Lineage to die for. Yet possibly the whole thing is an invention of Iolo Morganwg. Ah, you men who embellish our history and then move on. We owe our myths and legends to you. Today Treoda is on the maps and in the Whitchurch air. On the name plates of the roads and on the plaques screwed to the sides of houses and on the common itself, Gwaun-Treoda. Tre Oda. Oda's place. But who was this Oda? No-one knows.

Treoda castle stood on land behind the Fox and Hounds. Clearly a motte and bailey[21] structure once, and made of stone, but described as collapsed by almost everyone who wrote of it. Traces were few. In 1315 Edward II called it the ruined forcelettum de Blancminster. In the fifteenth century Owain Glyndwr burned it. Rhys Merrick in 1578 said it was 'decayd with scarce the foundation and Rubbish now remayneth'. On nineteenth century OS maps it is shown as a tump, a flattened mound, just north of St Mary's vicarage. By 1953 it is labelled as a castle mound and shown in the fields of Glan y Nant Secondary School. A low earth knoll in the garden behind Treoda House. But by the 1970s, when the Treoda flats to the north of the catholic church were built, and new maps drawn, it had all gone.

Treoda Castle would have been one of a line of Norman defence posts running from the Morganstown Mound, through the Rhiwbina Twmpath, Castell Morgraig on the Llanishen Crags, the towers along that ridge, and then down to the monster castle that is Caerphilly. Norman impregnability. The Welsh worried the invader. They still do.

Manor Way is the main artery north out of Cardiff. Overloaded with speed cameras, it's a mass of screech and air breaks and shuffle stop-start. British transport future shown at its worst in soft-spoken Wales. The name of the road flickers as it progresses. At the start it's Manor Way, then Northern Avenue, then Ash Grove. After that it becomes Manor Way again. For years it roared, cats eyes and dual carriage-ways, to end at nothing just before the Coryton railway. But then they found the money to finish it. Now it flows like a cracking whip all the A470 way to Llandudno. Who has travelled it and not cursed the road for its slow slow Norman slog. The Welsh way would have been on pony up through the woods and to become lost among the crags of Deheubarth before an invader's arrow could be loosed. Gareth[22]'s lower school stands to its west.

Whitchurch Comprehensive. Upper school on the old grammar school site next to the new Merthyr Road St Mary's Church. Lower School here, the 1939 mixed secondary school rebranded. I've got Gareth and his Assistant Head, former professional rugby player for both Neath and Nice, Steve Williams, accompanying me through the grounds to look for Treoda traces. Most of this northern triangle of former playing field is now taken up by new Powerleague five-a-side courts. Ten of them. Game of the age. All weather, floodlit, surface made from recycled road tyres. Club house with bar and multiple TV screens that show players kicking balls across endless green swards. The kids get access to all this during the day, Gareth tells me. Not the bar of course. Powerleague who paid for the development on a thirty-year lease make their money renting it outside school hours. High-speed accessible sport. Everyone wins. The courts have large signs attached to them. *Powerleague – Powered by X-box*. What does that mean? No-one seems to know.

Gareth was awarded an OBE in 2007 for services to Education. He kept it quiet but the *South Wales Echo* made sure the world knew. He's ebullient, accessible and seems to have a permanent avuncular smile. On MySpace the kids are demanding that he set up a website of his own so that they can 'adore him from a different perspective.' In my school we always hated the head. It didn't matter how good he was. It was a matter of principle. Gareth retires this summer. Perhaps they are waiting until he's gone.

At the top end, where the Whitchurch Brook has been significantly re-channelled to get it under Manor Way and then around the Treoda Flats, is the site of the now lost castle. Not even the slightest undulation in the surface remains to tell where it might have been. As ever, history totally wiped. No motte. No bailey. Nothing recalling the shapes they once held. Nothing to mark what once stood here. We view the spot from a bund built on school land to protect the housing beyond from Powerleague intrusion. There was a hockey court here once, Steve tells me. Redgra-covered hard core. And before that a sort of special needs hut teaching horticulture. Castle mound removed swiftly, ask no questions, in the rush of rebuild, post-war. The Norman past scraped flat. Couldn't do that today. The building of the Powerleague pitches required planning, consultation, more planning, permissions, Health and Safety action plan, an archaeological survey (found nothing) and then flood plain measurement, calibration and reconstitution. The arrival of the bund meant that less flood water could be accommodated across the school fields. The five-a-side courts had to be built 200mm lower to compensate. But does it actually flood here, I ask? Not that we've seen. Not yet.

RUPERRA

Winter high pressure. Sky clear blue. The fields are crisp with frost. In corners where the sun does not reach the earth is hard. Yesterday's seepings frozen across the roads. Ditches solid, bramble breaking through muck ice. The white stalks of last summer's grass bent and unmoving. Out here at the city's edge where the magnetic glow of urbanisation fades into the fields the world is a freer place. The globe warms but beneath my interlocked coats you wouldn't know.

This is not Cardiff but one of its rural outriders. Almost of the city but in reality actually not. The haze territory seen on bus timetables, in good pub guides and on the walking routes of the Ramblers. But if you live in the city then you can touch it, so it seems like it's yours. We've got onto the Rhymney Valley Ridgeway just past a set of notices protesting *No To Housing At Ruperra*. Keep the country clear. This is a bridle path, stopped by signs warning *No Vehicular Access* but covered with tyre tracks anyway. Ten minutes down it and the first set of four by fours overtake. Forest to our left, falling, sheep-filled fields to the right. I'm with Morgan again. He's wearing two hats against the cold, red wool and blue denim, plus a pair of giant gloves. He's explaining that all this ridge walking is turning him into a much fitter man. He needs this fitness in order to carry his equipment. What equipment? My new SLR and my tripod, of course. Heavy stuff. Morgan has taken up photography and has spent several months using the macro of a point and shoot digital to get into the trembling Rothko hearts of flowers. Now he has turned to bigger stuff and is intent on capturing waterfalls. Wants to slow them with a shutter that takes eternity to click. He has in mind the secret river rush of Sgwd Einion Gam. Einion, you know, anvil. The Twisted Anvil. On the Afon Pyrddin, one of the tributaries of the Nedd. In the Brecons.

The Brecons. Only people who don't come from Wales call these southern escarpments the Brecons. To the Welsh they are the Beacons. What else could they be? Morgan has bought himself a set of chest-high waders, rubber wellingtons (£6 from a garage, cut the tops off to get them to fit) plus a bulbous pack to keep all his equipment dry. He relishes the exclusivity of this venture. So long as you don't bloody write about this, Finch, there won't be any new visitors at the place for another ten years. See me out. How do you get all your equipment in, I ask? Plunging through water. Sliding over the stones. With difficulty, he replies. We stride on.

Ruperra Castle, where we are heading, is in that part of Caerphilly where the land bangs up against Newport and is overlorded by great all-powerful Cardiff. Border country. The rip saw accent may no longer be in evidence but economic dependence certainly is. Ruperra was built in 1626 by Sir Thomas Morgan, Steward to the Earl of Pembroke. The Morgan I am with is convinced that the castle was something brought here by the invading English. The Earl of Pembroke was given the county for his birthday, he tells me. Here son, said the Earl's father, happy birthday, have Pembroke. You exaggerate, Morgan. No, I don't. As the castle shades into view, a Jacobean wreck in the haze beyond the trees, Morgan returns the conversation to his birthplace at Onllwyn. The Choir went to Washington, you know, sang with Whoopi Goldberg. I think he imagines Goldberg to be a bit like

Aretha. Did they ever sing in Cardiff, I ask. No, but they went to Porthcawl.

The castle is a fake, fake now, was a fake when it was built. Never there to defend anything. It was destroyed by fire in 1785 and rebuilt with extra fake battlements added. The site is surrounded by a battlement encrusted wall. Never seen shots fired in anger even though Charles I stayed here straight after the battle of Naseby. The Jacobeans enjoyed castellation like we relish fake wooden beams and mock Tudor black and white gable ends. The building, with its southeast tower collapsed, is like the castle at Caerphilly but without the leaning grandeur. It is impressive in its isolated splendour. Its latter-day grey-beige render and weather-obliterated coats of arms are a perfect fit with the open and sheep-filled fields to the south and the hummock of forested Craig Ruperra to the north.

After a long history as residence for the Morgan family, including Godfrey Charles, First Viscount Tredegar who was in the Charge of the Light Brigade, the building again caught fire in 1941. This was while troops were stationed here. Everything went, including the roof. The then owner was the eccentric Second Viscount, Evan Morgan, poet and pet owner.[23] He had already turned down an offer to buy from William Randolph Hearst. Instead the castle was left as it was, stranded in the elements. John Morgan, the last Baron Tredegar, sold the building to the Eagle Star Insurance Company in 1956. It has spent the past fifty years slowly deteriorating: floors collapsed, glass gone, masonry coming loose, water goods stolen, ancient carved block and incised stone in a fallen heap. A romantic ruin.

That romance is still in place. Ruperra, now grade two listed with attendant rare bats and unusual newts, is unstable, and closed to the public. Polo player Ashraf Barakat bought the estate in 1998 with plans for redevelopment. Following Ruperra tradition his stable block almost immediately burned down. After some indecision about selling on he put in a redevelopment plan to turn the castle into apartments and to build what amounts to a brand new small village on land next door. New access roads would slice the countryside. The architecture of Thomas Hardwick would be compromised. Seventeenth century nostalgia for a chivalric past would be lost. The listed dairy blocks would sink under the onslaught of four by four car parking. The bats would leave or die. The newts would be depressed.

Local resistance is strong. Council Planners have rejected Barakat's approaches. But development is a long game. Barakat is appealing. The game plays on.

On the Craig Ruperra ridge above the castle the local conservation trust has replanted conifer with broad-leafed wood. The ridge was an iron-age hillfort in the time of the Silures and a Norman motte a millennium later. This was Castell Breiniog, a timber castle in the period of the Red Earl. Or maybe it was Castell Remni or even Castell y Ddraenen. History at this distance shades and shifts. The structure, the walls that survived eight hundred years, were rebuilt as a summer house in 1780[24]. The Trust have rebuilt them again now. In 2009 they are a spiral walled monument. From the top you can see Wales spread out. Morgan reckons that this place had to be completely forested before the farmers arrived. Cwm-Leyshon Quarry (dis) and ancient abandoned lead mines are in the distance. To the east the cluster of Draethen and above that Machen.

In the Hollybush at Draethen (Giant Flat Screen T.V. in the Snug for Sport and Entertainment – Sunday Lunch £8.00 – Chocolate Tasting Plate £4.25) Morgan, who hasn't drunk alcohol since 1957, has failed to get the Gaggia Espresso machine to deliver him a cup of hot water. He is making an explanatory map of Oakfield Street and Partridge Road using beer mats, the menu and a card advertising rugby matches. Here's the Blue Dragon Hotel, he points. They're threatening to turn that into apartments now. Blue Dragon, the cheapest place to stay in East Cardiff. European migrants littering its summer forecourt, beer cans in hand. Mis-spellings in most advertising. Folk club on Friday. A cultural loss. The Hollybush has finished its lunch-time sitting and the surplus Yorkshire puddings have been brought into the bar for free distribution among the locals. Bryson[25] would have engaged them in banter. Katz would have joined in the rush for free eats. Morgan and I don't bother.

LLANISHEN

A bloke called Chris Brown taught me about fighting. He came from Llanishen. Estate boy with aspirations. Showed me how to wrap the clips used to bracket tubular steel chairs together as knuckledusters. Metal fist. You could use it to punch marks onto walls. Not that I ever employed this skill. But at 14 it felt like one worth having. The haze of violence that follows our lives. A redness of menaced verbal and broken bone. Threat that stood behind walls, held sway in bar rooms, leant out at you when you least expected it. You lookin at me? Are you? Never a question worth answering.

In later life, Chris Brown down the red miasma river for GBH, blades and gouged out eyes, I went to Llanishen Leisure Centre to learn how all this violence ought to be done. The Martial Arts. Little to do with culture and reason. Not much to do with the spirit. Some of them with five minutes meditation at the start, or the end. Bow to the practice room then go home. A few with a layer of eastern mysticism. Aikido's unbendable arm. The eighteen arms of wushu. Chi flowing through the gates. Mostly, though, it was learning to kick high enough to take out teeth, to move fast enough to avoid the plunging knife, to hit hard enough to knock the branches off trees. I followed it for years. Could manage a sword, shadow box in shapes of incredible complexity, take a man down by touching his smallest finger. Could sweat, god could I do that. Learned also that the best idea was to cross the street and pass on the other side. Watch their eyes. Everything comes from that.

I drove there. Straight up Fidlas Road, left onto Ty Glas Avenue. Doors in need of repainting. Grass worn thin. On to the biggest and best of Cardiff Council's comprehensive leisure centre provision. This one with wave pool, extended weights room, dozens of squash courts and a fully featured skate board park like a set of giant unrolled gas pipes outside. Park. Go in. Dobok[26] on, start to move.

Today I'm walking. Martial arts forgotten bar the ability to get through a dense crowd without touching. Body still knows where all the others are. Set out from St Dennis's Well, Ffynon Denys, St Dene's pool, the scorbutic[27] curing pond in the centre of the oval, top of Roath Park Lake. Wattle and daub church here once, gone. Burial mound for the meditating dead still evident, just. No official sign anywhere. Memorial tree planted by the local historical society in

1993. God removed by urban creep. Llanishen, the district, bleeding
north into Lisvane and Thornhill and west into the newly developing
sprawl that was once the Royal Ordnance bomb factory, is bigger
than I'd thought. On Thomas Waring[28]'s Cardiff map of 1869 the
town already looks industrial and mighty. Grangetown, Roath,
Cathays, Ely Paper Mills, Llandaff Yard, all in place. The main line
north rushes towards the brand new Caerphilly tunnel. Llanishen is
somewhere beyond the vacant and empty heath. Trees. Sheep. Village.
Stream. Norman Church. Public house. Off the map. But not now.

As I go up Fidlas the rain starts. It's what you expect when you
rise north. Bluster and drizzle. The traffic is thick and stays so.
Lisvane dormitory dwellers go through here in their four by fours.
So does the whole of housing estate of Thornhill. Where the road
bends left to pass under the railway viaduct stands Bridge Cottage.
District ancient. 300 years old, 24 feet by 18, hidden behind
comprehensive fencing and tree growth. Impossible to photograph
unless you climb into the next-door MOT yard of Yapps Garage
and poke your camera through a loose piece of lattice like I do. On
a fence-affixed signboard the place is billed as a woodland retreat
offering craniosacral therapy, passive movement, yoga, and reflex-
ology[29]. One customer at a time I guess.

The atmosphere of alternative aloofness breaks as I round
towards Station Road and pass the double-fronted stop-me-and-get-
pissed frontage of Bargain Booze. Next door is where Stefan
Terlezki[30], to the right of Genghis Khan Conservative local and later
UK politician, once had his Cedars Hotel and a hand in the Phoenix
steak bar and Chinese restaurant. Terlezki was an advocate of
flogging football hooligans, removing civil rights from drug traffick-
ers, the return of the birch and introduced a bill into Parliament
seeking to replace May Day with a Bank Holiday on May 10,
Winston Churchill's birthday. In the 60s and 70s rarely did an
evening pass without Terlezki's Ukrainian face appearing in the *Echo*
in support of some right-wing local cause or other. He won Cardiff
West in 1983 from the late George Thomas and then lost it four
years later to Rhodri Morgan. The Cedars[31] has been replaced with
sheltered accommodation and the Phoenix has been flattened.
Signboards announce the imminent arrival of the Rhydes Court
stunning apartments. Capitalist this enterprise may be but the road
outside it runs red with disturbed clay.

Llanishen village, the centre, clusters around St Isan's Norman church and the quiz every Sunday, smokers under an umbrella near the car park, Church Inn. Llanishen Cards, Post Office, Darlows, Principality, Academy Hair Design, Co-op, Lloyds Pharmacy. All you need. At the church two men are struggling with a pew, one end in a wheel barrow the other on a skate board. Selling it, I ask? Nope. Putting it back. Been stripped and revarnished. Not all Christian institutions are in decline.

St Isan. Multicoloured rubble-stone. Part Dec. Part Perp. Quatrefoil in plan. Moulded. Arcade of short piers. Chamfered imposts. Cusped ogee heads. Standing saints. Fifteenth century when we really wanted it to be Norman. Rebuilt 1854 and again in 1907. Surrounded by tended graves.

Beyond is the Fishguard Estate, once council now largely privatised. You can tell by the care taken over lawns and entrance porches. Neat hedges. Plaster dogs on gateposts. I get the feeling as I walk through, south now towards the Glider Field (next to the Leisure Centre, used to train pilots in World War 2), that much of this place is unfinished. There are spaces where houses might have stood but don't, over large drives, plots of poor tarmac, full of parked cars, triangles of land undeveloped. Wouldn't last a minute like this nearer city centre. I asked at the Post Office if they had a local history book. They pointed me at Kimberley Terrace library, a converted shop, and it looked hopeful too. But being Wednesday it was closed.

Ty Glas Avenue with its hated eighteen-story twin-towered Tax Office at one end and the fought-over reservoirs at the other is the line which separates housing from commerce. I reach the blue mirror box of the Orchards, office outpost housing the Assembly, Camelot Group plc, Zurich Insurance, the National Lottery and the Higher Education Funding Council. Built in 1990, on the site of the Coal House, the industry's south Wales HQ until the days of the great falling apart in the 1980s. This is a building that tries not the be there,

reflecting what's around it, trees, playing fields, overcast sky, colouring everything blue. Norman Foster's idea. This one done by Wigley Fox. But you can't tell that unless you look it up.

I follow a tributary of the Nant Brook, the Licky, as its runs culverted, unculverted, in lost overgrowths of trees, squeezing across waste-ground, as it heads for the main event coming out from the twin Llanishen reservoirs just north of Ffynon Denis. Borderland – Lakeside, Llanishen, Heath. We knew just where all these places were once, now we don't.

I'm back where I started now. Isan's well, Dene's Well, Dennis's holy water. Quiet. Still there. Still ancient. Still holy.

notes:

1. *The Englishman Who Went Up A Hill But Came Down A Mountain* – 1995.
2. Known originally as Walnut Tree Quarry, named after the southern part of Taffs Well village. In 1841 Taffs Well had around 300 inhabitants mostly workers on the Glamorgan Canal but one or two quarrymen as well.
3. The system was excavated in 1912 by T E Lewis of Morganstown and again by M S Hussey in 1964. Hussey took out boulders, dug, suffered rock falls, and before abandoning the dangerous venture found a weaving comb, a needle and awl, and unworked flint.
4. Iron ore has been dug from the Lesser Garth since at least 1565. The tunnel on the north side descends some 400 feet to meet other tunnels from the east and the west. The pit was worked until the end of the nineteenth century.
5. Explorer 152, 151, and 166. The section east from the Caerphilly Tunnel can involve standing in wet forests trying to hold three maps open to make them gell. Path way marking is dreadful. Cross routes, diversions, forks and unmarked alternatives abound. There are gates across many sections along with buggered-up stiles that resist all attempts at traditional crossing. If you end up at the Maen Llwyd, the four hundred year old pub on the outskirts of Rudry, then you've missed a junction. Go in, have a pint, then retrace your steps and try again.
6. Llewelyn ap Gruffydd, ein llyw olaf – Llewelyn ap Gruffydd, (1225-1282), our last leader – the last leader of a united and independent Wales.
7. See *Real Cardiff One* page 81.
8. Castell Morgraig was excavated in 1895 by John Ward and a team from Cardiff Museum. They found battlements, lintels and extensive stonework. They failed to preserve it. In 1997 Jack

Spurgeon reported to the Royal Commission on Ancient and Historical Monuments in Wales on the castle's origins. His conclusion is that Morgraig is of Norman origin, dating from 1243. A defence against the Senghenydd Welsh marauding in from the north. His detractors claim the castle to be Welsh built facing south to threaten the Normans at Cardiff. A classic impasse. Eric and Morgan favour the Welsh. Reluctantly I'm more with Spurgeon. But I might be wrong.

9. Caerphilly cheese was never originally made in the town but sold at its market. Hand made in Wales today at Tregaron, Ceredigion although some local production has been instigated. Still sold at Caerphilly's Twyn Car Park farmer's market. Second Saturday each month.

10. Coryton House was built on part of Llwyn Mallt Farm by J. Herbert Cory (1857-1933), shipping magnate, director of thirty five companies, conservative MP for Cardiff and millionaire. After his death the building passed into the hands of the civil defence, then the GPO and eventually to BT. BT sold the land to Belway Homes in 2005. This wedge of brown field and trees between the Village Hotel and Leisure Club and the Forest Farm Nature Reserve is now Bellwood Park, apartments and family homes, orange brick, wood laminate floors. Coryton House in its lost glory slumbers among the trees, boarded-up but not yet vandalised, guarded by a uniformed Zimbabwean who wants to take my camera from me but fails. "They told me no photos." I assure him I've taken none.

11. The asylum was built to plans from Architects Oatley and Skinner of Bristol who had won the commission in open competition. Their previous experience included asylums at Surrey and Lancashire. Foundations were dug in 1902.

12. The hospital farms finished in 1953 when central government policy changed. Parcels of the land they occupied has been seeping off into the hands of speculators ever since.

13. Report of the Commissioners 1913.

14. In 1910 the Home Secretary, Winston Churchill, planned the forcible sterilisation of 100,000 moral degenerates. Didn't happen. Plans kept secret until 1992.

15. The Whitchurch gatehouse is now the Department for Clinical Psychology – Learning Difficulties.

16. Planned but never actually installed.

17. One pint, two pints, three pints. The mutation is different in each case.

18. Merthyr Road 2 miles, Newport Rd ? mile, Caerphilly 7 and something. Half the fraction has been vandalised.

19. PLU – Price Look Up.

20. *The Black Book on the Schwarz Retail Company* – Andreas Hamann und Gudrun Giese (2005) – selling cheap at the employees expense.

21. The motte (French – *clod of earth*) was a mound on the top of which was build a wooden (or later a stone) tower or keep. The mound was surrounded by a ditch with a fence on its inner side. Mounds were usually thirty feet high. The bailey was a nearby oval-shaped enclosed and defended space connected to the motte by a bridge. The Normans who seem to have invented this form of fort often found their ideas copied by the Welsh. Treoda Castle was built at the same time as others in the Norman defensive line – 1268-1271.

22. Gareth Matthewson. OBE for services to education. 'Safe Teacher. Walks around with a big umbrella' (RateMyTeachers.co.uk). Head of the biggest school in Wales.

23. Evan Morgan owned a bear named Alice, an anteater, a boxing kangaroo called Somerset and a Macaw called Blue Boy. He friends included HG Wells, Aldous Huxley, Augustus John, Nancy Cunard, Ivor Novello and Aleister Crowley. His poetry collections included *Fragments, At Dawn, The Eel* and *The City of Canals*. He drowned, aged 29, in the River Thames.

24. During eighteenth century development the Rev W Watkins discovered an erect skeleton here standing in a 2.5 m square room deep in the castle foundation.

25. Bill Bryson and his walking companion, Stephen Katz, from *A Walk In The Woods*, 1998.

26. The plain white costume of traditional taekwondo.

27. Scurvy.
28. Thomas Waring, surveyor and engineer to Cardiff, Canton and Roath Local Boards of Health, as well as Cardiff Rural District Built houses between 1874 and 1890.
29. www.marysyoga.co.uk
30. Stefan Terlezki, CBE, October 29, 1927 – February 21, 2006. Conservative politician, hotelier and chairman of Cardiff City FC. 'A happy warrior willing to fight hopeless seats' (*The Guardian*).
31. The hotel had an ignominious end. In its final entries Trip Advisor reported the Cedars as smelling of chip fat, with unbelievably uncomfortable beds, dirty cutlery, damp stains on the walls, horrendous decor, and blistered paintwork. Llanishen is probably glad it is gone.

BEYOND

THE LORDS OF CARDIFF

I've crossed the decayed Victorian splendour of Cathays cemetery, past the memorials to the lost greats of Cardiff's nineteenth century past. I've gone round the boarded-up chapel, skirted the health and safety fences, avoided the tapes and tarpaulins that keep the streaming Cardiff weather back. I've checked the council keeper's hut (empty), light on, leaflets and maps in their racks. I've crossed the road that leads to the Fairoak. Did you know there was one? Shattered remains in a labelled heap behind the railings, top of the flower park. Roath Flower Gardens. I'm at the end of Tewkesbury Place. Victorian Terrace. Two Nigerians on bikes. Woman with a pushchair the size of a bubble car. Dog on a lead. Tewkesbury – where is that place? Why is it celebrated here?

Tewkesbury, (pop 16,849)[1], is built where the Avon meets the Severn and it floods, often spectacularly. In the matter of Cardiff it is of forgotten but overwhelming importance. Is Cardiff twinned with this fine Gloucestershire township? No. Do we exchange civic formalities, play them at cricket, host their touring dramas, send them our rugby, receive their choirs, exchange stag night drinking crowds, mark them with a plaque in the historical fabric of our city? We've got Tewkesbury Place and its extension, Tewkesbury Street. That's enough.

When the Conqueror passed through Wales in 1081[2], he gave Cardiff to one of his lieutenants. Have this place. His cousin Robert Fitzhamon arrived sometime between 1089 and 1094 and started a castle[172]. He chose the obvious spot. The battered fort of the Romans

– strategically placed by the river and already full of stone. Fitzhamon, first Lord of new borough of Norman Cardiff. He had already founded a cathedral, the size of Westminster, on an existing religious site at Tewkesbury. Tewkesbury of the rivers. Commanding Tewkesbury. Tewkesbury the Norman power base. To fund his religious generosity Fitzhamon made swathes of Cardiff owe fealty to his new cathedral. Parts of the Roath farmlands (and almost all of Roath was farmland at this time) ended up being known as Roath Tewkesbury. They had to send everything they produced by pack horse the seventy miles up along the Severn shore. The Norman line rolled on. Fitzhamon was succeeded by Robert the Consul and then by a stream of castle-building de Clares. Four of them. Richard, Gilbert, Gilbert and Gilbert. After that came the le Despensers. Ralph de Monthermer. Richard Beauchamp. Geoffrey de Mandeville. Richard Neville. Their names repeat in the names of Cardiff Streets. All Lords. Running this place as part of the independent state of Marcher Walia. The Glamorgan March. The borderland, a buffer state between William's conquered England and a wild and warring autonomous Wales.

This period in the catholic medieval west of the Norman kingdoms was rich with internecine strife. The Lords, Earls and Barons fought with each other, made treaties, fell out, married each other's wives, made twisting alliances with Welsh princes. Loved. Lost. Assassinated each other. Were hung drawn and quartered. For infamy, for treason. This happened to Hugh le Despenser the Younger, the decadent traitor, whose quartered body was despatched from Hereford to the corners of the English kingdom – York, Bristol, Carlisle and Dover. His sawn off head was taken to the gates of London. With permission in 1330 his friends collected and reunited his corporeal remains. His widow Eleanor de Clare was presented with a bag containing his head, thigh bone and a few vertebrae. These were interred at Tewkesbury.

What The Lords Did

lost . hung . drew. sliced . sullied . shaved . cut . hacked . stretched . strangled . wrecked . executed . dealt . drilled . detached. disembowelled . burnt . broke . bust . cut off the genitals . desecrated . gouged . bled . red . bled. needled . crushed . caged . fired . infected . spiked . plundered . ripped . rushed . stripped . struck. defamed . loathed . bradawled . stabbed . blistered . locked . robbed . ate . spat . defiled . corrupted . dishonoured . beheaded . poisoned . shot . paid Lord God almighty such wealth as to ensure a gleaming place . endowed and endowed . bejeweled . said they prayed . probably did

This part of Gloucestershire is riddled with our past. Fitzhamon, Despenser, and de Clare: their remains are all at the Abbey. Distant Cardiff was never holy enough, never jewel encrusted, not filled with catholic light.

I get there in about an hour and half. A mile out I find a road sign to Walton Cardiff. I collect these places. Like a good psychogeographer and keen to top my visit to the minimal township of Cardiff, NY, I follow the track. It trails and winds. Pass four dwellings. A fifth. A seventeenth century timber-framed farm. Then nothing. St James Church, Walton Cardiff, abandoned 1975. Then I'm back in the country again. I stop a walker. Yes, that was it. Walton Cardiff. Embanked farmstead once owned by the Lord of Cardiff. Population in 1419 – twenty three. Today not much more. In comparison, Cardiff New York you are a city.

The Tewkesbury cathedral, the Abbey, is still the town's parish church. Restored. Alive. I park in the Vineyards Long Stay Car Park – *This Car Park is affected when the River Floods* reads the sign. Standing next to it on five foot brick plinths is the local cricket pavilion. The parking fee is £2 for four hours. A nun joins me at the pay machine. Do you have to pay for a whole four hours, she asks? I'm only going to be here for two. She returns to her Fiesta and drives off at speed.

The cathedral is palpably ancient and discretely restored. Decades of work by careful men with small trowels, by stone fixers, stone cleaners, repairers with the touch of watchmakers has happened here. On the edge of the town with open fields rolling beyond the past, several centuries have made hardly any impact at all. I am met, when I enter, by three men in dark blue, wound about with red harness, like punks with their webbing tidied and their Mohicans replaced with middle aged spread. Not everyone in Tewkesbury dresses like this, one of them says. We've been up there. He points to the east window above the choir. The Last Judgement and the Coronation of the Virgin Mary. Medieval fragments still in place. Lined now with Christmas candles. Used to get up there solo on a single ladder. Point on the top of it like a window cleaner's. Zip zip. But they won't let us now.

In the cathedral shop they tell me that Fitzhamon is in the choir. I am shown a hand-made map showing the location of the monuments. Could I borrow it? I'll come straight back. Sorry, no. I take a photograph and set off round the interior with my camera's LCD lit. The Reverend Canon Paul Williams narrates a six minute video in a booth in a far western corner. On it he calls the founder Fitzheymen. The historian John Davies insists the man should be known as Fitz Hammo. The winos on the Embankment in Cardiff don't care.

The monuments, when I locate them, cluster around the altar. Lost souls warming themselves on the holy fire. Untrammelled by contact with the twenty-first century, heated by Gurney coal burners, low lit, revered, silent despite intrusion. The location is a black hole in time. The de Clares, four of them, lie in a brass plaque lined row. Above them are the markers for three Despensers. Henry Beauchamp is between the choir stalls. Robert Fitzhamon is in his Founders Chapel on the left. Beyond is the great canopied memorial to Hugh Despenser the third, son of the traitor. Hugh in alabaster, dressed as a knight, next to his marble wife, Elizabeth Montacute.

These things have been here since the eleventh century, some of them. Trails of the past snaking forward. History you can grasp. Unaltered. But actually, no. Not everything is what it seems. Almost everything here at some time or other has been restored, investigated, taken apart, cleaned, refixed, reassembled and then taken apart to be restored once more. They've been right down there inside the memorial to the Founder. Taken his bones out, counted them, and brushed off the dust. Fixed the cracking sides of the stone memorial with new mortar and then with the addition of iron rods. When the iron corroded red and began to lever up the parts it was holding the rods were removed, the stones cleaned and the structure refixed with

stainless steel. How much of the Founder's spirit stayed to watch is unknown.

The brass plaques to the four de Clares were made in the nineteenth century. The earlier memorials, reputed to be jewel encrusted and made from precious metals, were desecrated before the reformation. Of them nothing remains. The grave of Maud de Clare, wife of Gilbert III, is below a large stone slab. It was once topped with a brass depiction of her form. Only the indent is left. Records show that the graves were all excavated in 1875. Stone coffins were discovered four feet down and found to be either smashed to pieces and their stone reused to provide wall foundations or were filled with rubble and gash. Only the bottom three inches of the stone of Gilbert I's coffin remained. Disrespect or more likely total disregard for what the twenty-first century thinks of as sacrosanct runs right through the past. The nineteenth century excavators[4] also found the grave of Isabel, Countess of Warwick. Like Tutankhamen's tomb this was discovered to be completely intact, the body still inside in its crumbling shroud. They resealed the grave and marked it with an inscribed brick. 'This grave was opened during the restoration of 1875, and, after being inspected, was reverently closed again and restored to its original condition.'

The brass diamond-shaped plaques inset amid the tiles of the choir and marking in Latin the legendary de Clares turn out to date from the 1875 restoration. Their inscriptions were composed by Mr Niblett, a Tewkesbury antiquarian. Death held no terror for him, it says above the Red Earl. He signed the Magna Carta, it says above Gilbert I. But he did not. He only served on an overseeing committee. Niblett didn't check.

Can we keep the past in a bottle? Seems not. Everything eventually falls apart.

Before I return I check out the town. Find Cornell's Antiquarian Books. The founder is in residence. Eating a cheese sandwich and pickle onion, ensconced behind a stock-laden desk. Big band music on a tape player. He sells me a stack of topography overstocks at a pound each. A few about Wales. Then Herbert M Thompson's *Cardiff*, from 1936. This has a fold-out chart in the back shewing the genealogy of the Lords of Cardiff from Fitzhamon to Richard Crookback. 1066 to 1509.

I take the old road back, along the northern side of the Severn. This is the way Fitzhamon must have come, with his invading army, on his horses. The road here twists and winds, is full of speed cameras and views of the flooding river. Flooding now as it flooded then. An arm's reach across. This is not the sea as it looks from home. The pubs are called things like the King's Head and the Severn Bore. Timber-frame old. Not Cardiff, not even Wales.

When I get back I check Thompson's book. Fitzhamon invaded by boat. Landed near Newport. Brought his force in and was once again the Founder. Hic jacet Robertus filius Haymonis hujus loci fundator, records Leland. Bound to be right.

notes:

1. According to http://www.tewkesbury.net/facts.asp
2. On a pilgrimage to St David's.
3. He might have done. William the Conqueror himself could have started the Norman motte and bailey which developed into the present day castle keep a decade earlier. The records of history waver.
4. Rev J H Blunt and Sir Edmund Lechmere.

THE PHOTOGRAPHS

All photographs by Peter Finch, apart from p.229, John Briggs.
Front and rear cover photographs by Peter Finch.

WORKS CONSULTED

Alston, David: *Into Painting: Brendon Stuart Burns*, Seren 2007

Celsa Steel UK, *Local Focus, Global Commitment*, Celsa, 2008

Chappell, Edgar L.: *History of the Port of Cardiff*, Priory Press, 1939

Chappell, Edgar L.: *Old Whitchurch – The Story of a Glamorgan Parish*, Merton Priory Press, 1994 (reprinting the 1945 Priory Press edition)

Chopin, Henri: *Poesie Sonore*, Jean-Michel Place, 1979

Codrington, Thomas: *Roman Roads In Britain*, Society for Promoting Christian Knowledge, 1903

Cooke, R.A.: *Track Layout Diagrams of the Great Western Railway and B.R. (W.R.) Section 46B Pontypridd-Cardiff*, Lightmore Press, 1996

Cooke, R.A.: *Track Layout Diagrams of the Great Western Railway and B.R. (W.R.) Section 43B Cardiff Docks*, Lightmore Press, 1996

Coverley, Merlin: *Psychogeography*, Pocket Essentials, 2006

Dart, Geoff: *A Cardiff Notebook,* Historic Records Project, 1988

Davies, John: *Cardiff A Pocket Guide*, University of Wales Press, 2002

Dicks, Brian: *Portrait of Cardiff and its Valleys*, Hale, 1984

Elborough, Travis: *The Long Player Goodbye - the Album from Vinyl to iPod and back again*, Sceptre, 2008

Fisk, Stephen: *Abandoned Communities - Temperance Town*,

Fletcher, J. Kyrle: *Cardiff – Notes Picturesque and Biographical*, Privately printed, 1930

Glover, Brian: *Brains 125 Years*, Breedon Books, 2007

Glover, Brian: *Cardiff Pubs and Breweries*, Tempus, 2005

Griffiths, David: *Portraits*, National Library of Wales, 2002

Hamann, Andreas & Giese, Gudrun: *The Black Book on the Schwarz Retail Company,* 2005

Holley, Fred, Vida & John: *Master of Hounds - Wyndham William Lewis Esquire, The Heath, Cardiff,* V A Holley, 1987

Hooper, Alan & Punter, John (eds): *Capital Cardiff 1975-2020 - Regeneration, Competitiveness and the Urban Environment*, UWP 2006

Howell, Ray: *Searching For The Silures - An Iron Age Tribe In South-East Wales*, Tempus, 2006

Hutton, John: *An Illustrated History of Cardiff Docks Volume 1*, Silver Link, 2008

Hutton, John: *The Taff Vale Railway Vol Two*, Silver Link, 2006

Jenkins, Simon: *Wales: Churches, Houses, Castles*, Allen Lane, 2008

Kidner, R.W.: *The Rhymney Railway*, The Oakwood Press, 1995

Lee, Brian: *The Illustrated History of Cardiff's Pubs*, Breedon Books, 2004

Lee, Brian: *The Welsh Grand National – from Deerstalker to Supreme Glory*, Tempus, 2002

Lee, Brian: *Welsh Steeplechase Jockeys*, Cwmnedd Press, 1993

Long, Helen: *The Edwardian House*, Manchester University Press, 1993

Morgan, Dennis: *The Cardiff Story*, D. Brown, 1991

Morgan, Dennis: *Memories of Cardiff's Past*, Breedon Books, 2006

Morris, Richard K. & Shoesmith, Ron: *Tewkesbury Abbey - History, Art & Architecture*, Logaston Press, 2003

Neal, Marjorie: *Rumney & St. Mellons - A History of two Villages*, Rumney & District Local History Society, 2005

Newman, John: *The Buildings of Wales - Glamorgan*, Penguin Books, 2001

Read, J.C.: *A History of St. John's Cardiff and the Churches of the Parish*, Pauline House, 1997

Rees, William: *Cardiff, A History of the City*, City of Cardiff, 1969

Thursby, Robert C.: *Eheda – Glamorgan Aviation*, Tempus, 2002

Thompson, Herbert M.: *Cardiff*, William Lewis, 1936

Walker, Mandy: *From Dowlais To Tremorfa - The Story of a Cardiff Steelmaking Company,* Tremorfa Books, 1993

Williams, Gareth: *Life On The Heath - The Making of a Cardiff Suburb*, Merton Priory Press, 2001

http://www.abandonedcommunities.co.uk/index.html

ACKNOWLEDGEMENTS

My thanks to the following people who all made an essential contribution to the book: Jonathan Adams, Kasim Ali, Shahida Ali-iqbal, George Auchterlonie, Nigel Barry, Andy Bentley, Bob Bosley, Tim Bowers, John Briggs, Stewart Burgess, Steve Burnett, Brendan Burns, Paul Cleverdon, David Dalton, Alan Davies, John Edwards, Stuart Emberlin, Cerian Evans, Mario Fiorillo, Morgan Francis, Trevor Gough, David Griffiths, Chris Guiver, the late Arthur Gummer, Nigel Hanson, Bob Hardy, Majid Karim, Zoe King, David Symons and Wiard Sterk at Safle, Brian Lee, Gareth Matthewson, Steven Madeley, Ian Meredith, Gary Rix, Eric Roberts, Lloyd Robson, Jennie Savage, Ben Soffa, Ian Symonds, Susan Tanti, Pat Thompson, Ian Wile, Andy Williams, Stan Williams, Steve Williams, Sue Wilshere. I might have missed someone and if I have then apologies. Let me know and at the next opportunity I'll add you in.

Earlier versions of the sections in Cardiff South that describe The Red House were originally commissioned by Safle on behalf of Westmark Developments as part of the public art project at the Watermark development on the site. The *Cock Hill* section first appeared in *The Western Mail*. *Agenda* published extracts from *The Creative East*. A version of *The Gardens* with typographic enhancements by Mick Felton was exhibited at the Waterloo Tea House in 2009.

INDEX

ABOUT THE AUTHOR

Peter Finch is a poet and literary entrepreneur who was born in Cardiff and still lives here. His lifetime output of poetry titles includes *Useful, Poems for Ghosts* and *Food* from Seren, *Antibodies* from Stride and *The Welsh Poems* from Shearsman. Seren published his *Selected Later Poems* in 2008 and will bring out *Zen Cymru* in 2010. He has written and published short fiction, criticism and a number of books on the business of writing including *How To Publish Yourself* (Allison & Busby) and *The Poetry Business* (Seren). His extensive web site is at www.peterfinch.co.uk

A former publisher and bookseller he is currently runs Academi, the Welsh National Literature Promotion Agency and Society of Writers. www.academi.org

Real Cardiff and *Real Cardiff Two* have both been Seren bestsellers. Peter Finch is currently editor of Seren's Real series which includes volumes on the conurbations of Llanelli, Merthyr Tydfil, Wrexham, Liverpool, Aberystwyth, Swansea and Newport. His is also the author of *Real Wales*. With Grahame Davies he has compiled *The Big Book of Cardiff*, an anthology of poetry and prose which concentrates on the revitalised city.

The author at the Waterloo Gardens Teahouse sitting below his portrait by David Griffiths. *Photo by John Briggs*

WHAT THE CRITICS SAID

This is a marvellous book – one of the very best books about a city I have ever read. It makes me feel terribly old-fashioned – superficial too, because I have never actually lived in the cities I have written about. I skip most of the poems, which I don't understand, but everything else in it is gripping me so fast that I have momentarily suspended my first ever reading of *Wuthering Heights*. **– Jan Morris**

Native Cardiffians now have the definitive guide to their city...the excitement of being one of the newest European capitals hangs light in the air. **– Kate Nicholson**, *Writers' News*

A wealth of information on the significance of familiar sites for those who live in Cardiff and an interesting insight into Wales' capital for those who don't, *Real Cardiff* is far more indicative of life in the city than the average tourist guide.

– Cathryn Scott, *The Big Issue*

The travel section of the Observer highlights Wales as a 'place to visit' in 2003. If you are persuaded, and would like a genuine flavour of the capital, read Peter Finch, who has studied the city in historical depth and quartered it on foot and will entertain you all the way. **– Sam Adams**, *PN Review*

The book's great strength is not in the macro but in the micro, in the deep, prolonged engagement with a particular place which has produced a richly nuanced, affectionate and sometimes exasperated portrait of a city. The beauty lies in the detail.

– Grahame Davies, *New Welsh Review*

Cunningly intermeshed with this cornucopia of useful and fascinating material is an account of how a young man who was something or other in the City Hall became an editor, a publisher, a bookseller, an arts administrator and a poet – the most surreally inventive and provocative writer we have – without leaving the city's limits.   **– Meic Stephens,** *Cambria*

In this book, Peter Finch gets the balance damn near spot on, casting the gentlest of aspersions, giving the knife a tiny twist where necessary, but always while staring you unwaveringly in the eye as a true poet. This is not just true poetry, however, it is also travel writing of the sharpest kind...Finch's particular skill is his supreme ability to weave the past in with the present, and to that end his illustrations are often exquisite in their sparseness.

– Mike Parker, *Planet*